How to Make the Stock Market Make Money for You

How to Make the Stock Market Make Money for You

TED WARREN

Copyright © 1966, 1993, 1998 by Ken Roberts

All rights reserved. No portion of this book may be reprinted in any form without written permission in advance from the publisher, except in the case of a reviewer who wishes to quote brief passages in connection with a review in a newspaper, magazine or journal.

Library of Congress Catalogue Card Number 66-26075

First Edition, First Printing 1966

Second Edition, First Printing 1993

Second Edition, Second Printing 1994

Second Edition, Third Printing 1995

Third Edition, Eighth Printing 2006

NOTE: The charts used throughout this book have been prepared by The United States Chart Company. They include everything Ted Warren wanted in a charting service. Call, write or fax for information:
U.S. Chart Company, 333 SW 5th Street, Grants Pass, OR 97526
Office: 541-955-2885
Stock Chart subscription: 800-230-7862
Commodity Chart subscription: 800-230-2427 Fax: 541-955-2889

PRINTED IN THE UNITED STATES OF AMERICA

Dedicated to the millions of investors and speculators who are striving to gain a little extra from our capitalistic system.

— Ted Warren
1966

Editor's Note
(1966 Edition)

There is no intent in the pages of this book to state definitely that the directors, management officials, owners or other employees of a company or corporation are the particular "insiders," "sponsors," or "manipulators" of the stock of that corporation. It is not the purpose of this book to identify thousands of ethical companies, their personnel or managing officials with abuses, but rather to point out that abuses do exist and that stocks are controlled by people—who quite plausibly may be far removed from the directorship, ownership, management or employ of a particular firm.

There is always risk in the purchasing of securities for profit. The methods presented here are not represented as being absolutely foolproof or entirely "safe," nor can there be any iron-clad guarantee of profit from following them. This approach to stock and commodities speculation is offered as a reasoned and practical guide to enhance as much as possible an individual's chance of success in the market.

Editor's Note
(1993 Edition)

This is a special edition of Ted Warren's brilliant work originally published in 1966. That first—and only—printing never reached the public, Mr. Warren claimed, because "the manipulators" bought it up and kept it out of public circulation.

Although it has taken 27 years for this classic manual to become widely available, the method it teaches is universal and timeless.

May this guide be your next step on the road to financial success.

— Ken Roberts

For further information regarding Ted Warren and his other works and ideas please contact:

The Ted Warren Corporation
128 SW "I" Street
Grants Pass, OR 97526
(541) 955-2779

Editor's Note
(1998 Edition)

A number of corrections, minor wording changes, and edits have been made throughout this edition.

Preface
(1998 Edition)

I don't take anything at face value. And I never suggest that other people do anything that I haven't first tried (and succeeded at) myself. Ted Warren's principles—the principles presented in this book—work. I know that from my own personal experience with both stocks and commodities.

They also worked for Ted Warren—a self-made millionaire who, starting with next to nothing, turned a skill at reading lines on a chart into several fortunes. Recently, before creating a stock course based on his principles, I put Ted's predictive ability to the test. I think you'll be interested in what I discovered.

For many years, Mr. Warren published his stock recommendations in the monthly TED WARREN INVESTOLATOR NEWSLETTER. One of the last issues, which appeared in November 1982, listed a number of stocks that he felt were about to take off. How well would an "investolator" following Ted's theories to the letter back in 1982 have done with his recommendations? This was what I set out to discover. I began by tracking down each of the 42 stocks he recommended. I used each stock's price as reported in the November 1982 Newsletter as the entry price. I then identified the date on which I believe Ted would have exited each market, based on clear sell signals that Mr. Warren used from the charts. Using a conservative estimate, I was able to identify this point for 39 of the 42 stocks. The remaining three stocks merged with other companies before a sell signal was given. For those stocks I used the closing price on the last day of trading. Finally, I calculated the profit Ted would have made on each of the 42 trades based on these buy and sell prices. Remarkably, every single stock rose in value, and the average *annualized* yield was 124%. (Compare that to the 15% yield most people consider "outstanding" for a mutual fund.)

Yes, Ted knew what he was doing. And fortunately for those with the vision to appreciate their value, he passed along his secrets in this extraordinary book. Take it from someone who knows from experience: You would be wise to learn its lessons well.

Happy Trading!

Ken Roberts

Table of Contents

Introduction   xv

PART ONE

How to be an investolator   3

How to buy in the lower price ranges   10

Consolidations: stocks preparing for a rise   29

Head and shoulders bottoms: Stocks building technical strength   47

Stocks that resist general market breaks   54

False support levels: Encouraging action that hides trouble ahead   68

Trend lines: Your buy and sell signals   74

Selling short   92

Why you should consider buying on margin   96

Volume: The important messages behind the figures   106

Stock splits   115

The Dow Jones trends   120

| Where you can obtain long range charts | 131 |
| Making the market make money for you | 136 |

PART TWO

Fundamentalists vs. chartists	151
Earnings and future prospects vs. stock action	164
Advisory services: A spider's web of conflicting claims and confusion	172
Two big advisory services: My predictions and theirs	188
The pro's and "con's" of investment courses	201
Why you can distrust trust funds	204
Advice from books?	209
The abuses of floor trading	216
My experiences while helping others to market success	227
Sample charts and comments	240
Fifty predictions from me to you	255

PART THREE

Poverty to wealth: My experiences in futures	269
What you should know about trading futures	288
Sample charts and comments	294

| Index of stock charts | 303 |
| Index of commodity charts | 305 |

Introduction

The purpose of this book is to pass on to you the knowledge of the stock market that I have acquired over a third of a century. This knowledge did not come easily to one with a sixth grade education. I was originally a common laborer, yet I was able to retire in late 1940.

I will teach you in simple language (the only kind I know) a reasonably safe method of buying securities and sound reasons for expecting a 200% or more rise. This method is, in my opinion, the only practical method—the key to stock market success.

I will teach you to think in a manner that most people never heard of—a method based on knowledge of market manipulation and the psychology of the public. By the use of readily available long range stock charts you will learn how the public reacts to various types of controlled price actions. These actions, like history, repeat themselves over and over; they may be relied upon and used with confidence.

In order to understand the technical condition or phase that a stock is in, you must learn to believe that every stock is under the guidance of "sponsors" who will manipulate its price movements in a way that will influence the unstable, emotional public into buying during the tops, and selling out at a loss. Who else but the public buys these stocks by the millions of shares in the top range?

Perfection in this field cannot be attained, there will always be some risk, but I will teach you how to buy securities when they are a bargain, and to hold with patience for the inevitable rise. To be successful in the market you must adhere to your original common sense concept of buying low and selling high. You must learn to recognize your own gullibility when it tends to overwhelm you and to cultivate patience, your best asset if you have it.

I will teach you the many pitfalls of the market. When you know how to avoid these, your success is partly assured.

There is, to my knowledge, no safer way of determining when to buy securities than following my instructions as outlined in this book. If you have been a long time "fundamentalist" you may find it very difficult to abandon your way of thinking and get aboard my train of thought. You need not be a "genius" nor have a "flair" to make money in the stock market, nor do you need a large amount of capital.

I will warn you of the hazards of short term speculating, but will teach you how to make long range profitable predictions. With patience and unemotional common sense you will discover that you have a road map to success in the stock market.

It has been said that you must know a great deal about the company in which you are about to invest. You may learn a great deal, but will this knowledge indicate with any degree of certainty what direction the price of its shares will move? Will this knowledge forewarn you that its stock is too high, may have become technically weak, and is subject to panic selling within a matter of only weeks? Of course not.

The fallacy of knowing a "great deal" about a company lies in the fact that this knowledge may be too little and too late. You may be years behind what the directors know. Also, a method of accounting may have been chosen that can exaggerate or hide the true picture until too late.

I will teach you that it is better to buy a second rate stock when it is unpopular and unwanted—by the public that is, and seemingly unable to rise, than it is to buy the bluest of the blue chips after they have soared.

I will teach you that "insiders" *can* control the price action of a stock and the emotional public more easily than they control the earnings of a company.

I will teach you how easy it is to avoid being a "high-level investor."

I will tell some very sound reasons for opening a margin account, instead of paying for your stock in full.

I will teach you to stand on your own feet in forming your opinion on the future course of a stock, instead of relying on the average broker or an advisory service. They are too unreliable. Some of the latter at times I suspect are merely touters.

I will teach you to ignore grandiose reports on the future prospects of a company. Too often they are also written by expert touters.

I hope you will forgive me if I am repetitious at times. But isn't repetition a proven method of teaching? Practicing a physical act, whether in work or sport, is necessary to be proficient. Surely repetition is just as important in mental training.

I wrote this introduction in October, 1965 while being checked through the Mayo Clinic at Rochester, Minn., previous to a minor operation. While minor, it did require a special skill which was developed at the Mayo Clinic.

The Mayo Bros. perhaps had little better background than many other M.D.'s have. But they must have had the drive and sincerity of purpose to put out the extra effort to help their fellow man.

In my own study of the stock market I had the drive to put out that extra effort, and I acquired an understanding that far exceeded my early imagination. It is now my sincere desire to pass on to you the benefit of this knowledge so that you may acquire some of the extra comforts in life.

While one may benefit from the knowledge and skill at the Mayo Clinic directly on the operating table, it is up to *you* to put out the effort to learn how to benefit from my thirty-five years of experience in the stock market.

There is nothing more difficult than success in the stock market, yet this success is attempted by so many who are so unqualified. But if you can read a road map, you can read my instructions and share in the benefits of our capitalistic system, under which has developed the highest standard of living ever known to man.

PART ONE

How To Be
An Investolator

DOING WHAT COMES NATURALLY. It is a strange fact that when the majority of people think pertaining to their stocks in a way that comes naturally, it is usually wrong.

If a person knows a stock has been lying quietly and low for a long time it is natural for him to question the reason that it stays there so long, even though it may be paying a high rate of return. He is suspicious that there are some detrimental facts about which he is not aware. So he passes up a bargain.

If a person does buy a stock reasonably low, but it drags along quietly for years, it is natural for him to get discouraged and sell.

If he does hold out for the duration of a long bottom, it is natural for him to feel lucky when he has a small profit and sell. If he is the type that held on past this first stage, it is natural for him to fall into the mistake of thinking it will go higher, no matter how high it goes, especially if he is watching it closely and reading all the rosy reports and opinions on it. Then after it has hit the top and he has failed to sell, it is natural for him to think it will come back up and he will set his selling price too high. If he was lucky enough to have sold a stock in the top range or soon after, the thinking that comes naturally will induce him to buy it too soon on the way down, because it appears low compared to its recent high.

If he is alert and watching for a stock about to have a fast rise, he will naturally buy one that has just shown some activity on the upside and then, soon after he bought it, it reacts, and the more time it spends during this reaction, the more natural it will be for him to think that he made a mistake and he will take a loss. When a stock has had a fast move and heavy buying is taking place it is natural for him to think that the majority must be right, and he will buy. Mob psychology has infected him and he is being led to slaughter with the rest of the lambs. Then it comes naturally for him to be slow about making up his mind that he made a mistake, because he was so positive that he was right. Now wherever he takes a loss it is natural for him to think it is going lower and his losses will not grow larger. And in this case he is usually right. If he made a quick decision to sell at a loss, shortly after buying his stock, it comes naturally for him to think that he made a mistake if he sees a following rally. If he should have the stamina to carry a stock down and into a dragged out bottom he may sell it because he has acquired a hatred for it, a reversal of his emotions from an earlier time when he had a large profit on his stock and he fell in love with it. During panic selling, the thinking that comes naturally is to sell. During weak appearing rallies, such as followed the 1957 and 1962 panic it becomes natural to think the market cannot go up.

When a person failed to take a fair profit at a certain price, it comes natural for him to sell it when it again reaches that price. More often than not this is wrong.

When considering buying stocks it comes naturally to think in terms of fundamentals. For the average person that is a handicap. Forget the fundamentals and pick your purchase from the long range charts where you can see when they are on the bargain counter. If you do not use charts it comes naturally to ask your broker to suggest a good stock. Don't. Ask him to suggest a sound stock that is priced reasonably low instead. And believe it or not, it comes naturally to listen to tips and rumors.

Does all this seem exaggerated? Take my word for it. It is not. I learned it the hard way.

WHAT IS AN "INVESTOLATOR"? In the stock market there are two distinct classes of people, the *speculators* and the *investors*. The percentage of casualties among the speculators is unbelievable. Over a period of time they have little chance. They are very much like those who bet on the horses. They tell about the times when they win, but seldom mention their losses. How often have you heard someone say, "I know a fellow who plays the market, and he does pretty well." It is a safe bet that he only gave an impression that he did "pretty well."

There is some element of luck among investors, the timing of their purchase being the most important. Was the stock high or low when he had the impulse to buy it? The earnings of some very good companies can turn sour; others can come up with some very pleasant surprises. The average investor's luck depends a good deal on the source of his advice. It takes a certain amount of courage in customer relations for a broker to recommend a stock when it happens to be going through a period of low earnings, or is selling at a deflated price.

The first stock I ever bought was Case Threshing Machine (CTM), known today as J. I. Case. As I look back now I realize the underlying influence that caused me to pick this stock. The word "Case" was the first trade name of which I was ever aware, with its impressive eagle sitting on a globe of the world. As a young boy in a farming community in South Dakota I always looked forward to threshing time and the fascinating sight of the huge steam tractor majestically pulling along the even larger grain separator with ease. I even thrilled at the sight of its winding tracks across the stubble fields. I was also influenced by a fact that I already knew, a little more basic, but not much; someone had told me that the stock market was "very low." I wish someone had told me that it was going lower, much lower. I found that CTM was selling below $120 a share, nearly $400 below its 1929 high of $509.

I had saved money while working in logging camps out of Seattle and was now working on the assembly line in the old Ford Motor assembly plant near Lake Union. I had worked hard for my money and I had a vague idea that I wanted my money to work for me. Until now it was very vague. At least I had the beginner's common sense of thinking in terms of buying low, and had not become infected by the speculative fever which can become compulsive. The symptoms of this too-common ailment show up in their worst form when they cause the trader to buy during a fast rising market.

I opened an account of $1,000 to begin with, and bought 35 shares of Case Threshing Machine at $118. I cannot recall why I didn't go the limit and buy more, as buying on a 15% margin was common then. It was not long before CTM touched 133 where I had a profit of over $500 — on paper that is.

I had always known my limitations as a relatively uneducated farm boy and laborer, and was happy on this job as a production worker. About all I knew was hard work. I never squandered money, having learned the value of a dollar the hard way. At this time I was getting the high wages of $7.20 a day, very high for what could be termed as common labor. About this time I began to take a dim view of the labor approach to making a living. My job was turning sour, or was it I who was turning sour on my job? I had just discovered an easy way of making a living; or so I thought. I was hooked. I had become a speculator. But it did not occur to me in such words. I thought in terms of buying low and selling high. Very good logic. I had a lot of experience behind me before I realized that logic is a factor that is displaced by emotion when you become a stock market speculator. A speculator's emotions are influenced by watching the tape, and the daily quotations. He does his trading by that, and he thinks it is good reasoning at the time. Fear, hope, wishful thinking, rumors and mob psychology are also emotional influences that guide him. Also, I had not yet learned that the casualties among speculators are very close to 100%.

Anyway I had my sights set much higher for CTM and did not sell. There was no reason for my unsophisticated mentality to even guess we were headed for a depression. I had never heard of such a thing.

A few weeks later I sold out CTM with a loss. In my first venture in the jungle of Wall Street I frightened quickly. Now the pattern was set.

A person should never buy a stock just because he likes it, or because he happens to have the money available at the time. Before making a purchase he should check its current price in comparison to its price range in the past. The simple way to do this is through the use of a chart. The very best of stocks have price drops or *reactions,* often as much as 50% or more after a large rise. It is far better to wait until you can buy more shares at a lower price with a higher rate of return. Patient waiting can be worth a lot even though you miss two or three years of dividends. There are many reasons why an investor may need the money and so decides to sell. The difference between taking a loss or profit is whether or not the purchase was made while the stock was in its high or low range.

The investor enters the market with patience and slowly collects his dividends. The speculator enters the market with impatience and eventually loses. I would like to see the speculator forget his great ambition to get rich quickly. His imagination goes to extremes, but he thinks it is sound reasoning. His emotions also run to extremes as the market fluctuates. As these fluctuations control his emotions, most of his trades are based on them. When he takes a loss it is because he is afraid of a further drop in price. When his losses are piling up on him, he is probably losing sleep. When he sells, it is a form of relief. Now his losses can not grow larger. Often, he sells near or at the bottom of a dip and when the price rallies he condemns himself for making that mistake. He has lost his position. So invariably he buys back on a rally. If it is only a rally, he soon finds himself again with a loss and again will sell. This can happen several times in succession and can happen in both a rising market and a falling one. This is called being *whipsawed*.

When a speculator has purchased a stock, especially if he has held his stock for some time, he is apt to take a profit too soon. It is impossible to beat the market taking small profits. On the other hand if he has held his position beyond the small profit stage there is a strong tendency to set his sights too high. His usual reaction then, is to think his stock is going higher. He sees extremely heavy volume and boiling action or violent fluctuations on his stock. Instead of associating this with other top actions that he has seen in the past it only blinds him into over-confidence and wishful thinking. Nearly all that he hears and reads about the stock is favorable. Any comment that is unfavorable he ignores. The compelling influence of the market action can be powerful. He is beyond any logical reasoning; even his best friends can't influence him, if they disagreed with him, but usually they have been caught up with the same line of thinking.

If he was lucky enough to have sold out near the top, he may start "feeling for the bottom" far too soon. When the stock has dropped 25% it may appear cheap to him, and of course he can be right at times, but "feeling for the bottom" is an expensive way of finding a bargain. Usually when a stock has reached a bottom range the speculator has become too pessimistic to buy it. Also, if he does buy when it reaches the bottom range, he is buying too soon. There is likely to be a long wait ahead before another rise. Discouraged, the speculator will invariably sell, usually at a loss. By now you should be aware of the fact that I am against speculating. You are right. If the speculator can take the advice that I am able to pass on he can save himself from these speculative headaches and financial losses. Making money in the stock market can be done as a speculator if you know how, but gaining this knowledge is probably one of the most difficult skills to acquire.

The average investor who sits tight through it all is less affected by the hot and cold waves of emotions that the speculator goes through. He leads a more serene life. His mind is not diverted so much and can give better attention to his regular occupation and family. I have seen the time when I was reluctant to go on an extended camping trip with friends when I expected critical action in cotton futures. The investor, as you see, can even enjoy his vacations better.

My purpose here is to get the speculator to simmer down and acquire the patience of an investor. The speculator is inclined to think of the investor as a "fuddyduddy," too slow a thinker to be in his fast company, but the pitfalls are too numerous for the speculator to cope with and he can rarely escape them all. Now, if he will admit defeat and join ranks with the investor I will try and be a little more on the positive side. I will admit that I have sounded quite negative on the subject of speculation, and will also admit that it has been purely intentional.

I would like to coin a word that will describe a new category of shareholder. This person would be classed between the investor and speculator. The best idea that I can come up with is a combination of the two present classifications. I would term a person in this third classification an *investolator*. An investolator would buy like an investor should — and sell like a speculator hopes to. He should have the patience of the investor but with his sights set for a large, long term capital gain.[1]

It should not be very difficult for the investor to change to this new investolator category, but once he has — and gets used to the change of pace, he must be very careful not to be attracted into the role of a speculator. The speculator will find it more difficult to be converted and stay converted. He has been used to making many decisions. He will be inclined to watch the market too closely and may fall back into his old habits. If this happens, he had better join "Speculators Anonymous"!

---

[1] Capital Gain is a term used by the U.S. Government to describe for income tax purposes a profit gained from the sale of stocks, real estate properties, et cetera (other than by a dealer), which have been held for 18 months or more, and that is taxable at a lower rate than regular income.

To be an investolator, you must also be chart conscious. I do not mean that you should keep daily charts and try to interpret each juggle and curlycue. It almost takes intuition to understand why certain actions discourage a person into selling and other actions incite him into buying. Few can begin to interpret these short term actions.

The charts you will study in this book are "long range" charts. Many of these charts show curves that, from a money making point of view, are as attractive as some of the curves pictured in *Playboy*. While the curves you see in *Playboy* are formed by nature, the curves you see in these charts are formed by the machinations of the stock market, and the emotions of the public.

You will be fascinated by these pictures because you will see at a glance whether stocks are in their high or low price range. You will really become price conscious. Stocks that you may have been thinking of buying because they were "good" stocks you may easily recognize are too high.

If you will study these pictures with an open mind, I will show why the "sleepers" are the bargains, and that they are the ones that have the largest potential profits.

How To Buy In The Lower Price Ranges

THE LONG RANGE STOCK CHART. If a novice in the stock market was to leaf through this book he might be dismayed by the number of charts. He might jump to the erroneous conclusion that these charts are something too technical and complicated for him to understand. Actually they are simple and clearly show the past price range of a stock over a period of many years. Also they show the formation of patterns of action over a given time which indicate that the price change to follow will be similar to earlier patterns.

Curtiss Wright Corporation (CW)

You will see in the chart of Curtiss Wright Corp. (CW) that each charted line shows the price range of the stock for a month. The first row of figures below the years indicates the earnings for each year. At times there is a "−" ahead of the figure, indicating a deficit for that year.

At the upper right corner is the ticker tape symbol (CW) used by brokers. At times there will also be an "amex" which indicates that the stock is traded on the American Exchange; otherwise it is traded on the New York Exchange.

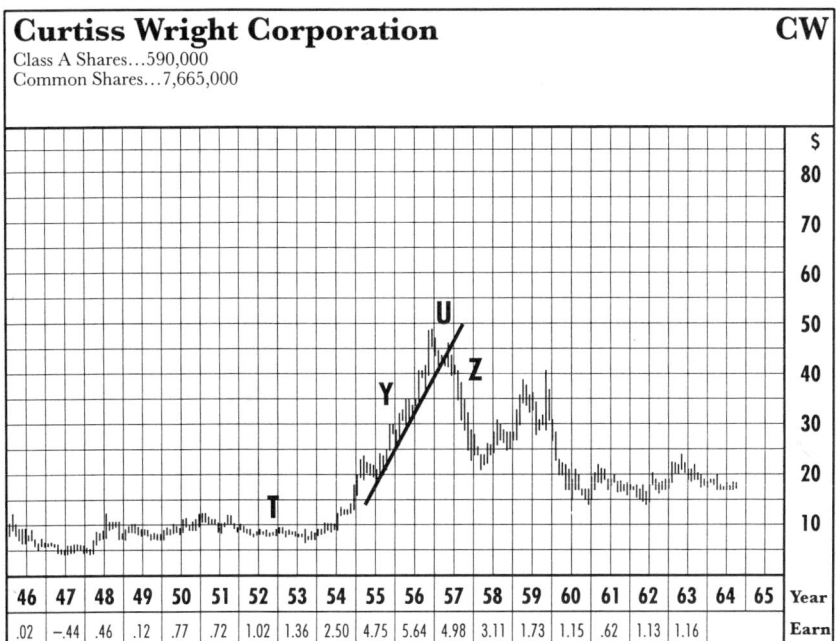

THE FOUR PHASES OF THE STOCK PRICE CYCLE. The stock prices of every company fluctuate through a cycle consisting of four phases. In the chart of Curtiss Wright you will notice, in order, the *base*, (T); the *rise*, (Y); the *top*, (U); and the following *drop*, (Z). This cycle can be compared to the growth of an apple tree. The quiet, low-level period called the base can be termed the *accumulation* period, similar to the dormant period of the tree during the winter. The rise of CW is called the *markup*, analogous to the period when the sap is flowing in the tree and its growth is well underway. The top range is called *distribution*, resembling the time when the fruits of the tree are harvested and the growth ceases for the season. The inevitable drop in price which follows is known as *markdown*, during which phase the leaves and uncollected fruit of the tree are dropping.

Remember these terms:
base — accumulation
rise — markup
top — distribution
drop — markdown

Notice that Curtiss Wright is beginning a new cycle in the base range.

While the cycles of a year, or steam and gasoline engines are exact, price changes are so variable and inconsistent in time and amount that few have learned that these cycles do exist. By the use of graphic charts, using the monthly price range of a stock, it is often possible to see by certain patterns of price actions over a period of years what phase of its cycle a stock is in, giving you a clue to what its next phase will be. These price cycles do not just happen. They are guided just as surely as you guide your car in traffic.

The two charts of Gimbel Brothers, Inc. (GI) clearly show the tops of one cycle in 1937 (A), the top of the next in 1946 (B), and a third cycle that has not yet ended (C). It may end with a violent boom and bust along with the rest of the market similar to the 1929 debacle when GI topped at 24-1/8 and the low came in 1932 at 3/8.

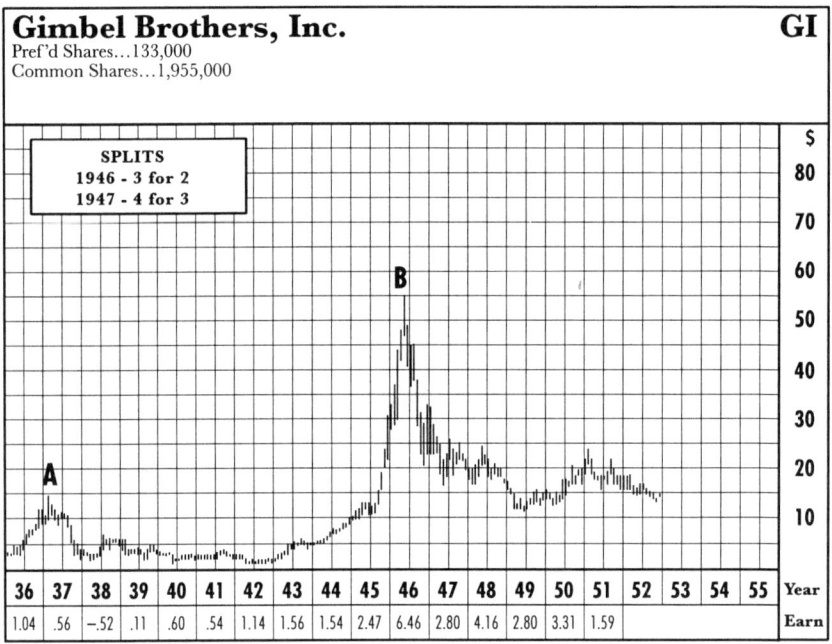

BASES. A base is formed during a period of accumulation. This is when the insiders and others "in the know" are buying the stock at bargain prices. Sound bases are easily seen when the prices of stocks have been extremely quiet in a low range for a period of at least three years.

A stock is never a bargain unless it is in a range where it is changing from weak to strong hands, changing to those who KNOW what they are doing, and

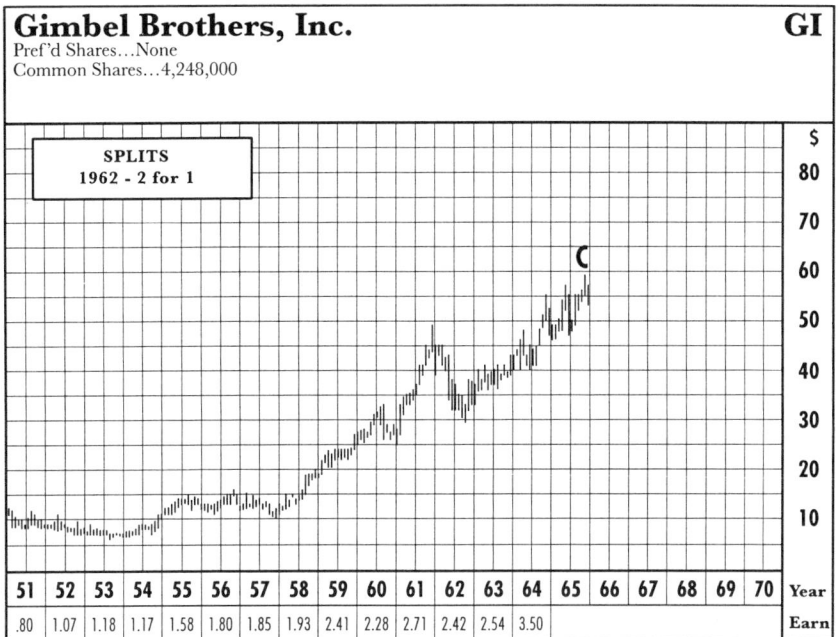

why. It is up to you to determine, with the use of charts, *where* that range is. It may be extremely low, or at times it may be near the all time highs of a stock, far above the previous bottom range. In this chapter I will explain only the bases in the low range.

In order to determine what phase of its cycle a stock is in, you must understand the public sentiment concerning it in the past and at the present. If you can determine this, you will know what it will do in the future, given time. To understand this you must realize that the price action of a stock is what influences the public to be bullish or bearish.[1]

Anyone building a temporary shack in the woods would not put much effort into building a really sound foundation under it. But if a person was to observe a very deep excavation in which an extremely solid foundation was being poured, he would know that a high rise building was being built. An expert architect could even make a fair estimate as to how many stories it would be. Anyone would know that this extensive foundation was not being built for a mere shack. But few people realize that a quiet base of many years is the foundation for a high rise, not for a mere rally. You, as an investolator, can learn to develop fair judgment in making an estimate of how much of a rise

---

[1] These are terms commonly used to describe a person's optimistic (bullish) attitude toward the market, or his pessimistic (bearish) attitude.

can be expected from the various types of bottom actions, and the time involved during these actions. These foundations are not made with concrete and steel; their built-in strength is derived from inducing the public to sell out. The higher percentage that are sold out, the sounder the base. It's as simple as that.

There can never be a sound base, unless a large percentage of the public has for one reason or another sold out. This is accomplished by price actions that are discouraging to them. Many different illustrations of this may be seen throughout this book.

Sunshine Biscuits, Inc. and Parmelee Transportation Co. completed typical bases in 1942. Similar patterns of actions will be just as sound in the future as they were thirty years ago. It is up to you to watch for them and to recognize them for what they represent. Seldom will a broker or advisor point them out to you.

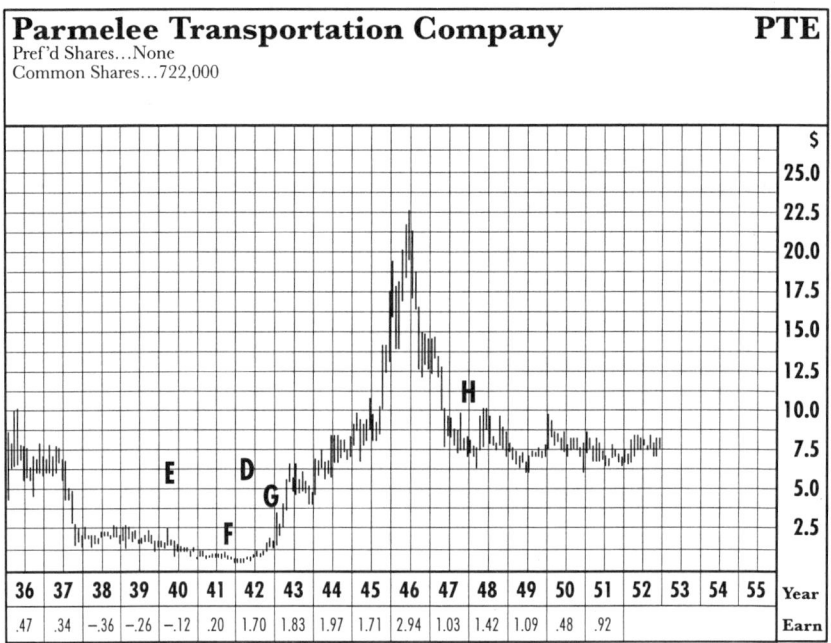

Parmelee Transportation Company (PTE)

This base action was the most common pattern with slight variations ending in 1942 (D) when nearly all stocks were under accumulation. The sponsors of this stock no doubt picked up many shares during 1938-39 when the discouraged public were selling out with heavy losses because the company was operating in the red. (Note the —'s, which indicate deficits during the years 1938-39-40 in the earnings line.)

The pessimistic public sold heavily after the Germans invaded France, Belgium, and the Netherlands in May, 1940 (E). The insiders picked up their best bargains after Pearl Harbor in December, 1941 (F). This final shock caused more weak shareholders to sell out.

The final two years of this five-year accumulation period were distressing to the public. It is not necessary to have a Pearl Harbor, or for the company to be in the red to distress the public. Any extremely quiet action, especially if it is in a downtrend, worries the majority into selling. The perfect signal to buy came at 75 cents when the downtrend was broken in 1942 (G).

The beginning of the next cycle in PTE was in 1947 (H) with a seven-year base.

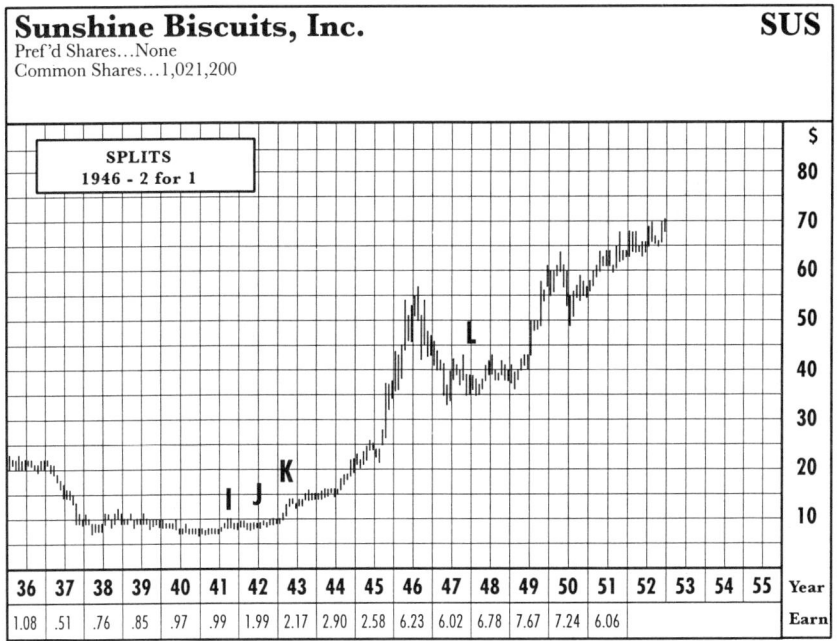

Sunshine Biscuits, Inc. (SUS)

SUS had a perfect five-year accumulation base. It made its low a year before Pearl Harbor. After its small rally in late 1941 (I), it then spent a year quietly acting as if it was too weak to go up (J). This is one of the important highlights of market psychology for you to learn.

When a stock *appears* unable to rise above an apparent "resistance level," this is almost positive proof that it eventually will, because this action induces public selling. The perfect buy signal was at 10 (K) when this resistance level was finally broken.

The more than two-year base in 1947-48 (L) proved to be a good one, but this action was not long enough or the type that you could have complete confidence in.

During these long quiet periods the manipulators are quietly buying while the public are selling their stocks from fear that they will go lower, or in disgust—at a loss. These bases have been forming periodically over the years, but few people recognize them as such. Shouldn't it be obvious that these bases were in a low price range? These quiet actions give an almost positive assurance that they will be followed by a very profitable rise, profitable for those investolators who will sell when they should.

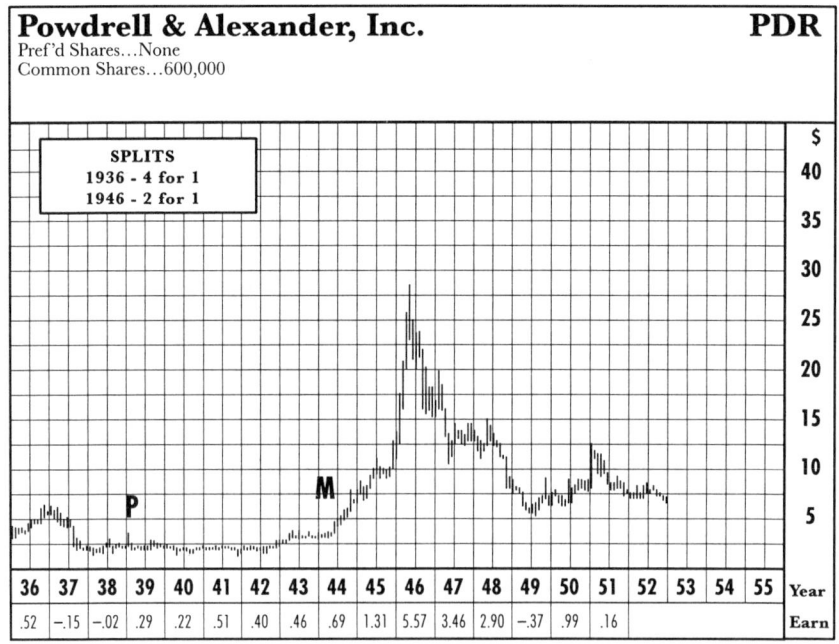

Powdrell & Alexander, Inc. (PDR)

Note that the bases of Powdrell & Alexander, Inc. ending in 1944 and of Parmelee ending in 1954 are almost identical in action and period of time involved. The only notable difference is that the last

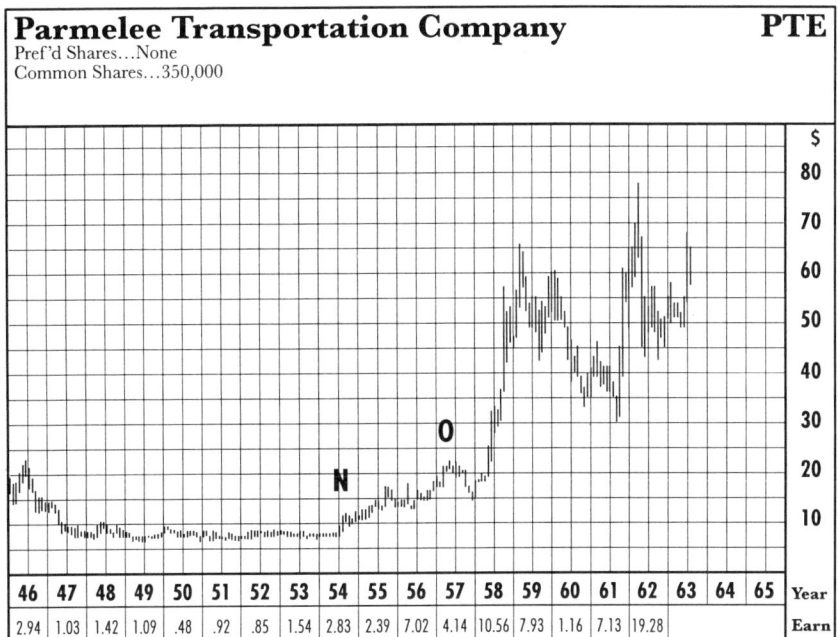

eighteen months (M) of the base of PDR took place slightly above the previous price range, while the last 18 months of PTE remained in the same price range. PDR developed a fourteen-month resistance level that as usual proved to be false. These two charts should convince you that very often stock price actions are only history repeating itself. A base similar to these and others that are pictured as strong bases will be just as sound and reliable fifty years from now in other stocks as they were in the past.

When I refer to a "buy signal," I mean that when the price moves above certain types of past action for a long base, it invariably signals an upward breakaway from that action. Usually, it is the very beginning of a 200% or more rise that will require several years to take place.

As an investolator, on occasion, you should adopt a method of buying often used by speculators, especially if you are out of contact with the latest quotations. For instance, if you had not bought during the base of Parmelee Transportation Co. ending in 1954, as the price rose to 8 (N) you could have placed a "stop-buy" order at 9.[1] This was the buy signal when it rose above the previous highs during 1952.

---

[1] A stop buy is an order that you may enter for a period of up to thirty days, but is removable. When your stated price is reached, your order becomes an "at the market" order and is executed at once. This order may be cancelled or changed at any time.

Another good signal was at 18 (O) in January, 1957. A stop buy at 23 would have caught the fast rise perfectly. As long as there has not been too large a rise, or a distribution action has not taken place, a stop buy can be used with reasonable safety.

The Powdrell & Alexander base had two breakaway signals where stop buys could have been strategically placed, at 2-1/2 (P) and 4 (M). If your money is idle, why wait for these signals? The long period of quietness is signal enough that the rise is to follow. Why wait? If, as often happens, there is a final shakeout, you must ignore it, and hold on with determination.

To be a successful investolator you must learn to recognize what kind of action is discouraging and then form a *contrary opinion*. You must learn to ward off the pessimistic sentiment that is bound to rub off on you. When you have mastered this you will have stepped out of a jungle of uncertainty. Self-confidence will have arrived. Your outlook will be comparable to mine when, as a child after hurting myself for the first time, I failed to cry. This was a big milestone in my life; I felt that I had outgrown a childish weakness. A milestone in your life will be the time when you have learned to immunize yourself against the influence of market actions and are able to think in terms that are opposite to the general public.

The late Mr. Bernard Baruch has been given credit for saying that nobody can tell whether stocks are too high or too low, and that nobody can determine what they are worth. It could be said that a stock is worth what someone is willing to pay for it. At least the buyer could believe this. But most likely the motive for the purchase was the belief that the price would go higher, no matter what its current price. And as so often happens, a seller will sell his stock far below its real value or its value based on its earnings. He does not really have a logical motive for doing so. He is frightened. He can't stand the pressure of holding his stock while visualizing the possibility of it going lower.

Only a blind person could fail to see whether many of the stocks as shown in the long range charts are either too high or too low. Just a comparison between the two extremes should be enough.

It can be said that a stock is never too high to buy if it is going higher or is never too low to sell if it is going lower. Many times a trader will have been correct when buying at a high price or when selling low. But would he have sold at a profit when the opportunity presented itself, or bought back at a lower price after having sold? Surprisingly often, he would have failed to follow through. This course is too risky to follow.

The problem is to decide when a stock is low enough to buy or high enough to sell. At both extremes the stock is under or over priced. By the use of long range charts you will learn to simplify this problem to a degree that most people will not realize has been possible.

The purpose of this chapter is to show how easy it is to determine the difference between a stock which *appears* to be priced low and one that is really low. Most stocks may appear to be low compared with their recent highs long before the real bottom has been reached. To avoid buying when a stock only *appears* low, *never buy during a downtrend*. It is as simple as that. Your guess could be right. But far too often you would be wrong.

As an investolator the odds will be weighted heavily in your favor if you *buy a stock after a low price range or base of several years, especially, after it has turned extremely quiet for many months*. Study these charts carefully.

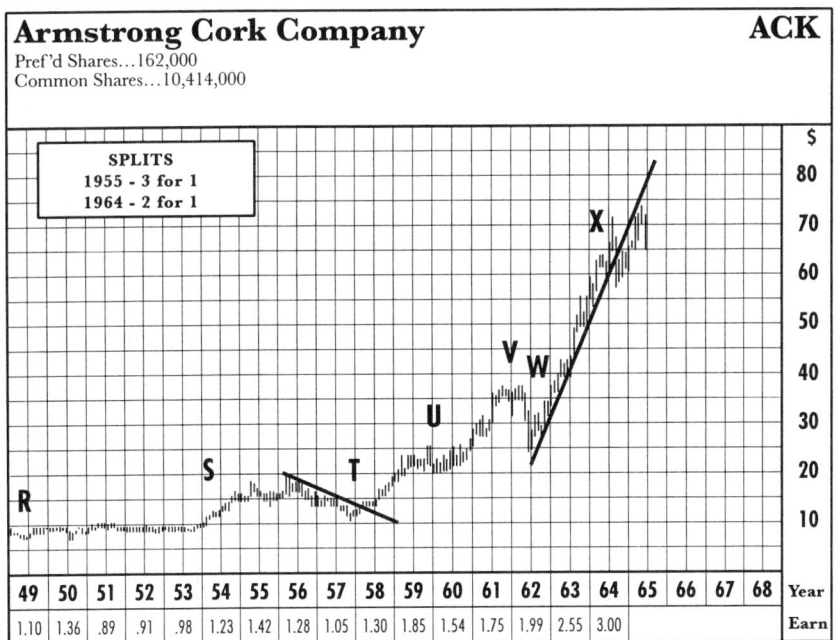

Armstrong Cork Company (ACK)

From the sound base of ACK which extended several years previous to 1949 (R) you should expect at least a 200% profit if you had bought it at $9. Moving above 10 (S), a positive buy signal was given. The next five years only strengthened it technically when more people sold out. You would then be justified in raising your sights another 100% from its base price of 9.

Another buy signal was given at 13 or 14 (T) when the two-year downtrend line was broken in early 1958.

The next consolidation of nineteen months around 22 (U) again strengthened its technical condition. You now would be justified in expecting at least another 50% rise for a total of 350%. ACK now had a total of sixteen years of accumulation and consolidation. The main rise or markup was still ahead.

The next rise to 37 (V) was too slow to be distribution, and was only 12 points above its last consolidation period. Too soon to sell. Then came the sharp break during the panic selloff in 1962 (W). Here is where an investolator must reassure himself that ACK had not yet topped. The action around 35 was too quiet for distribution.

The sell signal came at 60 (X), when the two-year steep uptrend line was broken in September, 1964. You must accept this sell signal. To fail would be folly in most cases. A 550% profit was taken if bought at 9. To expect more would indicate blind greediness. You could have sold at 70 six months later, but there was no reason to expect a secondary top.

To the average market addict my explanations seem contrary to popular opinion. After giving my version of why certain long range actions give the stock technical strength (because the weak holders are selling out), he will invariably ask, "What makes you think the stock will go up?" He looks at quiet bottom actions with suspicion. He looks for a fundamental reason for it being so low. Is the company's business dropping off? Maybe they are going to cut their dividend. When a person is in that frame of mind, it takes a lot of explanation to convince him that the stock is sound and that it is selling at a bargain.

Anaconda Company (The) (A)

It is sometimes difficult to determine when a stock is making bottom, such as seen in the chart of Anaconda. The time element on each dip is too short. Why guess when there are sound bases to be seen? Leave the guessing to the speculators.

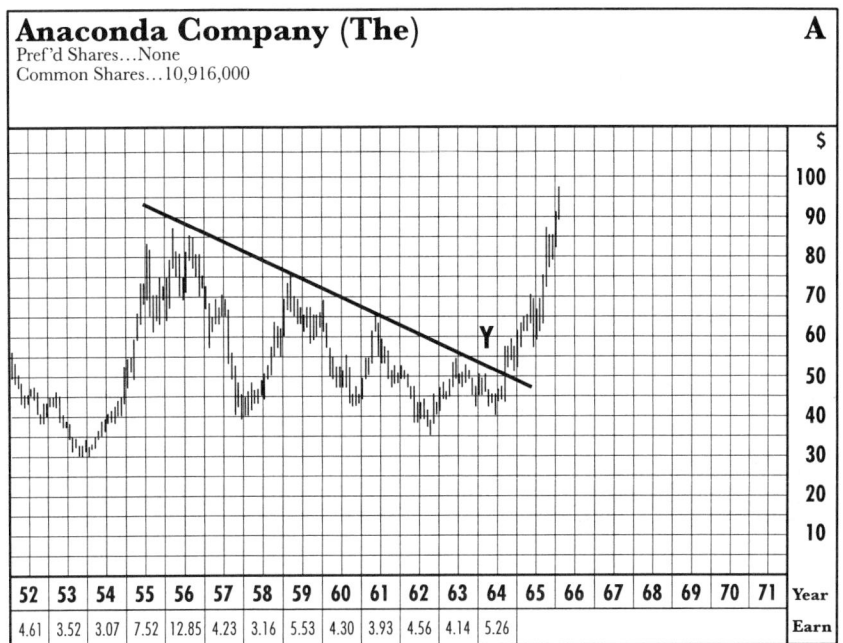

The nine-year downtrend line when broken in September, 1964 (Y) gave the buy signal when the price crossed 50. Long trend lines like this eliminate much guesswork.

I have had you concentrate on *long* bases. Some stocks have had very good rises after a bottom of less than a year. Anaconda Copper for instance. It is not necessary to have a long base, but it helps. Anaconda is very speculative. When copper is low the reasoning is that the earnings are bound to be low also — so the speculators sell their stock. Their selling is concentrated near the bottom. When copper prices are high, the theory is, and rightly so, that the company's earnings will be high also, so again the crowd is wrong. They buy near the top. Continue to concentrate on the long bases for a buying spot. You can see these, and positively. You are only guessing at the others. You will notice that while there are healthy rises that develop from these quickie bases, seldom do they have a rise to the extent that those with the long bases have. Generally then, *it is obvious that the sounder the base, the better chance of a large rise.*

Besides buying low and often avoiding the worry of holding a stock at a loss, here is an example showing the importance of buying low. Suppose you had enough cash to buy 200 shares of stock at $5. In time you were able to sell at 25, a profit of $4,000 or 400%. But suppose you procrastinated until later and bought it at 10. Perhaps the action at 10 appeared more positive than it did at 5. You consider it is still a safe buy at 10 because of its quiet consolidation action. With the same amount of money you now can buy only 100 shares. And selling at 25 you have made only $1500 or 150%. Besides missing out on the $2500 profit, you missed a lot of dividends, providing it paid any.

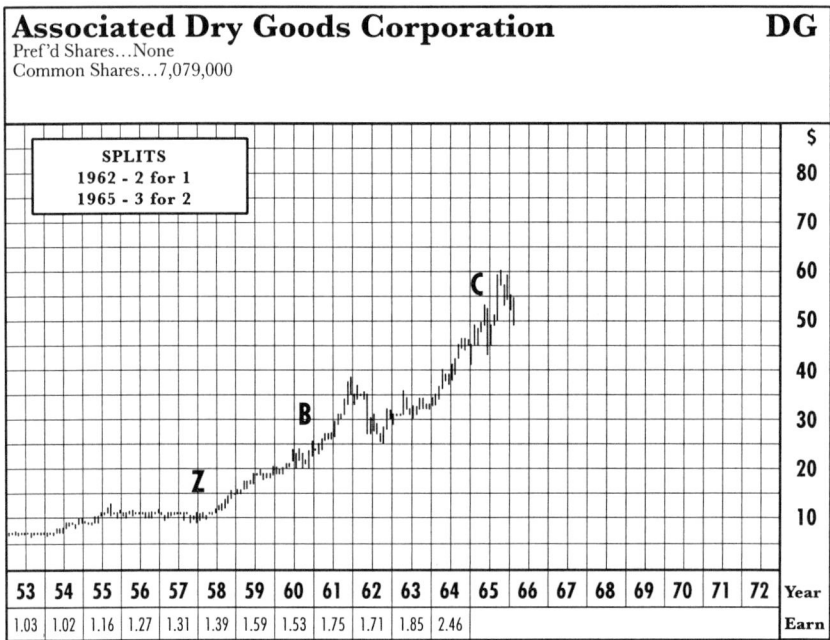

Associated Dry Goods Corporation (DG)

After writing the last paragraph I looked for a chart that could fit this example. Change the buying figures to 10 (Z), and 20 (B) and you will see that Associated Dry Goods fits my word picture perfectly. The sale price is 50 (C). This should impress on you the importance of buying low. But do not get carried away by this attitude and start bidding too low. When you see the right formation, buy *"at the market."* This term is used to explain the situation when the buyer does not want to risk bidding for a stock at a lower price. It may not sell down to his bid price.

Vanadium Corporation (VCA)

The very lack of rallying ability of VCA above the fourteen-month

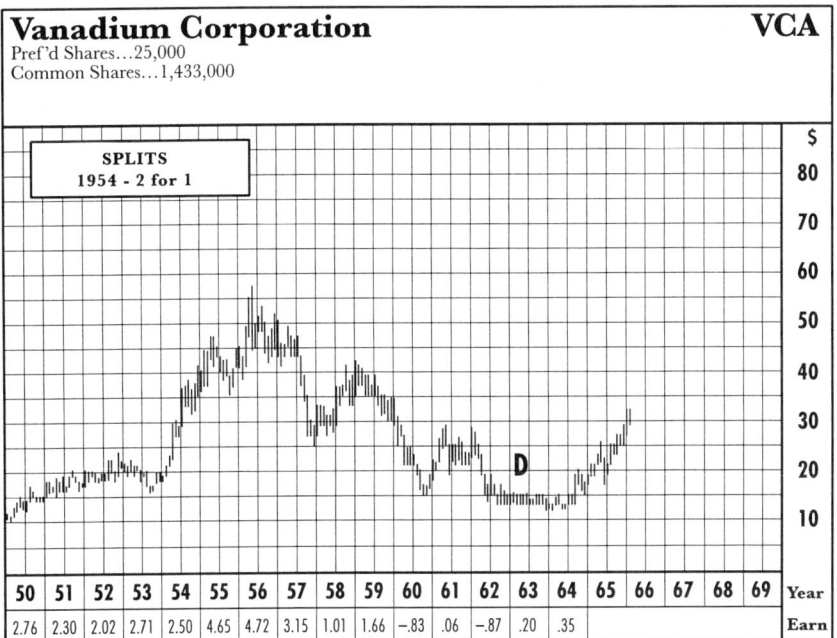

false support level in 1963 (D) is action that is very depressing, and worries the shareholders into taking losses for fear it will go lower. This action does not just happen. It is guided this way for the purpose of appearing weak. Notice the two waves of strength at previous higher levels, which baited the public to buy back after many of them had sold out previously during weakness. This also, did not just happen.

Plenty of stock came out for sale around 14 during this quiet period. When selling slowed, the price was let down merely by withholding purchases. When the price broke the support level, a new wave of selling came out, and more bargains changed from weak to strong hands.

This base began with the 1962 panic selloff and continued while the general market was rising. Notice the difference between this sharp break in 1962 and its continued weakness, proving the stock was in weak hands, while such stocks as Briggs & Stratton, Columbia Broadcasting, Dr. Pepper, General Motors and Greyhound proved to be technically strong, or in strong hands, by recovering quickly. While VCA began its base in 1962, another stock, Evans Products ended its base. This is the advantage of having mixed trends in stocks. There is nearly always a bargain, and by the use of long range charts, they may be seen.

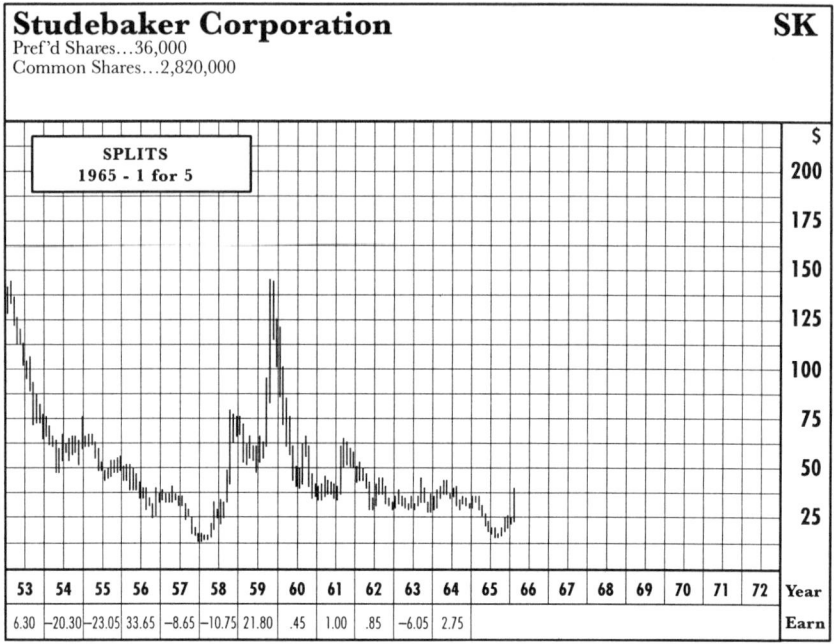

Studebaker Corporation (SK)

The chart of SK remains the same as it did before the 1-for-5 reverse split. The difference is that the price lines have been increased five-fold, and a shareholder who previously owned 100 shares, now owns only 20, but at five times its former value.

When the 1-for-5 reverse split was announced the shareholders were affected bearishly and they sold heavily. The price break was even worse when the new price of 27-5/8 came on the ticker tape. The stock was then under accumulation *below* the false support level at 30. The discouraged public were then taking heavy losses.

Metro-Goldwyn-Mayer, Inc. (MGM)

An investolator must learn to recognize that just because the price of a stock apparently stabilizes after a large drop, it does not necessarily mean that it is under accumulation. This four-year period of MGM (1948-51) was too active (E). Very little time was spent in the lower part of its range. The numerous rallies gave the impression that there was an effort to move it up. The final rally carried above a resistance level giving a false buy signal as it did so. The average chartist would automatically have accepted it as such and been hooked. But an investolator

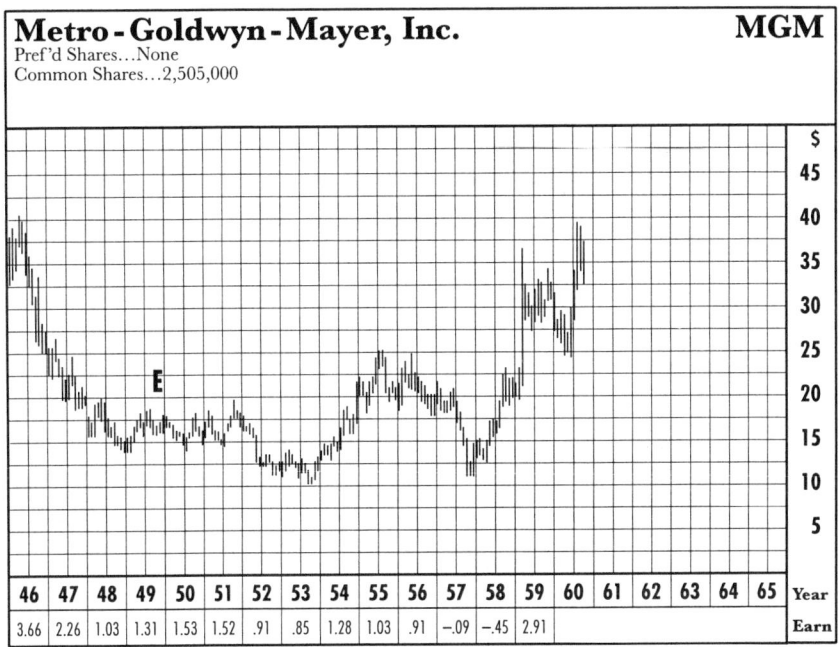

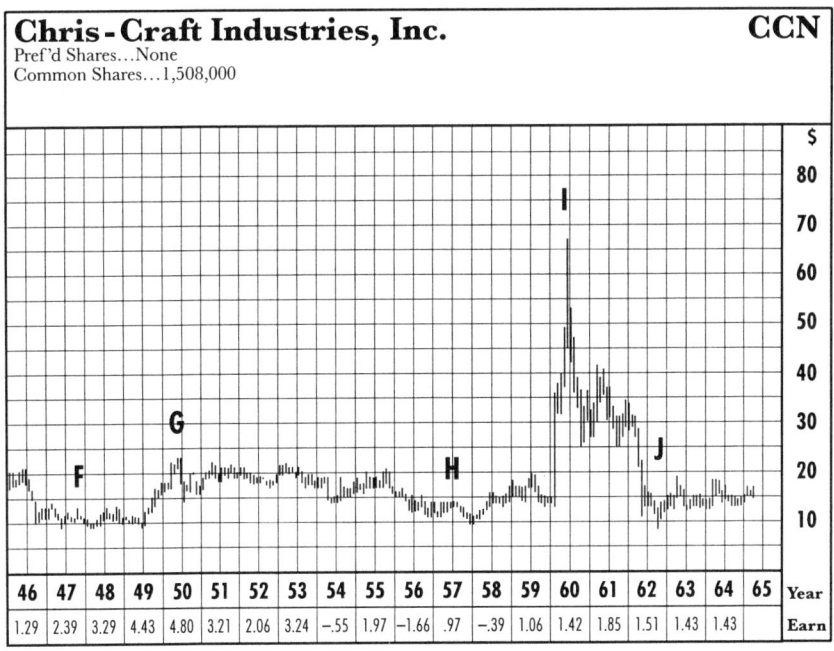

should realize that this action was too buoyant for a base. The weaker the rallies, the more a sound base is indicated. It is then that the public is induced to sell out.

Chris-Craft Industries Inc. (CCN)

The 1947-49 base of CCN appeared to be a reasonably sound base, but apparently was not (F). Did this apparent accumulation action fail to induce the public to sell according to plan? This could be true, because the earnings were far higher than on the previous top. The following rise was only 100% above the base price of 10 (G). Did the sponsors then believe that they could accumulate at a higher level? Certainly that quiet action around 20 all those years did not appear to be distribution. Again perhaps the high earnings were attracting too many investors. With the aid of deficits and passed dividends, the sponsors were able to induce many to sell out over a four-year period at a lower price (H). Now there was an incentive to move it up which they apparently did not have during those years of extremely high earnings ratios. So now they really made hay by inducing the speculators to bid the price up over 350% to 66-1/4 when the earnings for the year were only $1.42 (I). The speculators took an exceptionally bad beating, selling as low as $9.00 two years later (J).

How would you as an investolator have fared on this action? If you had strictly followed my instructions you may have had the courage to buy during the final quietness in early 1949. If not, you should have bought at 14 as it rose above the recent highs. When the squeeze was put on the shareholders by cutting, then passing the dividend during the mid '50's, you should not have allowed this to worry you into selling. Certainly there could not have been heavy distribution which would warrant a larger drop. This example of CCN is about the worst that could happen to an investolator.

On the fast rise you would have to make a quick decision to sell. You should have had the nerve to hold on to at least 40. If you had sold above 50 you took a chance of not selling at all. Hesitating too long in deciding to sell on this kind of a move may leave you holding too long. Note that CCN soared when earnings were only $1.47 but did not rise above 23 when earnings were $4.80.

Chicago Yellow Cab Company, Inc. (CYC)

It is not fair to show only charts of those actions that turned out perfectly, or near perfectly for the investolator. An investolator must be prepared for disappointments while waiting for his stock to get underway. Following the logic of an investolator there may be none that would

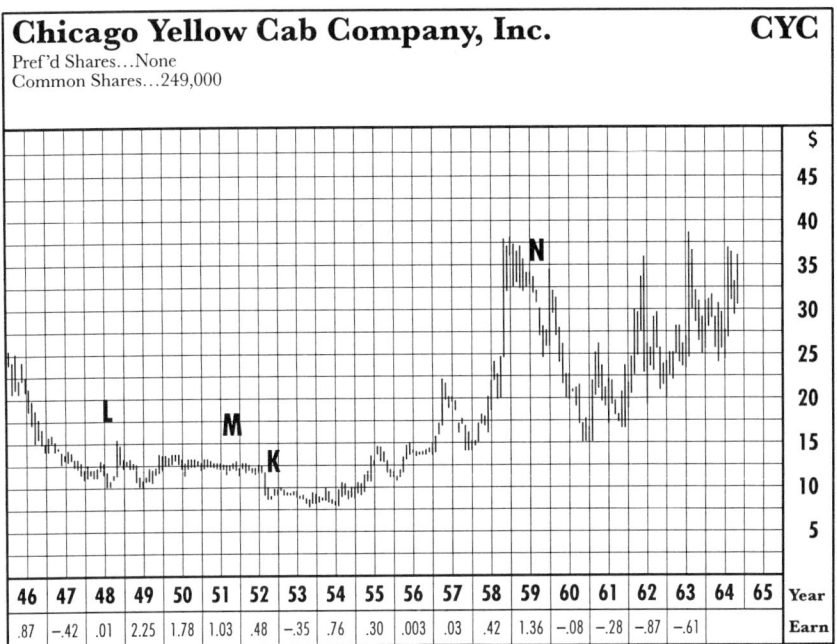

have tricked you worse than CYC, had you bought it during the quiet period in early 1952 (K). The following break would have frightened you. Had you sold at a loss, you would have lost your position at a price where it would have been better to be buying. Had you bought another stock, you may have had to wait even longer for it to get under way to its ultimate top. Moral: an investolator should NEVER sell at a loss.

Let's analyze the CYC action previous to this two-year quiet period. The 1948 action did not appear healthy (L). The sharp rally from 10 to 15 after such a short period of time near the 10 level had the appearance of enticing the sold out public to buy back into the market. In other words, a stock remains risky when it rallies too sharply when there has been no substantial base. When it rallied again from 10, after having spent only a few months in this low level, it had the suspicious appearance of having a false support level, especially at an even figure such as 10, easily noticed by the majority who then became confident buyers. So far not a good picture, not enough quietness in its low range. This was not the action that induces the public to sell out, which is necessary for a bottom action.

The two years of quietness around 12 (M) could easily have been mistaken for the final period of an accumulation base. With the coming of reduced earnings, the price was allowed to really drop into the bargain basement, and selling by the public was no doubt very heavy.

On the following rise you should have sold CYC around 35. If not you should have sold when the false support level at 32 was broken (N). The exciting 13 point rise kept the speculators steamed up and in a buying mood for nine months, with the hopes of seeing another fast rise. It is beyond their concept to understand why the rise should come to a dead stop. They do not understand that the smart money smoothly and obligingly filled the demand as usual after a fast rise while the public's sights for selling was set from one to twenty dollars higher.

From charts like this, you will realize that it is not necessarily high earnings that stimulate buying at high prices; it is the high price that stimulates.

Why should CYC rise to 38 when earnings were low, while it could not rise above 13-1/2 in 1949-50 with high earnings? Because there was not enough stock in strong hands in 1950 to warrant a large move. By the end of 1956 this condition had ended. The accumulation period was now complete. It was now only a matter of good manipulation as this chart of CYC demonstrates. When you realize that the manipulators have patience, you must learn to be patient with them.

Also you must be convinced by studying these charts, that the speculators lead a tempestuous life. That is not for you.

Backed by the logical use of long range charts you will develop the strength of mind to buy when you should and to sell only with large profits. If nothing else you should be able to keep yourself out of serious trouble.

Consolidations:
Stocks Preparing for a Rise

There is no better proof that a stock will go up, than when it acts as if it can't. Consolidation action of a stock means just that: It is consolidating its gain in price for a further rise. During a period of consolidation the technical strength of a stock is being improved. It is action that tends to impress the public that the stock has lost its ability to rise further, often by developing a perfect resistance level that after a time seems impenetrable. This is the way the majority are impressed, and many will then sell out.

In the past are hundreds of consolidation actions of varying periods of time and levels, all above their bases, all proving these resistance levels to be false. This is one of the easiest actions to interpret, and it is then a simple matter to form a contrary opinion.

Schenley Industries, Inc. (SH)

SH, after completing a perfect base in 1941 at the $3 level (O), had three shorter than usual consolidations on the way up. This rise produced a possible profit of 2500%. If the average, unsophisticated person had held this stock that long, he would have missed the top, because he would have expected even more. Following the rules of an investolator you may have voluntarily sold on the fast rise to 29. Following another rule, selling when an uptrend line was broken, you would not have.

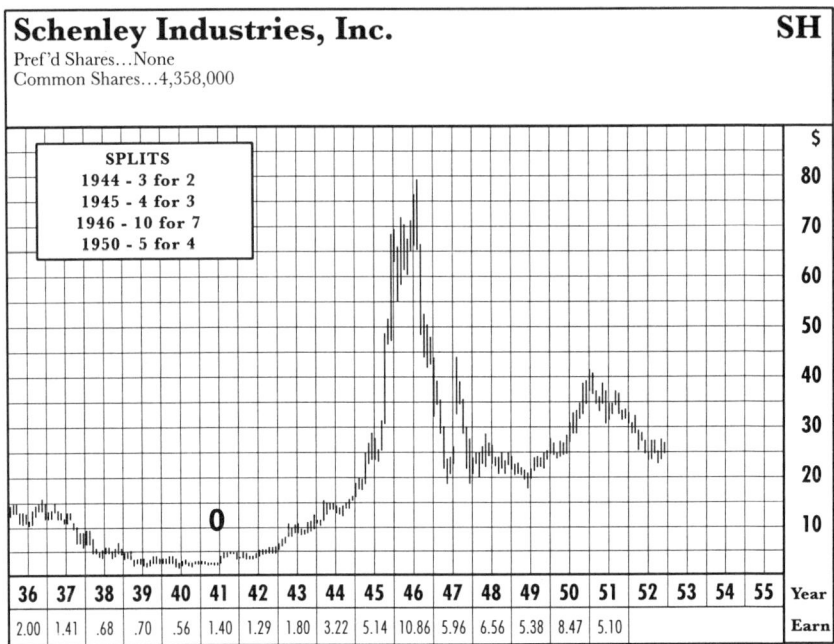

The two prerequisites were fulfilled: the fast rise, and the more than 200% minimum profit to be expected from a sound base. If you held beyond that you would have been lucky. An investolator should never have lost his head and carried his stock too long on this one.

A consolidation of one to three years, only moderately above the base price, gives the investor an ideal opportunity to buy before its completion. Timing of a purchase can be perfect when a stock breaks out on the upside, an almost positive indication that the big rise is again either getting under way, or moving up a step to a new consolidation.

Pfeiffer Brewing Company (PFB)

The extreme quietness of PFB in 1942 ended a perfect base at 2-1/2 (P). After three short consolidations, which appear to be three perfect steps, PFB developed a nearly two-year consolidation that ended with a false start in 1947 (Q) when it broke out on the upside. This false start earns its name because of the fact that the price fell back into its former level. This is a common maneuver to impress the shareholders that the price rise was unable to continue, again inducing more selling.

If you had been waiting for a breakaway buy signal in 1947, it

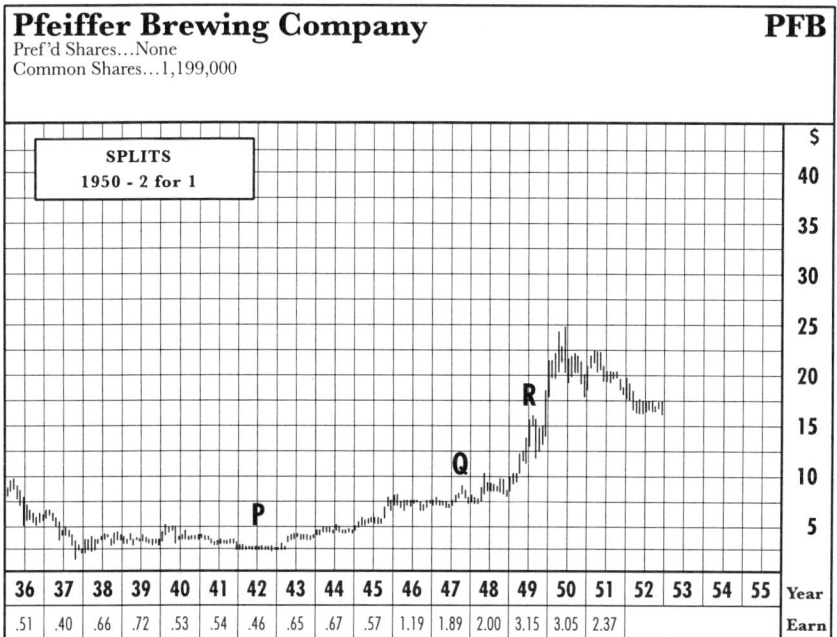

came at 8-1/2 during this false start. As an investolator you should not have been disturbed by this premature purchase, only disappointed. From a study of tops you well know that the recent actions on PFB could not have been distribution, because they have not been active enough, and therefore the important markup must be somewhere ahead. The next and final consolidation ending in March, 1949 (R) had a more irregular pattern than most, but the action indicated that it was only another step during its markup.

You would have been justified in selling at 15 after a 500% markup. If you had been fortunate enough to have held it into the next rise, there should have been no doubt about selling it. Only doubt, at what price? It has since sold below 4.

Associated Dry Goods Corporation (DG)

Associated Dry Goods had two three-year consolidations which gave it great technical strength. This enabled it to be moved up to 57 in 1961 (S), on 5 cents less earnings than in 1946 when the high was only 18-1/2.

These consolidations were nearly perfect, with the latter having a final shakeout, or false move, which can always be expected. At times

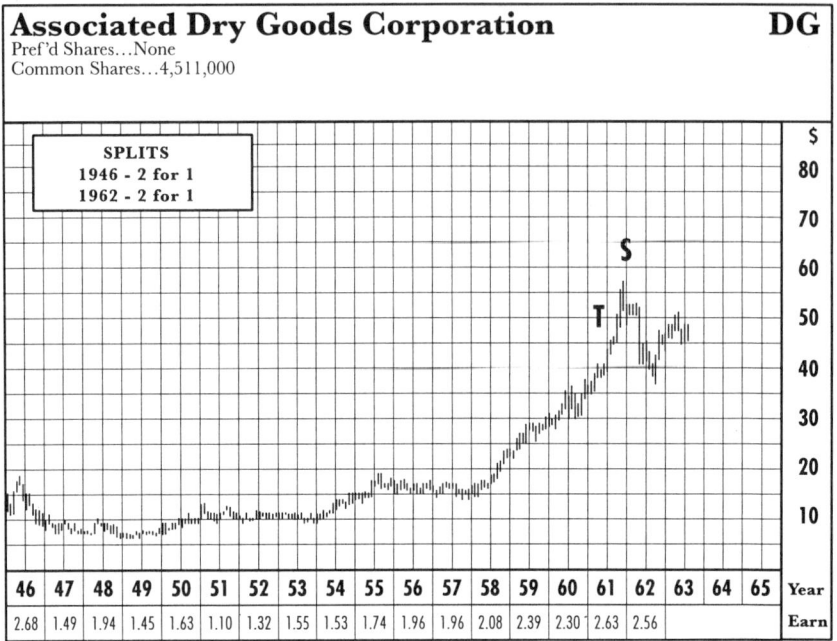

these false moves may be more drastic and of longer duration. Object: a final attempt to frighten shareholders into selling.

The slow, sluggish recovery following this shakeout gives the tape watcher (one who watches price changes closely in the brokers' offices) and others an impression of weakness. This very dullness and weak appearance indicates to an investolator that there is a great buildup of underlying strength. If an investolator should ever become excited, it is when he sees actions of this type.

The cue to sell came after the two-month fast rise in 1961 (T), either to sell "at the market," or when the steeper uptrend line was broken in early 1962 at about 50. Because of the two long consolidations, a higher than normal rise was expected. Neither qualifications for a selling point (amount of rise or speed) had been fulfilled previous to the 40 level.

The long term, high level consolidations of six to ten years are tremendously strong bases for very large rises. Few people, I am sure, recognize them as such. Not even active traders. The active traders cannot visualize that far ahead because they don't check back that far on past actions; nor would they be able to properly interpret this long term action if they did.

From these bases it is safe to buy at new, all-time highs when the price moves out on the upside. But few know this, and the price usually moves up in a sluggish manner, often dropping back below its former resistance level, giving the impression that it lacked sufficient buying power to continue higher.

Remarks such as this can be heard in brokers' offices during a setback of this type: "It tried to go up but couldn't." The Borg-Warner chart shows this type of action. This action does give a weak appearance, but believe me, as profit taking by the public takes place, it is overcoming its "weakness" by the week. Its strength will only be apparent and convincing to the majority at far higher prices.

Naturally, like the bases, the consolidation actions will vary a good deal. Don't expect all consolidation bases to show perfect resistance levels. They are probably the most effective for the purpose for which they are meant and they should be easily seen by an investolator. Study the various consolidations pictured. All are effective in inducing the public to sell out. The more "ragged" ones only make it slightly more difficult for the investolator to pinpoint the timing of its purchase.

Borg-Warner Corporation (BOR)

Borg-Warner has the most convincing *false resistance level* of all time.

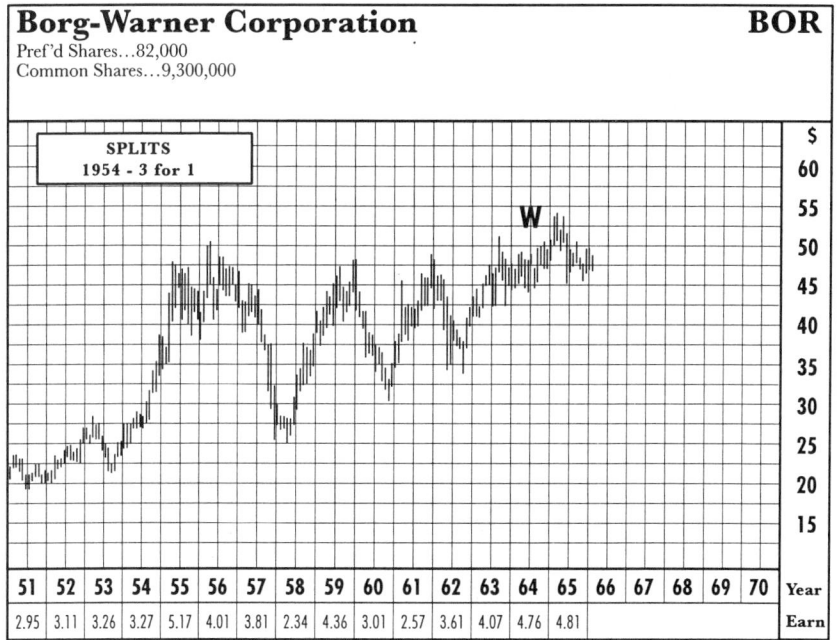

That final quiet period below 50 in 1965 (W) was the tip-off that this formation was about complete. Much stock will have been bought by the smart money. Many people were happily taking a profit at this level, happy in the thought that their decision was so easy to come by. Isn't it common sense to sell a stock that does not act very well, and obviously cannot go up? Isn't selling it the smart thing to do? You can't go broke taking a profit (so it is said).

During 1964 I was recommending Borg-Warner because it had a perfect consolidation with a flat top. I visualized its recent action as a perfect launching pad. I would consider it a waste of time digging into the fundamental aspects of the company in order to confirm my opinion, because it would make no difference to me whether they were rated excellent or poor. I would hold to my positive opinion that this stock was being groomed for a big rise. In March, 1964, as shown in my sealed predictions, I doubted that the price would break out on the upside until 1965. The breakaway came on February 2, 1965. After selling at 54-1/4, it fell back to undergo more discouraging action below 50. I had no way of foretelling this. This action indicates to me that there are still too many weak holders in it. When BOR again sells above 50, following the 1966 general market shakeout, it should really be on its way up.

The basis for this thinking is an understanding of this grooming process, a process during which the stock changes into strong hands.

My March, 1964 predictions on BOR were not merely wild guesses. I try to think in terms of what action at this time will best serve the purpose of the manipulators. A further quiet action in this upper range would induce the public to sell out. Not a difficult deduction. Nearly all bases, high, low, or consolidations end with a quiet period. Patience by the public grows thin in this final quiet period. An investolator who really understands this simple picture, knows that this is prime buying time—a genuine bargain stock, although it is not in a low range.

The terminology to describe these long range resistance levels by the "wise guys" around brokers' offices is that there is "too much stock for sale." This is true, and remains true, until completion of the consolidation period.

During the early tops it is the smart money that represents the oversupply, but when the resistance level has become obvious to the public, then it is their stock that is "overhanging" the market.

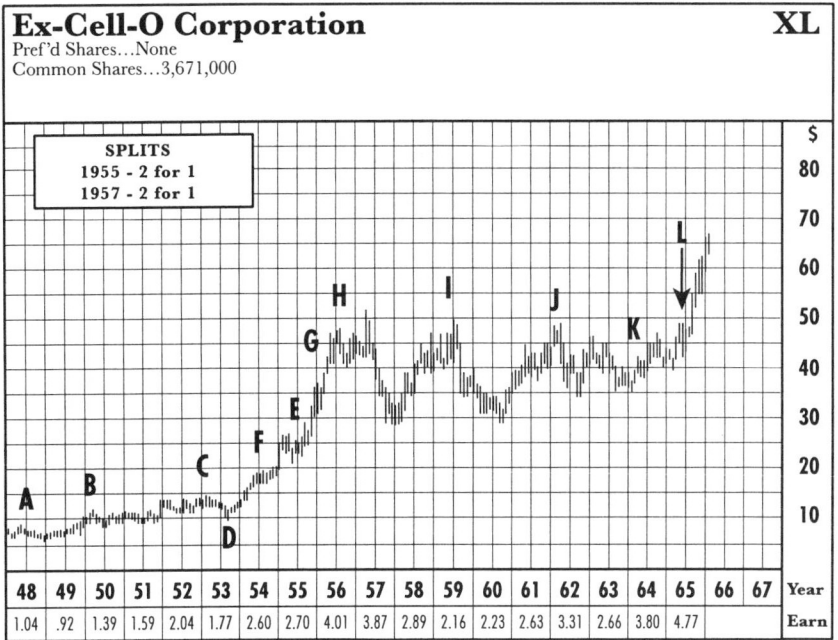

Ex-Cell-O Corporation (XL)

Rising from a sound base (A), XL had a perfect two-year consolidation (B). After a moderate rise, another two-year consolidation (C) ended with a final frightening shakeout (D). An investolator who can recognize that a sound foundation has been built should never allow a shakeout to frighten him into selling. (E) and (F) represent two short periods of consolidations. XL had now entered its markup phase which ended when the uptrend line (G) of over 45 degrees was broken. A sale should have been made below this breakthrough at no less than 42.

If you had not bought XL during its bottom range, your cue to buy was at 9 in October, 1949. During the last half of 1951 it was now obvious that this was consolidation. It should have been bought then or at 12 when the price broke out on the upside. Another signal to buy came in February, 1953 at 14 when it broke through the resistance level. This proved to be a false start and was followed by the shakeout. This shakeout is where most speculators would have sold out. You as an investolator must have the courage to hold on, knowing that the manipulators of this stock have not yet sold out. Your next buy signal came at 15. If you had the confidence acquired from the knowledge of XL's past action you may have bought any time during 1953 and early 1954.

In my opinion based on hindsight, the sponsors probably sold only part of their holdings during tops (H) and (I), and certainly very little at (J). At (K) it was now certain that XL was building up a sound high level consolidation base. It could safely be bought at any time here. The perfect buy signal came at 50, breaking the false resistance level at 49 (L). It will rise to at least 150 and will no doubt be split. XL has since risen to 66-3/4 and has dropped back under the influence of the 1966 shakeout.

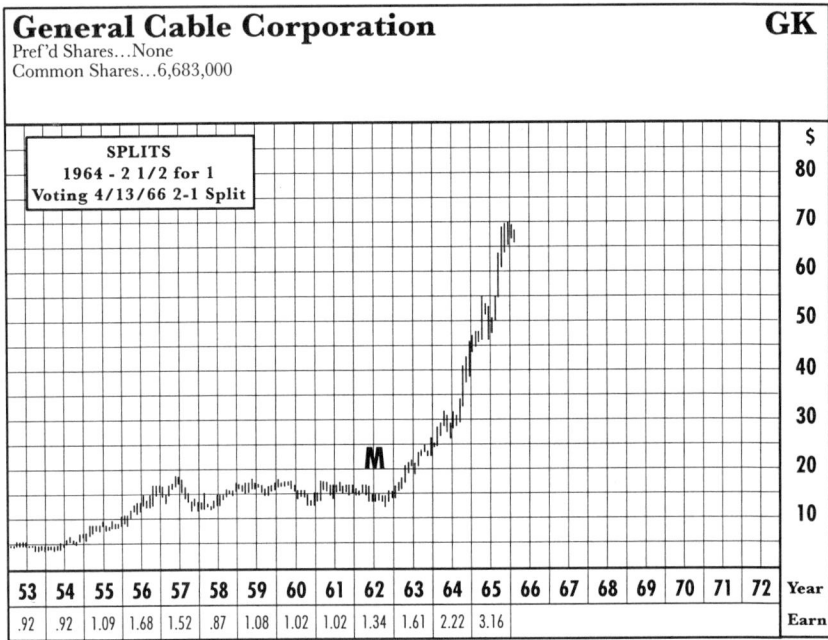

General Cable Corporation (GK)

The rise of GK has more than fulfilled positive predictions that I made in early 1962, based on its high level consolidation.

I gave a lecture on the stock market at the Los Angeles Adventurers Club, of which I am a member. Among other positive predictions, I told them that GK would have a large rise from this base, subject of course to a small setback at any time before doing so. Two of the members bought it. The 1962 panic did cause it to react (M). As this book goes to press, it has sold as high as 75, and it has positively not reached the top. I know this because the volume of daily trading has increased only moderately. The insiders cannot sell out until the public are buying heavily. The speculators have not yet become excited. They have not yet been given the bait. Another split is now being processed.

General Motors Corporation (GM)

GM had an unusual two-level consolidation period of over seven years. The second four-month flat top below 60 (N) really confirmed the bearish opinions at that time around the brokers' offices. The 1962 break proved them right (O). That's what they thought, until the positive bull market signal came when GM proved its technical strength by being one of the first to sell at new high prices following the 1962 panic selloff. This is one of the most positive cues that a substantial rise is about to get underway. It led the way into a new phase of the longest bull market in history.

Crown Zellerbach Corporation (ZB)

ZB had a false start in 1952 from its slightly ascending two-year consolidation (P). A false start becomes more common as more traders learn to buy on these "breakaways." The following downturn was for the purpose of convincing these traders who "jumped the gun" that they were too hasty, and also to induce other nervous shareholders to sell out. This selloff should never concern you as an investolator. You have a sound reason for your confidence. These sound bases and consolidations are not illusions.

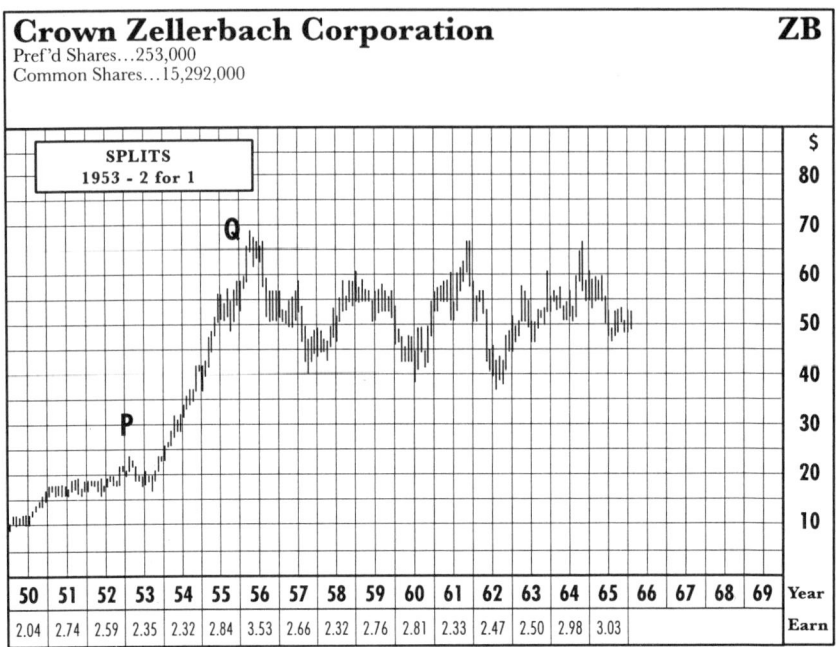

If you had held on to ZB until the perfect uptrend line was broken in 1956 (Q), it would have been a sale at 60. If you had bought at 10 in the base range, you would have had a 500% profit on twice as many shares as you would have had if you bought it at 20 in the consolidation range, from where you would have had only a 200% gain.

Note that because of the 2-for-1 split and the 50% stock dividend the price of 20 in 1952 was 60 and the action would appear more active than the present chart would indicate.

As this book goes to press it appears that ZB is forming a ragged high level consolidation. If there is a year of quiet action in the near future it should be a safe purchase. It should be a bargain even as it rises through the 70 level.

Carrier Corporation (CRR)

The three-year action of CRR around 40 (R) appeared to be perfect consolidation, but it turned out to be a very rare top action. It is doubtful that much more stock had been sold to the public at the end of three years than had been sold to them during the first year on this top. The six-month drop in 1955 actually appeared to be accumulation action. It is difficult to induce the public to buy after the rise has

apparently stalled. The anticipation of higher prices is being lost. Perhaps too many people were quietly buying in anticipation of an air conditioning boom. If so, they were right far too soon.

My version is this. Instead of allowing the price to drift downward in a more common manner, it was held up until the timing was right to coincide with the 1957 panic selloff. Breaking down sharply from that top level brings out very heavy selling. Perhaps more shares were bought on this action than would have been on a drifting downward action. Each manipulator does it to suit his idea of what is best. Note that there was also the 1962 panic selloff during this unusually active base.

Normally an investolator should be buying in the latter part of a three-year consolidation period. But buying should be considered only when the three-year consolidation has taken place after a small rise. The consolidation appearance of CRR took place after a large rise. Buying on a high level consolidation should never be considered until after a minimum of six years, and then only if the last year or more has been quiet action.

Mead Corporation (The) (MEA)

MEA has built a terrific high level base with a nearly perfect resistance level at 50.

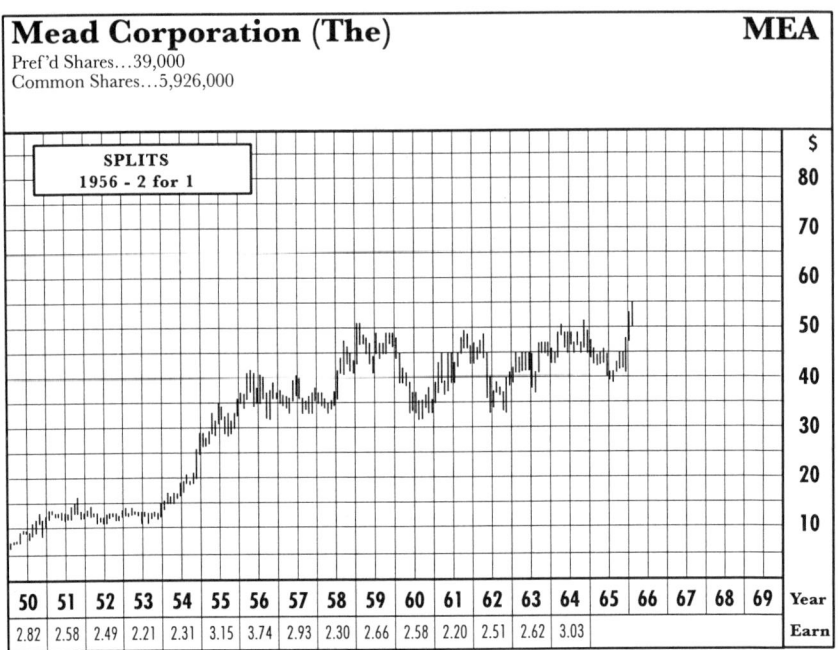

Notice the earnings during the first five years of this consolidation are almost identical to that of the three-year consolidation of 1951-53, below 14. Here is proof that earnings do not necessarily control prices. Just before publication MEA made a false start to 55, then fell back giving my readers a final opportunity to buy it at a bargain.

Firestone Tire & Rubber Company (FIR)

When a chart has a triple top such as FIR shows, it matters little what type of action appears during this period. It must be consolidation for a further rise. No doubt there was some distribution on the first two tops, but the overall picture shows more action indicating accumulation rather than distribution. Why else the triple top false resistance level?

The FIR picture indicates a very sound, high level base. Buy any time "at the market" or when it rises through 52 for the "breakaway." Time only can tell whether it will have a false start. This breakaway will probably occur *after* publication of this book.

TRIANGLES. There are charts where both an uptrend and downtrend line are formed at the same time during a period of years. When these

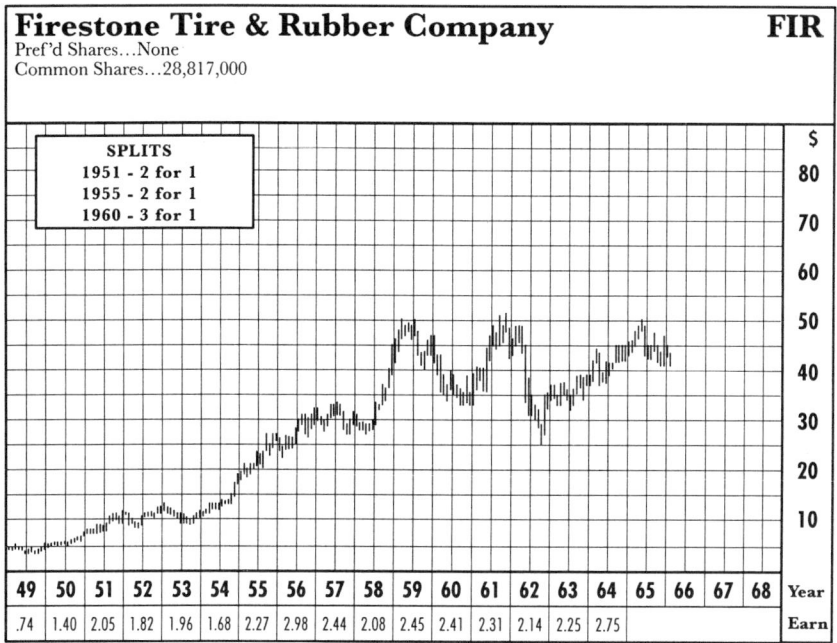

lines meet they have completed a *triangle* or *coil* from which a large rise will begin. In effect they are similar to a high level consolidation. Often the price will break below the lower trend line in the form of a false move, or common shakeout, BEFORE the rise.

During the latter part of the coil the price fluctuations narrow down to a quiet range. The majority of the public just does not buy during this dull type of action, so this cannot be distribution. It must be accumulation. The manipulators are buying back what they sold on the first two tops.

A long term triangle is a positive indication of a large rise to follow, but it may not be as large as that from a quiet base of many years. As usual, as from any base, do not expect the rise to show speed to begin with. That would stimulate buying by the public at the wrong time. At this stage the slow rise and apparent sluggishness is intended to encourage profit taking or selling by those earlier buyers who are now happy to sell out without a loss.

Buying on the completion of a triangle should be an easy decision for an investolator to make, but to succeed, you must have the patience and determination to hold for a large rise. The risk is almost nil.

Woodward Iron Company (WOD)

The price of Woodward Iron in its apparent struggle to move upward from the 1962 panic selling low point, influences the majority to believe that its slow rise is a sign of weakness. This rise was with an extremely light amount of daily trading; some days there was no trading. Perhaps the reasoning of the public subconsciously is, why should they buy or hold this stock when obviously few others want it?

This long term triangle, to an investolator, is a perfect picture that insures a very large profit. From this point on, all it takes is patience and an ability to ward off any bearish influences. A rise of 200% from its apex should be easily reached.

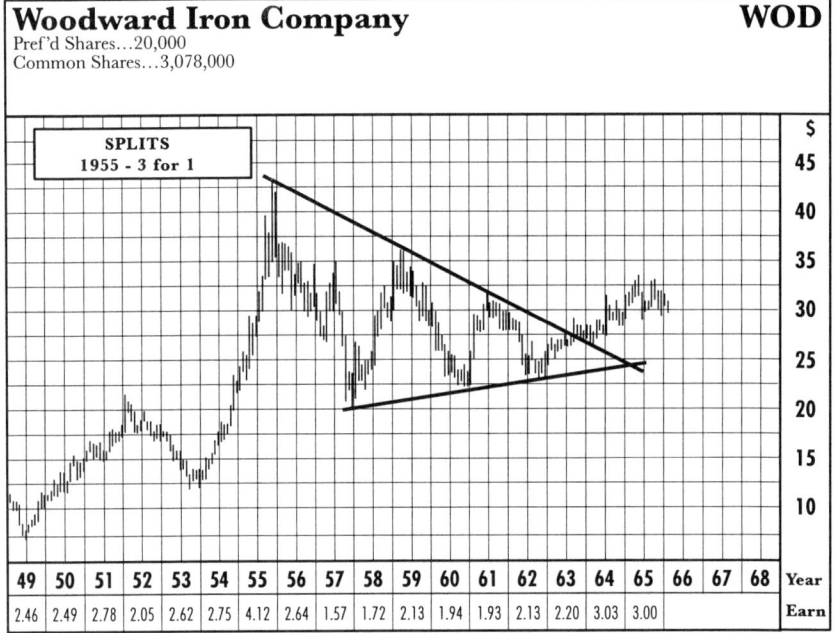

New York Central Railroad Company (CN) and KVP Sutherland Paper Company (KSP)

When you see the triangle of New York Central proving itself, shouldn't it be obvious that the shakeout of KVP Sutherland Paper in 1965-66 is duplicating the final 1962 shakeout of N.Y. Central? The price of KVP should rise far above the old high in 1955.

CONSOLIDATIONS: STOCKS PREPARING FOR A RISE   43

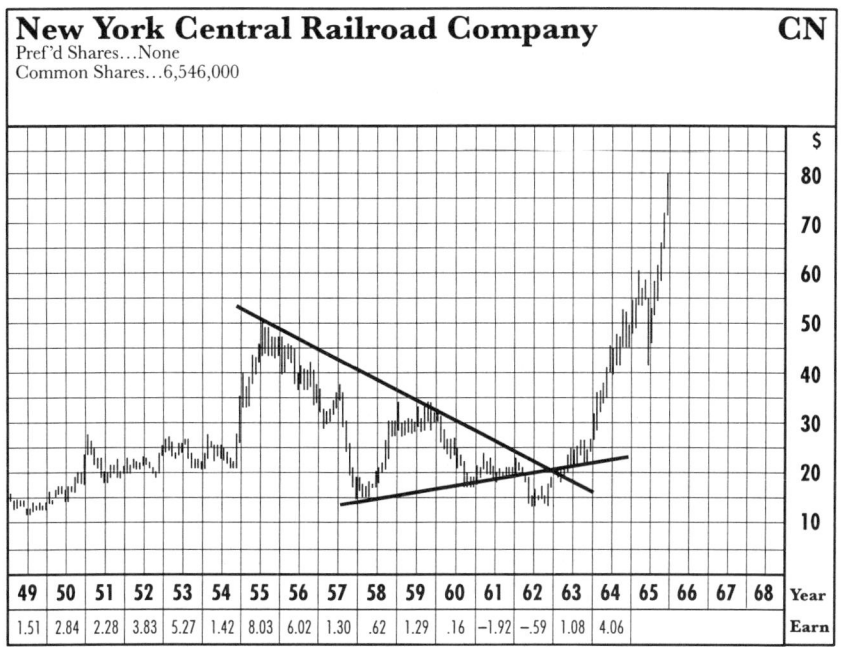

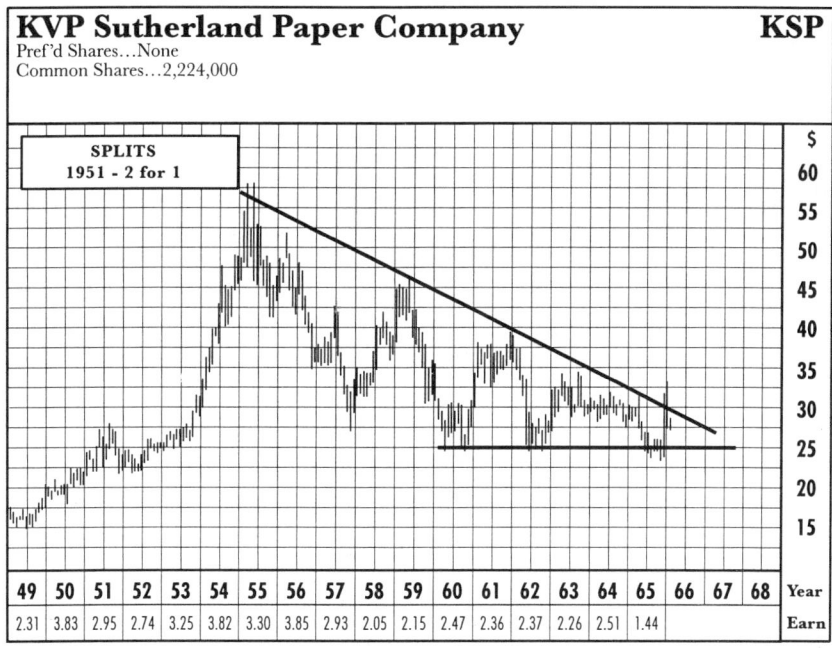

Central Soya Company and Eagle-Picher Company (EGP)

Time will tell if the price rise from the shorter triangles of Central

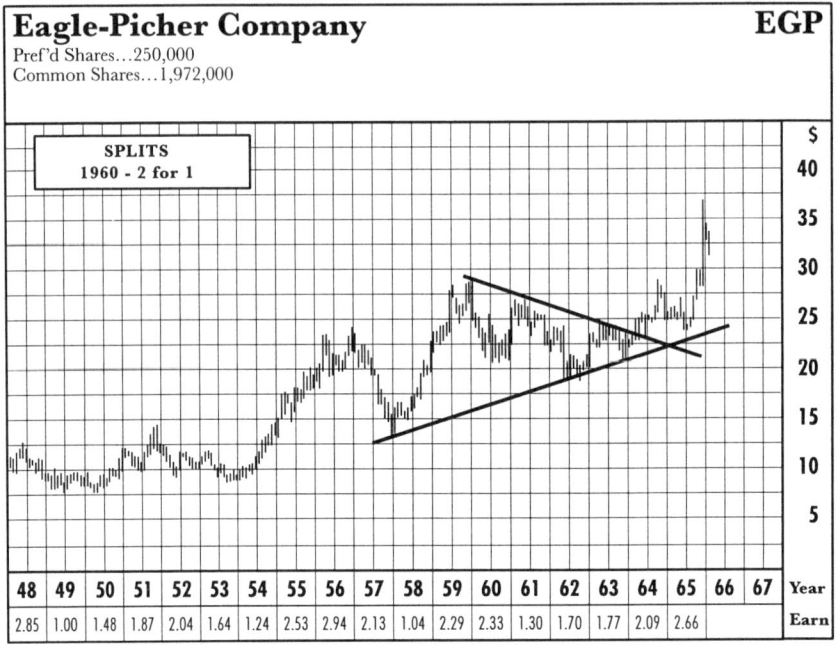

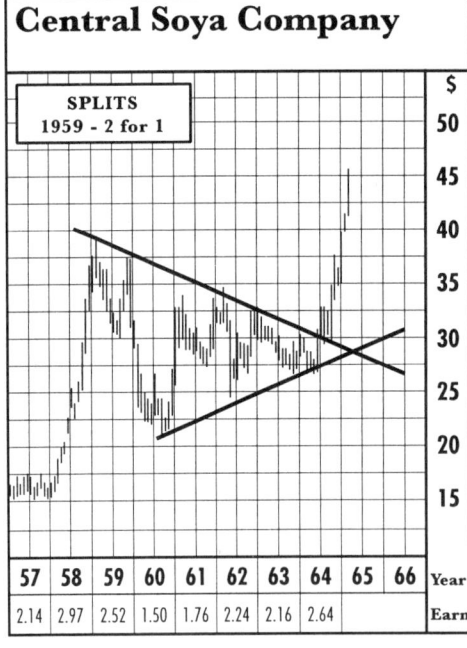

Soya and Eagle-Picher will carry as high percentage-wise as those of long duration.

Canadian Pacific Railway Company (CP)

You may think that the perfect triple bottom of Canadian Pacific Railroad would have built up confidence among its shareholders, but they were too far apart to have this effect. The shareholders on both sides of the border were influenced more by the apparent inability of CP to rise. It is this apparent weakness that actually gives strength to a stock. CP will sell above 100 before the end of our bull market.

Kelsey-Hayes Company (KW)

From a mere glance at the chart of Kelsey-Hayes Co. you may have overlooked the imperfect triangle. This is just as sound as a perfect

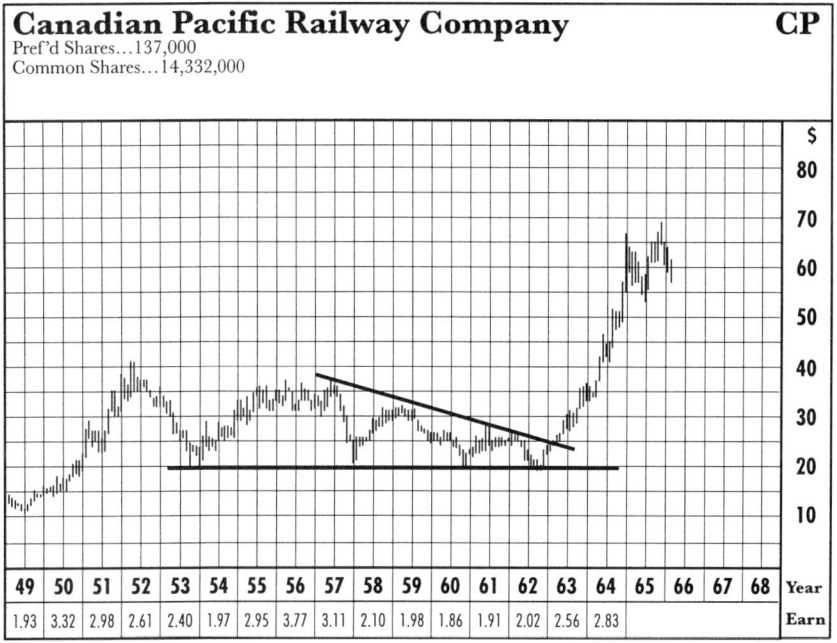

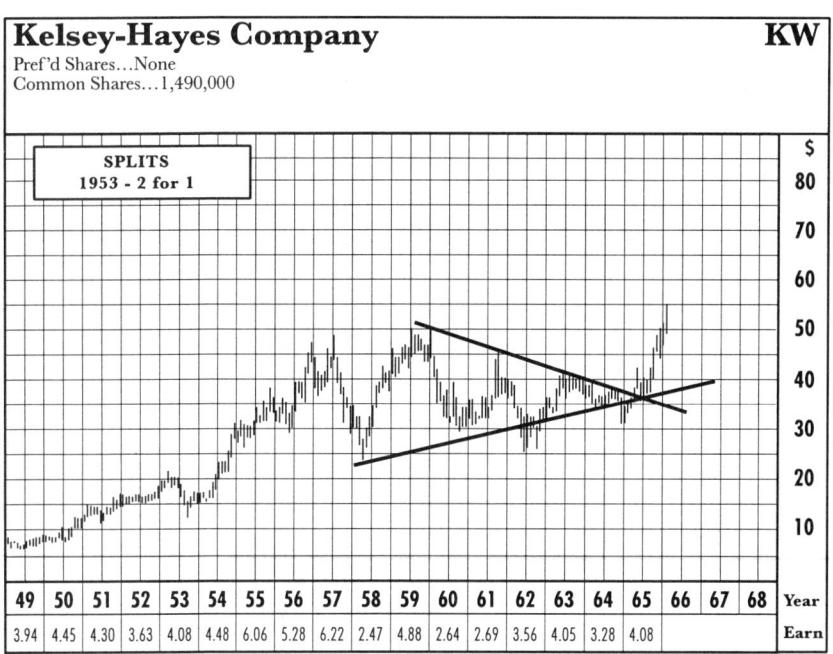

one. That was an unusually sharp final shakeout before the final turn-up. A shakeout accomplishes more than shaking out weak holders. Because of this show of weakness, others are more apt to be willing sellers as the price rallies to higher levels.

It is important not to overlook these triangles as they appear in the action of a stock. Overlooking a triangle is overlooking future profits.

Head and Shoulders Bottoms:
Stocks Building Technical Strength

A head and shoulders bottom is merely an inverted "head and shoulders" top, and is one of the oldest formations known to chartists. In length of time, its formation can vary from a few weeks to over ten years. The speculators who use charts are always alert for these formations. Of course they seldom notice the long term ones which an investolator would be interested in.

The depressing influence of a head and shoulders bottom, which is so necessary during accumulation, lies in the fact that the public are frightened during the first shoulder and the head. During the second shoulder they sell in fear that the price will drop down again. They have lost hope in its ability to go up.

United Shoe Machinery Corporation (USH)

The head and shoulders bottom of USH in 1957-58 is a perfect formation in which the public became very bearish during the first or left shoulder. They were then inclined to panic and sold heavily on the 25% further break. This formed the head. During the right shoulder at approximately the same price level and the same time period, the public who still held through the recent fright are now inclined to sell because the slowing down of this rally leads them to believe that this is

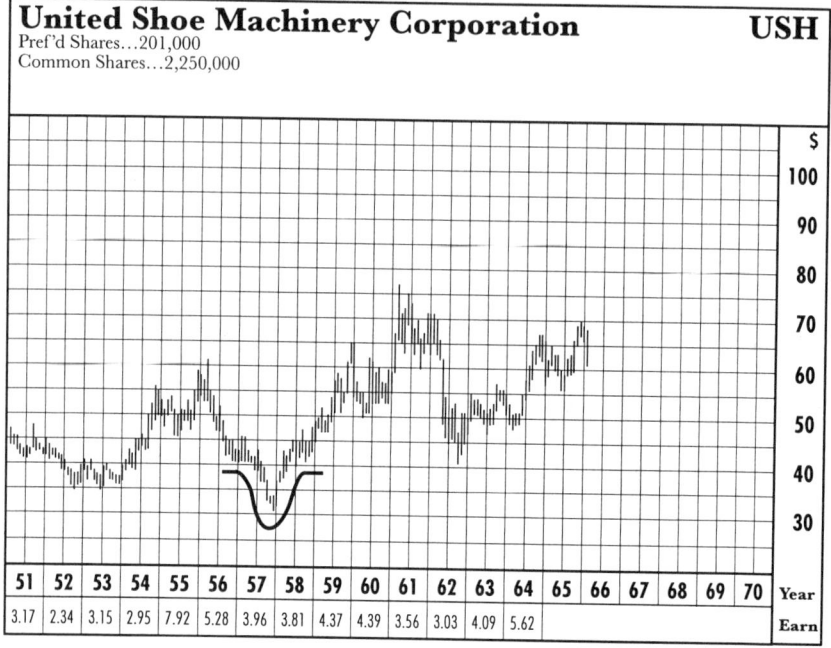

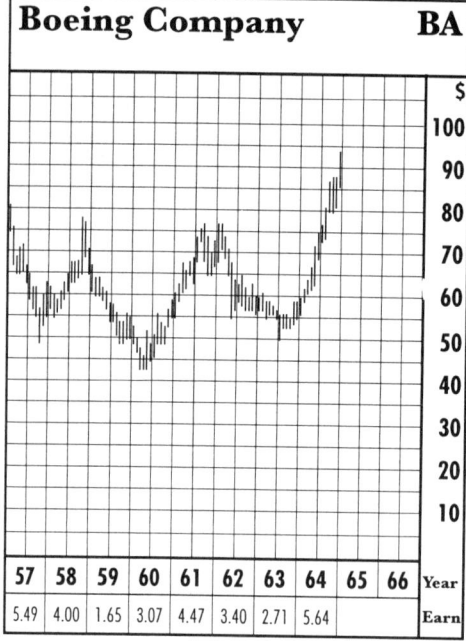

only a rally. They have lost confidence in a further rise. And so another accumulation period was completed.

Head and shoulders bottoms do not have the value of long and quiet bases, probably because there is seldom as much time spent during the period of worrying out the public. You would not be justified in expecting much over a 100% rise from them. Of course if it is in conjunction with another base formation, then you may raise your sights in anticipating a larger rise.

There is practically no way of anticipating a head and shoulders bottom until it is nearly complete, so you certainly would miss buying during the head, its lowest price level. In fact, the completion of its head amounts to the same as the breaking of a downtrend line. Buying at a time when the trend line is fairly steep is not a safe policy. (This is further described in the chapter on stock trends.)

There are not many head and shoulders bottoms to be found in a really low base, probably because there are far better base actions that accomplish the purpose of inducing the public to sell out.

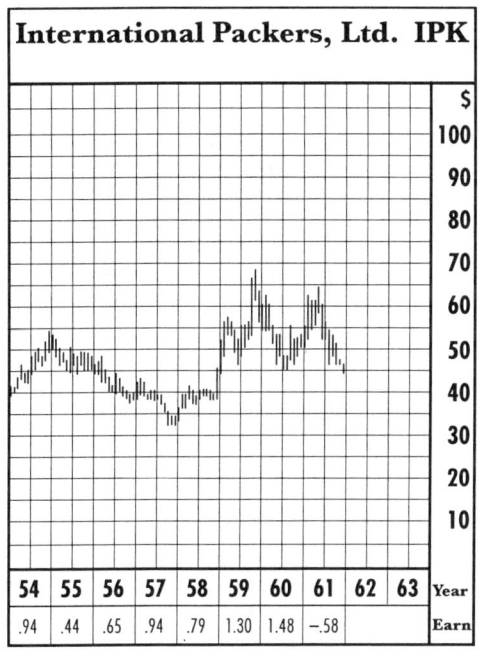

Boeing Company (BA) and International Packers, Ltd. (IPK)

Boeing Co. in 1959-60, and International Packers, Ltd., in 1957-58, developed good head and shoulders bottoms. Both proved to be sound enough for a moderate rise.

A head and shoulders bottom need not be on the true bottom. More often they may be seen far above the original base of a stock. These actually serve the same purpose as consolidations. When one is seen it adds a good deal to the original technical strength of the stock. One may be certain that the stock has not yet been under distribution.

Republic Steel Corporation (RS)

The head and shoulders bottom of Republic Steel in 1953 (S) really added strength to this picture, following so closely to the two-year consolidation. It really was similar to consolidation. It added technical strength to an already strong stock.

Note the action in 1949 (T) which could be called a head and shoulders bottom, but could be better described as a V-bottom. This action also could be said to be the final shakeout of a three-year base. Whatever you prefer to call it, it served its purpose well.

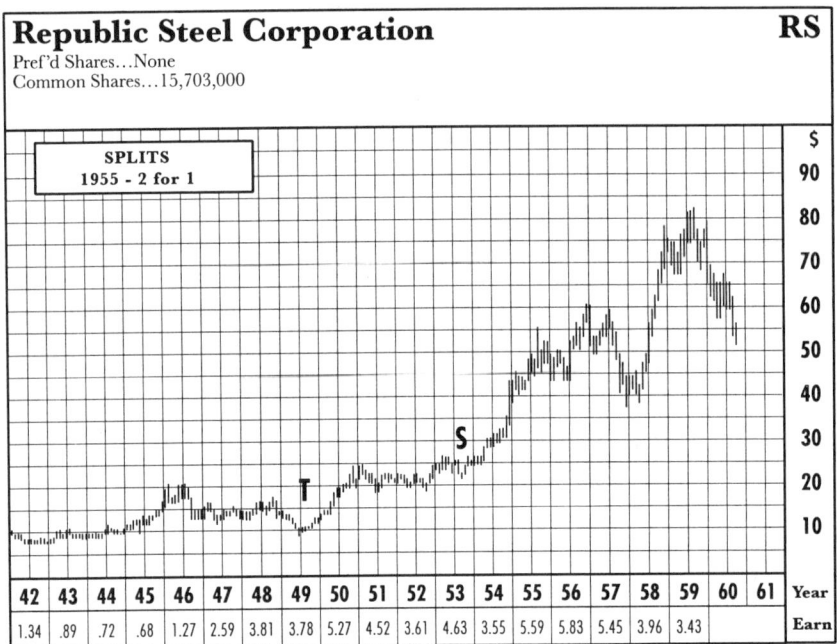

Continental Oil Company (CLL)

From a sound base ending in 1942 and a three-year consolidation which included a head and shoulders bottom, CLL did not move up very much during the 1946 market top (U). Certainly its previous sound action justified a far larger rise. An investolator should not have hesitated buying this on the setback in 1946. CLL was slow in making new highs but it did resist the selloff in late 1946. Another head and shoulders bottom developed in 1948-49 which gave further confidence in its technical strength.

Where you would have sold is debatable. You should not have considered selling below 50. You may have become nervous and sold in November, 1951 when the trend line was slightly broken (V). The fast rise above 60 should have triggered you into selling before the trend was broken.

American Can Company (AC)

The nearly eleven-year head and shoulders bottom formation of AC is probably an all-time record in the matter of time. This picture really shows the value of this type of action when the sponsors believe they have too much company and are determined to get rid of much

HEAD AND SHOULDERS BOTTOMS:
STOCKS BUILDING TECHNICAL STRENGTH

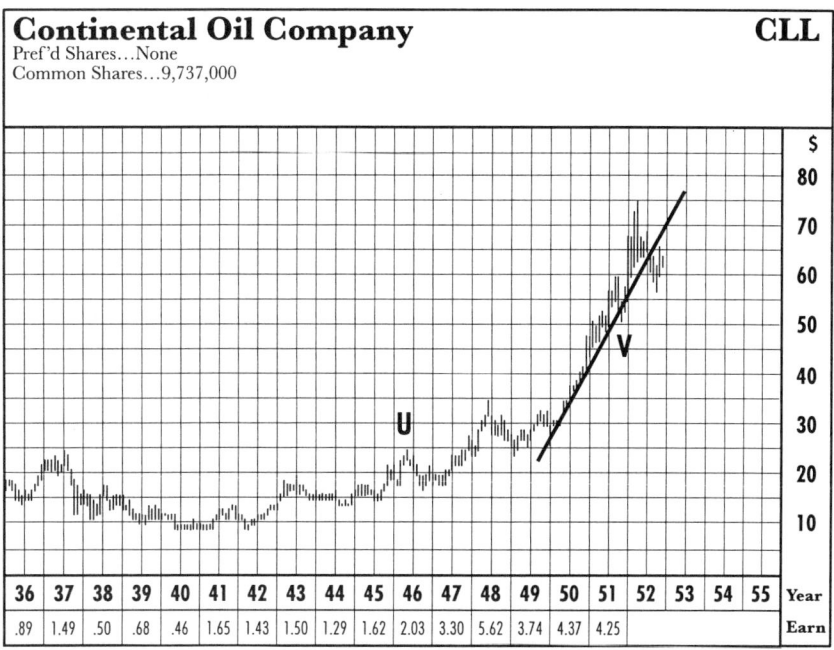

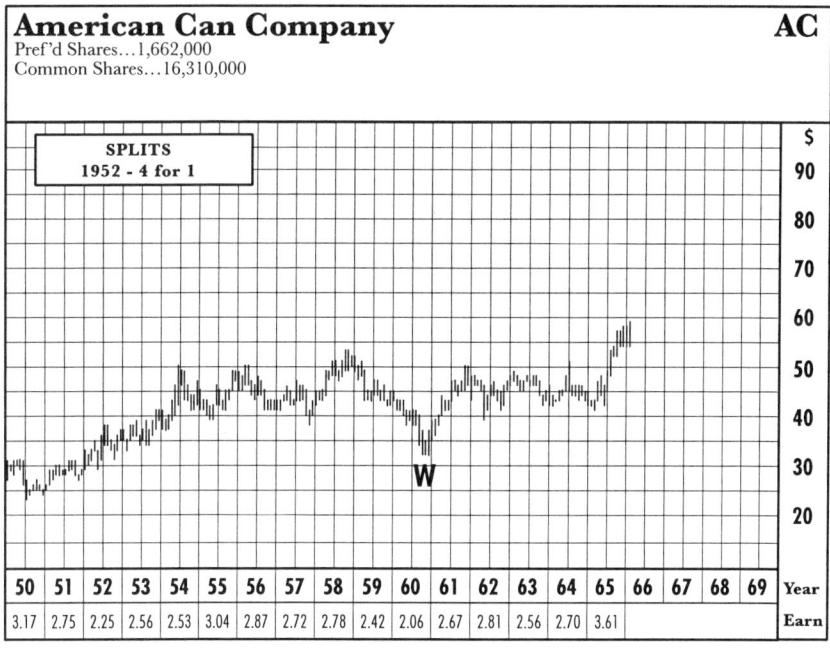

of it. The sharp shakeout of 1960 (W) accomplished a good job of this. The four-year right shoulder gave the appearance of being unable

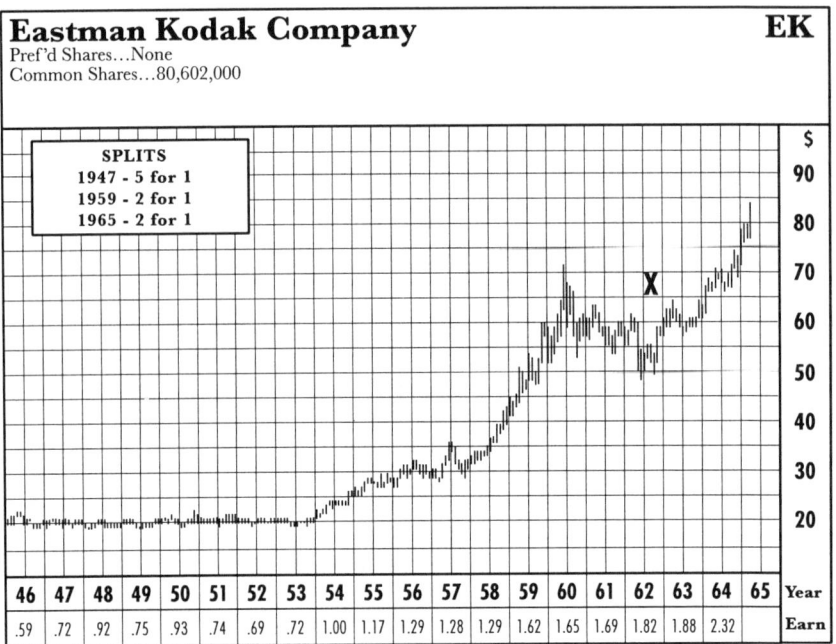

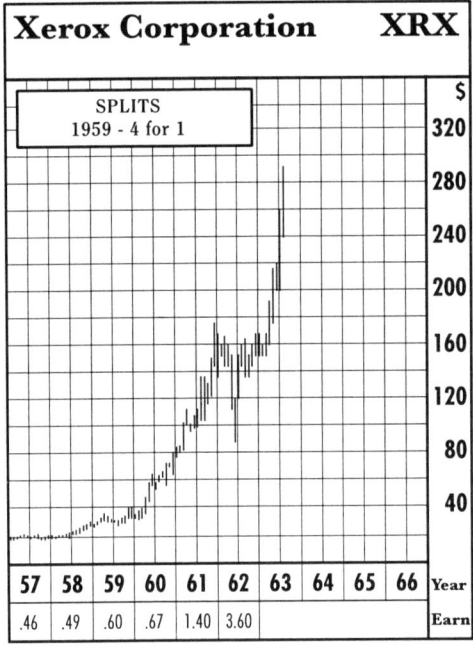

to carry above the left shoulder. With the memory of the shakeout (head) and the apparent lack of strength, the public reasoning is very inclined to be bearish. This action can be considered more of a high level consolidation.

Notice the earnings record of AC has been exceptionally steady despite a rather jagged stock picture.

Eastman Kodak Company (EK)

The head and shoulders bottom of EK during 1961-63 (X) took place far above its base.

This is an example proving that the price of a stock should never be considered by an investolator. Your opinion should be based entirely on the past actions of a stock. While EK was a bargain at 124 (before it split) another stock may be dangerously high at 24, even though it may be a sound company.

Xerox Corporation (XRX)

Xerox Corp. formed a near perfect head and shoulders bottom which included the 1962 panic. The quick recovery and quietness in the upper range with a false resistance level above 160 gave a sound base. An investolator would have sold about the time it first hit the 160 range or when it broke the uptrend line. This is one situation where you were justified in considering buying back at a price above your sale price. Normally, this is a very risky procedure.

Stocks that Resist
General Market Breaks

There comes a time when panic selling hits the stock market as in 1946, 1957, and 1962. When the public panics, for a period of a month or so, it is a rare stock that does not drop in value. Some will merely sag, while others will break wide open. For others this break may be the beginning of a long, drawn out accumulation base. Never consider buying these weak stocks after a sharp break no matter how low they may appear. This chapter will teach you what type of action to watch for at a time like this.

Following the rules of an investolator you would have sold most stocks in 1946. Steep uptrend lines were broken all across the stock charts. The 1946 top was a genuine distribution top, whereas distribution took place in only a portion of the stocks during the general market tops since 1946.

After selling a stock you will naturally be an eager beaver to get back into the market, and rightly so. But do not allow yourself to get carried away by your eagerness. Rather than buying stocks at what appear to be low prices after a general break, check the charts closely for those that resisted the general market break. They attract very little attention by their action, but they show one of the most positive indications of internal technical strength. Heavy selling fails to develop in these because the majority of Milquetoasts and Nervous Nellies have

STOCKS THAT RESIST GENERAL MARKET BREAKS

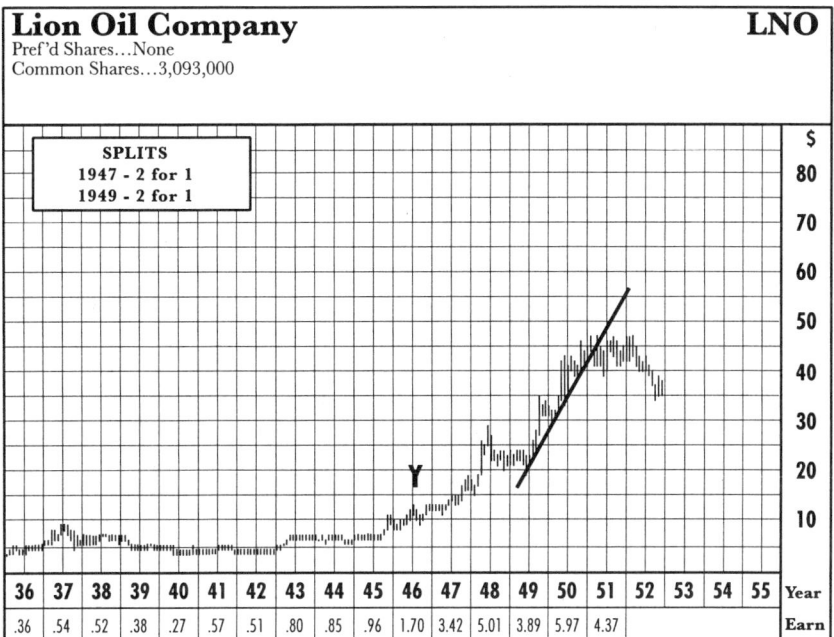

long ago sold out. The selling that does appear is well taken by the smart money.

Lion Oil Company (LNO)

Lion Oil showed outstanding strength when it resisted the 1946 break (Y). Lion Oil previously had a perfect three-year base; then during the next three years while nearly all other stocks were being marked up, it went through a perfect consolidation pattern. It failed to follow the general market rise but was actually strengthening its own position. In 1946 while others were quite active and under distribution, it moved up only moderately.

Besides resisting the general market break when it came, it proved the upside was the line of least resistance when it made new highs three months later. It was now a safe purchase at this higher price. How much better this would have been than if you bought others on the lows of 1946 when most were only entering their accumulation bases. While these bases were "maturing" you were gaining a good profit in Lion Oil.

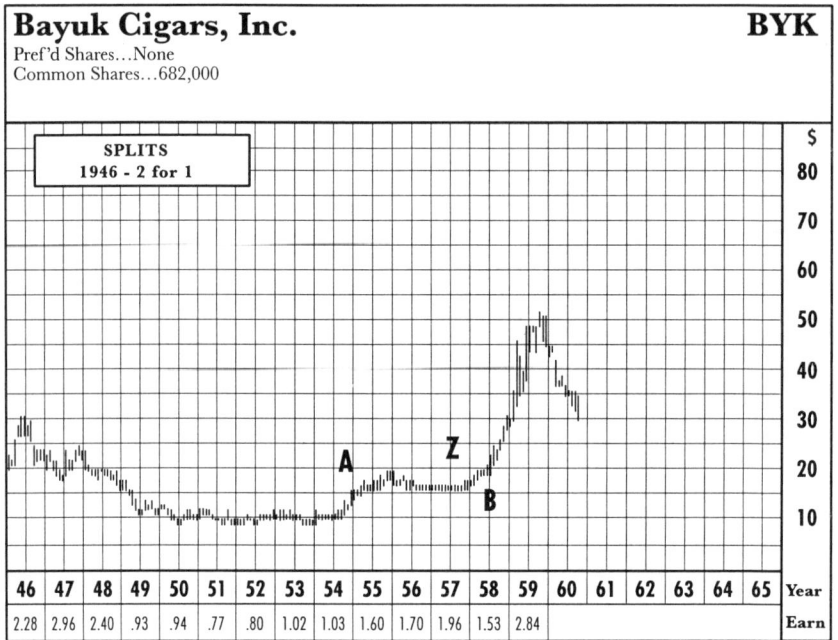

Bayuk Cigars, Inc. (BYK)

This stock showed an extremely strong resistance to panic selling in October, 1957 (Z). BYK sold below its consolidation with a final shakeout two months before the panic, then held firm in the face of it. Two perfect buy signals appeared at 12 in 1954 (A) and at 18 in 1958 (B). On a perfect base and consolidation period (as shown here) it is not necessary to wait for the buy signal. Note the previous perfect accumulation base of BYK.

Beatrice Foods Company (BRY)

Beatrice Foods Co. (BRY) sold at new lows below its consolidation one month after the panic selloff (C). Four months later, it made a new high when it made its breakaway.

Strangely, BRY spent much more time in consolidation than it did during its short base. These consolidations really build up the strength for continued rises. They are especially important when they resist a general market break. They present a safe purchase when perhaps there are no others available.

Anchor Hocking Glass Corporation (ARH)

Anchor Hocking Glass Corp. held up well during the October, 1957 panic (D), then immediately rallied into new high ground.

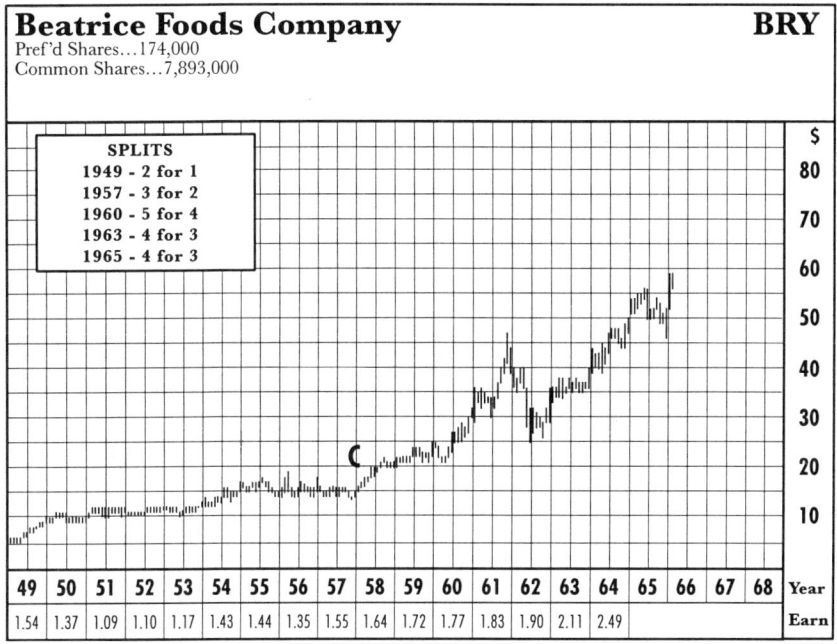

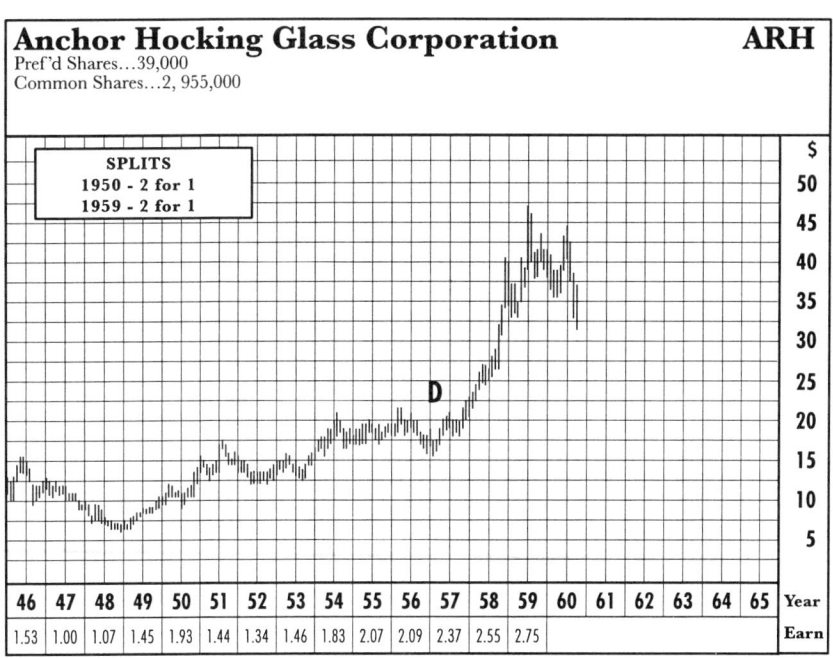

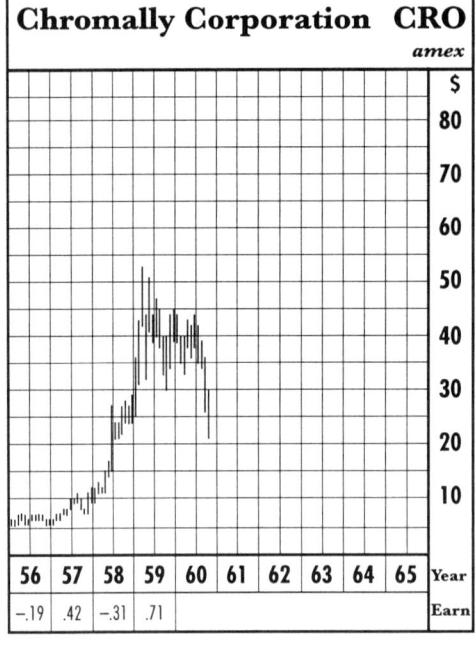

Corn Products Company (CPG)

Corn Products Co. showed great strength by resisting the 1957 general market selloff (E). Also in the face of the late 1960 general market selloff, CPG sold higher each month (F).

Chromally Corporation (CRO)

Chromally Corp. was the leader by making new highs the next month after the 1957 panic (G), then rose over 150% during the following year when it had a deficit of 31 cents. Never allow deficits to concern you. It is the action that should be your guide.

Collins & Aikman Corporation (CK), and Crown Cork & Seal Company (CCK)

Both were perfectly safe buys when they firmly resisted the general

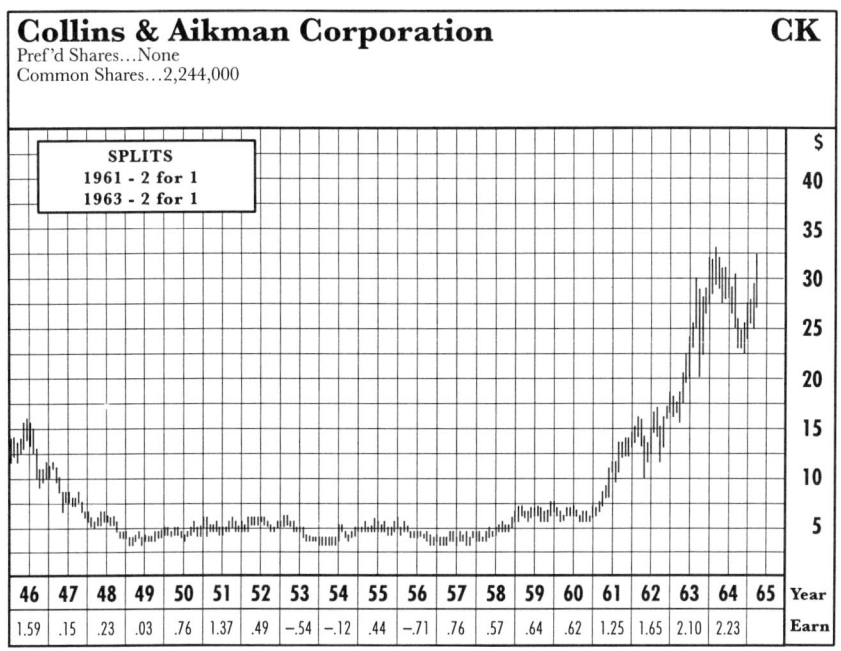

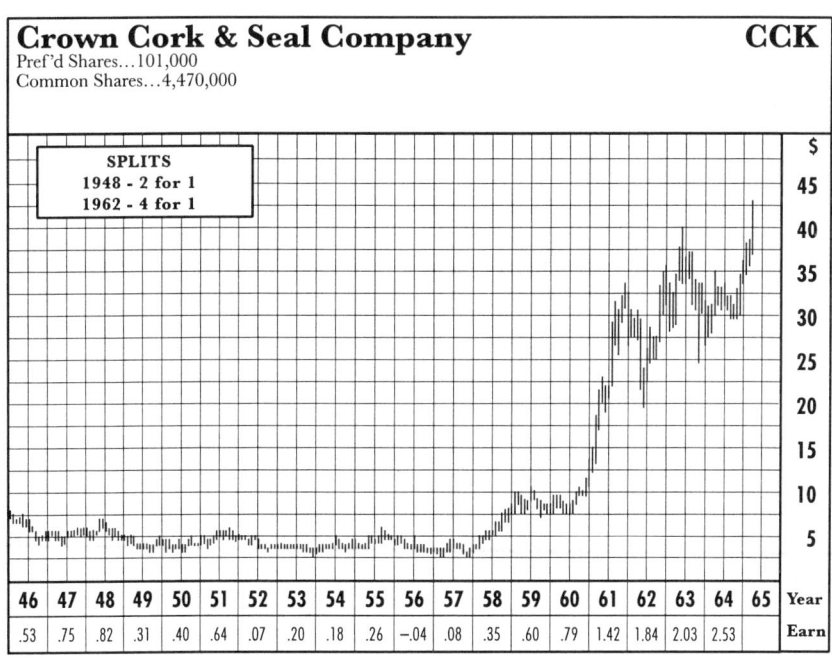

market's severe shakeout in both the 1957 and 1960 general market selloff.

Note that CCK rose 1900% without paying a dividend.

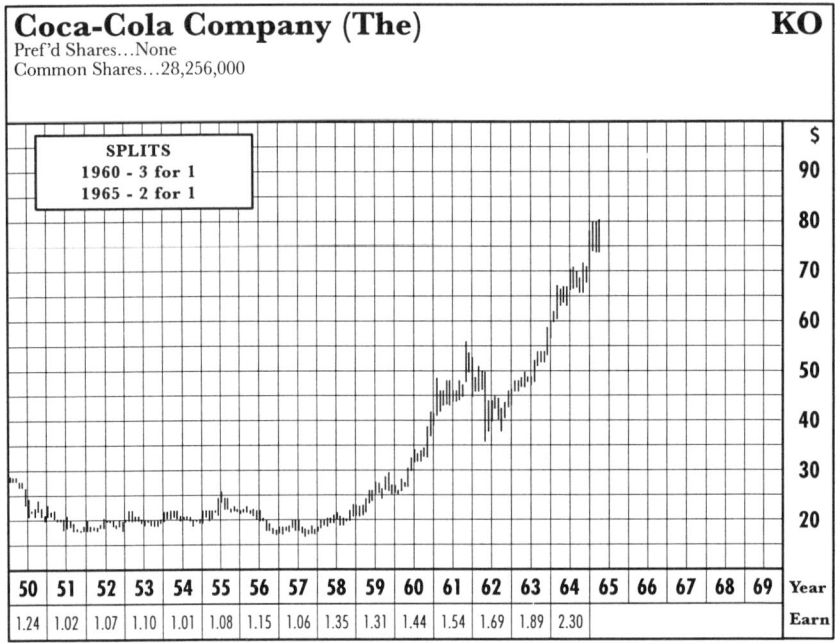

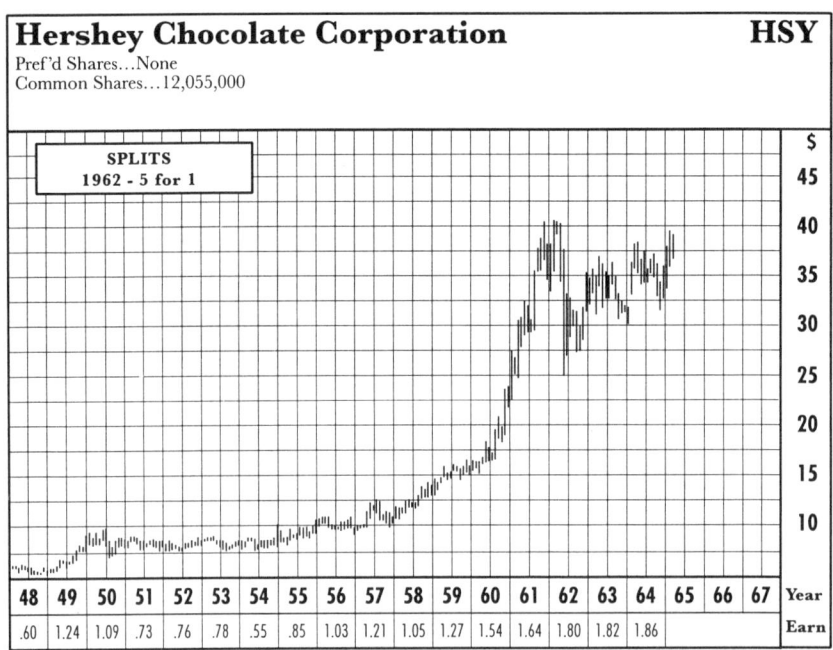

Coca Cola Company (KO), and Hershey Chocolate Corporation (HSY)

Both of these actually swam against the tide during the 1960 break. Also both showed individual strength by recovering quickly after the 1957 break.

At the time of publication HSY appears to be in a high level consolidation. Watch for that year or more of quietness in its upper range which will indicate that it is nearing its completion.

The panic selloff in 1962 was so severe that even most stocks that were in a strong technical position sold down sharply for one month, but they recovered quickly.

Nearly everyone involved in the stock market watches its actions, whether they are chartists or not. The market opinions of most shareholders, although they are not aware of it, are influenced by market action rather than by fundamentals.

Isn't the 1962 market break proof of this? Did not public sentiment change from bullishness to not mere bearishness, but into being unreasonably panicky in only two months, from March to May? Did the fundamental outlook of our corporations change during this time? Of course not. It was only public sentiment that changed.

The largest drops in 1962 were in those stocks which were technically weak. Again those stocks that resisted the selloff were the ones to watch for.

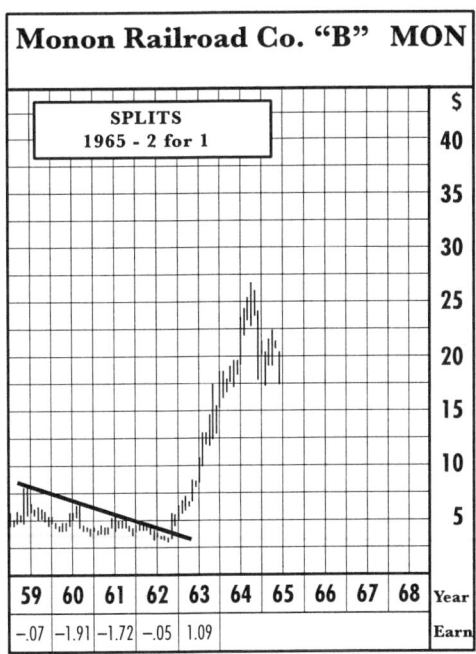

Monon Railroad Co. "B" (MON) and Monogram Industries, Inc. (MGP)

There are those who may argue, "Wouldn't it be better to buy those that had a severe drop or those that had dropped considerably before the 1962 panic?"

It would have been better if you had bought one like Monon Railroad Co. "B." But these were few at that time. It had a typical three-year downtrend line,

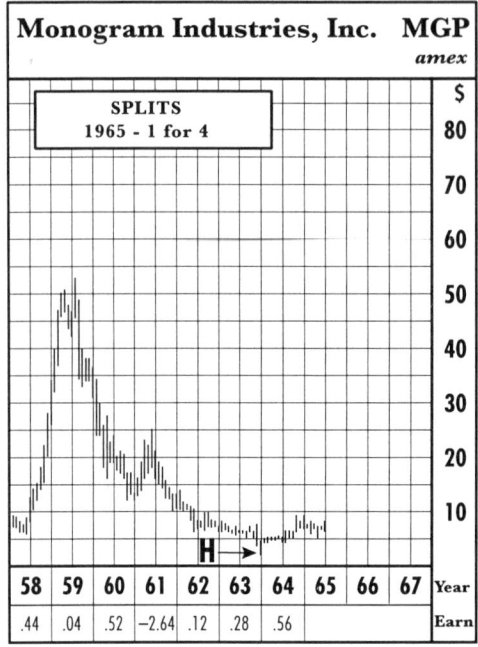

ending with a final shakeout. The breaking of this trend in November, 1962 was a perfect buy signal. But by this reasoning, you would have bought Monogram Industries, Inc. at about 7, and far too soon. You may have been very nervous when it sold below 2 (H). It was a far better buy at the same price two years later. It was still a good purchase at 10 three years later.

Briggs & Stratton, Columbia Broadcasting, Dr. Pepper and Greyhound proved their underlying strength by making new 1962 highs after the market's violent shakeout. To see signs of technical strength you must be aware of these

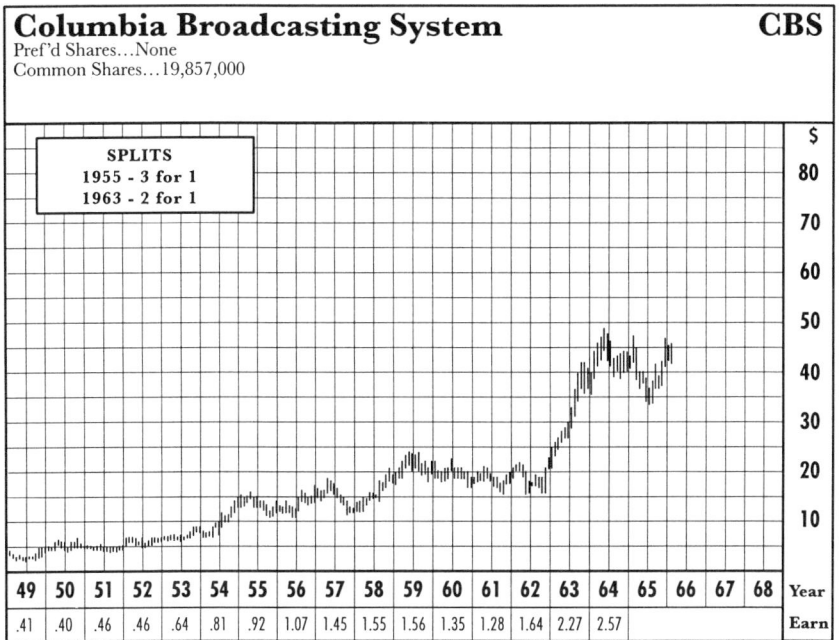

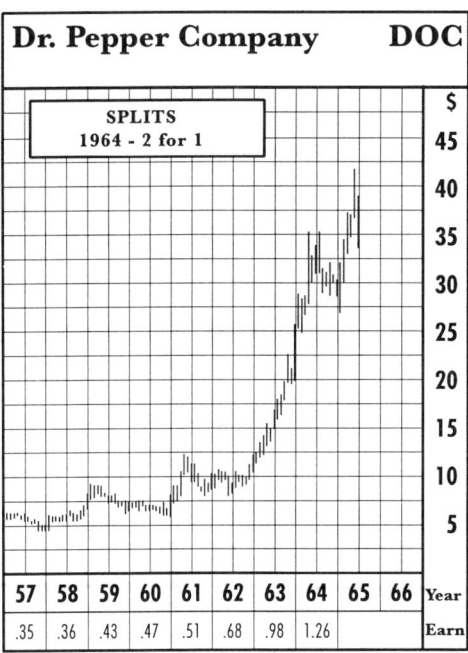

actions and the importance of the timing. There is no fundamental study or set of statistics that can give you these clues. You can see them only through the use of charts. You must watch and compare what is happening to other stocks. Study them as if you were a general in the field of battle watching for a strategic move, and watch for those formations that have proven themselves in the past. If you are unable to become confident in pictures like these you have failed to understand the term "technical strength." Without "technical strength" a stock cannot have anything but a minor rally.

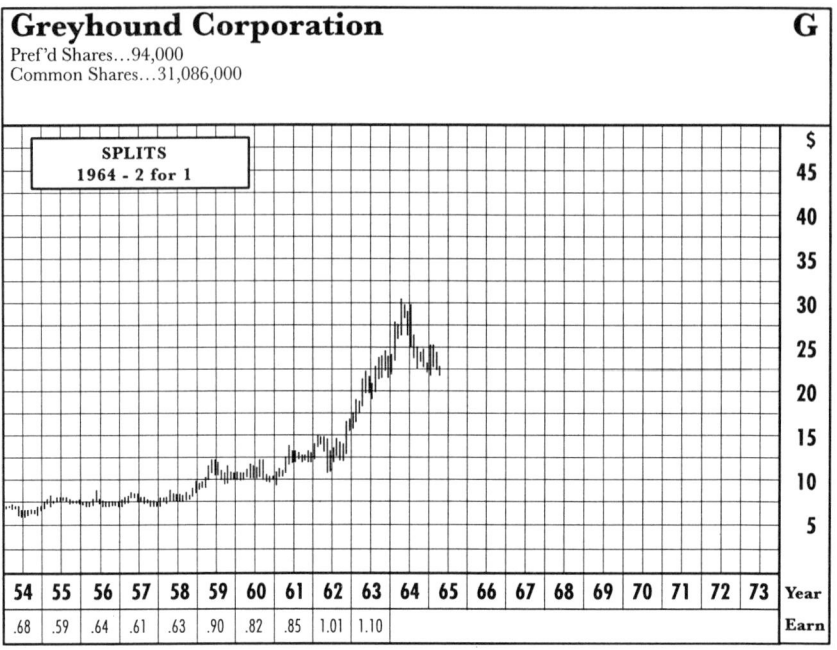

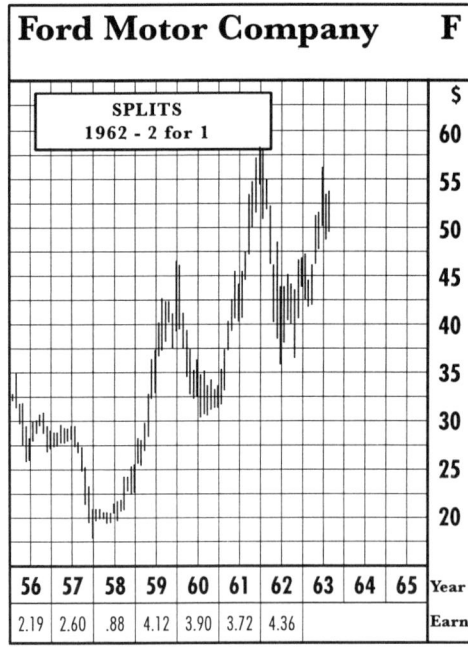

Ford Motor Company (F)

The price action of Ford Motor Co. after the stock became public will demonstrate what I mean. The public demand was so great for the offering that brokers were forced to ration it. But public demand after it was on the open market failed to stimulate it to more than a minor rally. Why? Because there was no one prepared to move it up. The stock was held by the public and it was therefore technically weak. It was natural then for the disenchanted shareholders to sell when it failed to rise. This was just what I predicted would happen at the time. When enough shares were picked up by the smart money on the following decline, the price was marked up to where the public originally thought it would go. An investolator must realize that a *fair percentage of the public must be sold out before a stock has a chance for a profitable rise.* Otherwise there will be no sponsors. Those who do not understand this may be doomed to be emotionally inspired and given false courage for various reasons at the wrong time and price. Timing of your purchase is all important. If the time is right, the price must be right.

As long as the market contains so many mixed trends, at almost any given time there will be stocks that should be bought. Many of them will give the cue to buy through actions such as I have described to you. When you make a purchase after seeing one of these strong actions, rarely will it prove to be wrong. Perhaps disappointing before proving itself, but seldom wrong. Learn to buy when a stock shows quiet strength, not during the violent displays of strength in the high ranges.

My success has come from the many mistakes I have made in the past, and I am trying to give sound conservative advice that I have gained the hard way. Don't let anyone sway you with their knowing talk about the fundamentals of a company. They fortify themselves with "facts" to bolster their opinions. The fact is that they often pick the very facts that will coincide with their opinions. These in turn were probably formed emotionally on the basis of the price action of a stock or the market as a whole. Who else but these people buy high and sell low?

Chrysler Corporation (C)

The Chrysler chart shows one of the most outstanding endings of an accumulation period to be seen. It had nearly everything to be found during a bottom action. The long slow downtrend, the quiet wearing out action in 1960-61 (I), followed by a double top (J) and the sharp shakeout during the 1962 market break (K). The following rally stalled at the previous resistance level of 15. Here was an unusual picture. Three positive buying signals appearing at one time: breaking the long downtrend, going above the triple top false ceiling and rising above the head and shoulders bottom. Sixteen was the perfect buying price on this breakaway.

Normally an investolator would have sold Chrysler in the upper 40 level. The fast, three-month rise (during extremely heavy daily trading) to 49-7/8 should have alerted him to sell out. Eventually it sold at 67-1/2

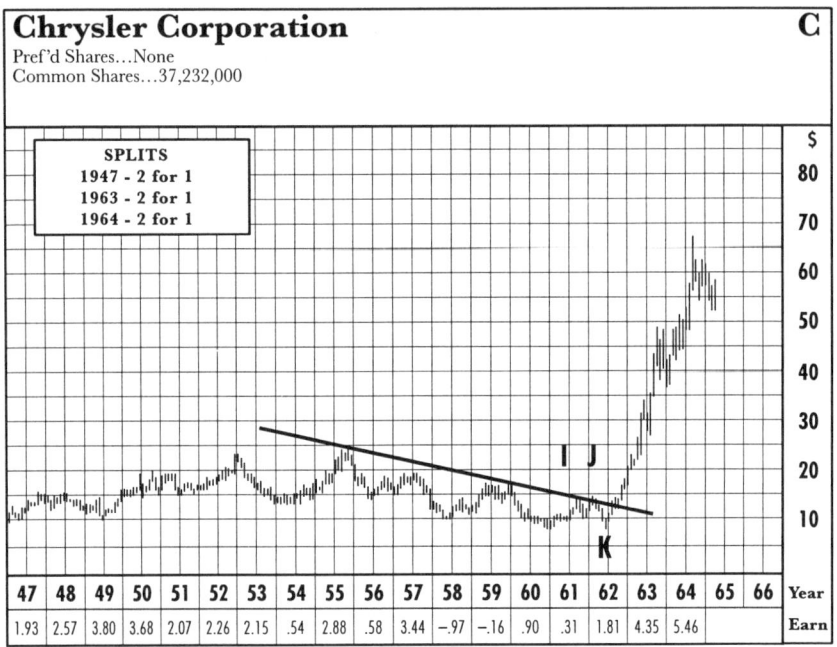

on a reduced amount of trading, but this was too much to expect. When you hold out for that extra rise, four out of five times you will find yourself holding the stock too long and too late.

Learn to recognize the variety of bases, consolidations, trends, false ceilings, false support levels, false starts and shakeouts. There are internal changes which take place, all of which have an important bearing on the future action of a stock. If you can detect these formations, you will acquire the "know how" in forecasting stock price movements.

How many times have people timidly bought only a fraction of the shares which they really could afford because they lacked confidence in their choice of a stock or the economic condition of the country? By the use of long range charts they should be able to pick a bargain. Forget the question of economic health of the corporations or the country. Your only interest should be, has the stock action been acting in a way that has been worrying the shareholders into selling? Does the stock now appear to be in strong hands?

There may come a time when a study of the charts will indicate that there are no bargains available and that the whole market is too high. If you have sold out, you must decide to stay out. Sit back and watch the profits go by. Later you can watch the prices melt away. That can be the means of avoiding heavy losses. That is really more important than making money in the market. Many people fare very well without capital gains, whereas losses could leave them destitute.

False Support Levels:
Encouraging Action That Hides Trouble Ahead

The chart on Thor Power Tool shows one of the best examples of a false support level during the years 1961-64. During this period there were three fast rises that indicated attempts at inducing the public to buy the stock (L, M, N). Notice that during these years there was little time spent in the lower price range. There were no accumulation periods. Whoever was responsible for its particular activity bought only the necessary amount to give it support in the area of 25-1/2. Two rather feeble rallies in 1964 were the last attempts at distribution before the truth became known that the company was in trouble, and the price dropped 50% below the false bottom.

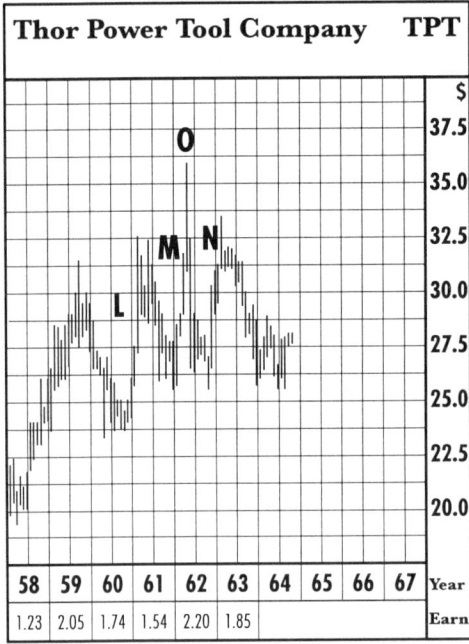

FALSE SUPPORT LEVELS:
ENCOURAGING ACTION THAT HIDES TROUBLE AHEAD

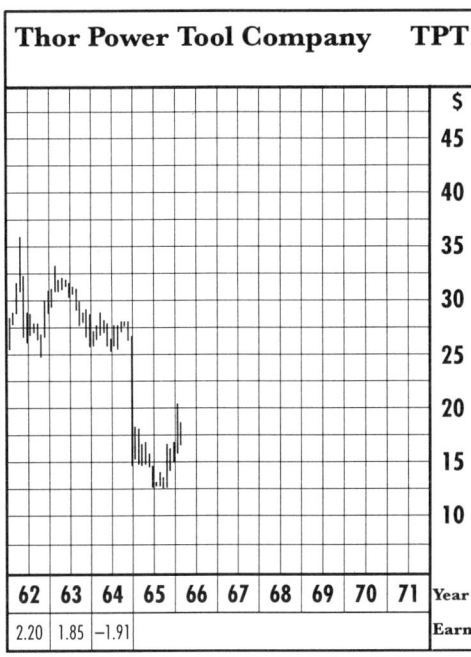

In September, 1964, the board of directors of TPT announced an agreement for the sale of their company to Stewart-Warner for the price of $28.40 per share, and later on asked the shareholders to vote their approval of this sale. In literature that was intended to influence a favorable vote, it was said, "In the light of earnings for 1963 and the first six months of 1964, recent market prices of the Company's stock of $18.45 per share as of June 30, 1964, the Board of Directors concluded that the price fixed in, and the terms of the agreement, which were arrived at as a result of arms-length bargaining between the officers and directors of the Company and Stewart-Warner, were fair and in the best interest of Thor Stockholders."

This "arms-length" phrase sounds as if someone was wary of the deal. In fact from subsequent events, one might suspect the whole agreement was a hoax.

The audit of December 31, 1964 proved to be far different from what was reported for the first nine months. In their annual message to their shareholders they said, "It was a year of great disappointment. The results of the audit of Thor's operation which was made in connection with the proposed sale of its assets and business to Stewart-Warner Corporation led your board of directors to agree to terminate that agreement." Certainly they had no thought of putting something over on Stewart-Warner, but the public were certainly baited by the price appeal of $28.40 per share.

Obviously, in the case of Thor Tool there was no way for a fundamentalist to become forewarned that the price props would be pulled, but a friend to whom I had given a few pointers in long range chart reading, and who had an open mind, recognized how perfectly the price of Thor Tool was being supported at 25-1/2. He became suspicious enough to sell his shares just before the big drop. I had previously explained to him that perfect support levels are usually phony. After the big drop he told me all about it. He had received a phonograph record from Thor Power Tool praising the company and its products. This could very well have been used for advertising purposes, but more than likely it was a come-on to buy the stock. He sheepishly admitted that the record had influenced him into buying it.

A well-known commentator was hired as the narrator of this seventy minutes of monotonous corn. There were a number of people, all mentioned by name, from a schoolboy to various contractors, all praising the worth of Thor Tools. Of course there was a bit of "name dropping" including Diamond Jim Brady who was alleged to have been involved with the company in its pioneer days. The record told of the long service of many of their tool makers, how their super salesmen were bound to increase sales, and one person was amazed at how fast the company had grown in the last few years, setting records every month. A fair percentage of people who listened to this record were certain to be brainwashed into buying the stock.

The clincher came when an unnamed character with an unusually convincing voice told of buying 25 shares for $967 in 1917 which increased to 630 shares worth over $19,000. He stressed every angle from which he benefited from this stock. He told of receiving $1,008 a year in dividends, paying him more than his investment in the first place, for a total of $31,775, and that the dividends and value now totaled over $50,000. He told of reading now and then in the financial pages of amazing growth of someone's stock over a number of years, but didn't recall many instances more outstanding than Thor Power Tool. Why was this shareowner unnamed? Probably because he was nonexistent.

Apparently someone recognized that the company's future was not so bright, and made a concerted effort, by both touting, and manipulation of the stock prices, to induce public buying of its shares. One may wonder if the sellout was fully successful.

In 1965, the Thor Power Tool Co. filed suit in circuit court against the estate of its late president and three former officers. The company charged the defendants with concealing the true financial condition of the company from other directors and shareholders and operating it for their own personal gain.

This is an example of how an alert chart reader, still a novice, was able to suspect that a bad situation was shaping up even before part of the management knew that trouble was brewing. Certainly there was too much price activity in the stock to indicate consolidation.

In the February 1, 1966 issue of a periodical entitled "Better Investing,"[1] David L. Babson, President of David L. Babson and Co., Boston pointed out the difficulties now facing the fundamentalist in the area of analyzing a company report in an attempt to discover the real worth of a firm.

He says:

The net income reported to stockholders by a corporation is the universal yardstick used in appraising the value of its shares. Most investors place implicit trust in these figures as an accurate measure of the relative rate of progress being made.

Following the 1929 crash and its regulatory aftermath, shareowners had reason to believe that, in the future, much greater reliance could be placed on reported earnings. For a number of reasons, however, even today published income statements cannot fully be accepted at face value.

Accounting Practices

Although outright misrepresentation is now rare, trends in accounting practices and tax laws have widened management's latitude in selecting the policies which determine the amount to be reported as "earnings per share." As a result, company reports are often just as hard to evaluate as they were back in the Roaring Twenties.

1. Impact of Recent Tax Liberalization: Changes in the tax laws in the past decade have brought about a great diversity of corporate reporting practices. In 1954, companies were allowed to use accelerated depreciation methods in computing taxable income and, three years ago, were permitted to adopt generally shorter "lives" of plant equipment.

In 1962, Congress also initiated the "investment credit," whereby purchasers of new equipment are given a tax reduction equal to 7% of the cost (3% for utilities). About this same time, manufacturing companies as well as retail establishments were allowed to use the installment method of reporting earn-

---

[1] The National Assoc. of Investment Clubs, 1300 Washington Boulevard Building, Detroit, Mich. (A non-profit organization.)

ings (which indefinitely defers for tax purposes a portion of the income from installment sales).

New Rules

As intended, the new rules on depreciation, investment and credit sales have made a significant contribution to the current strength in capital spending. Unfortunately, they have also opened a Pandora's Box of confusion for company executives, security analysts and investors alike. Disagreements within the accounting profession have prevented it from establishing uniform reporting practices under the new laws.

As a result, corporations have pretty much gone their own way in handling these items. The methods by which "shareholder earnings" are determined seem to depend largely on the relative conservatism of management. Some report depreciation, taxes and earnings on the same basis both to Internal Revenue and to shareholders and spread the 7% investment credit over the full lives of the related equipment.

Reserve for Deferred Taxes

Other managements do not charge as much depreciation against earnings in their reports to stockholders as they do for tax purposes. However, they offset the favorable effect on net earnings by including in their income tax accrual a "reserve for deferred taxes" equal to the temporary tax savings.

At the very aggressive end of the spectrum are some which take full advantage of the new tax benefits without setting up deferred tax reserves. Many other variations in accounting policies arising out of the new tax laws bring about differences in the level of reported profits. The result is that the published earnings of companies, even within the same industry, may not be comparable . . .

If this is true, and there is general agreement among the most diehard fundamentalists that it is, what chance has the average trader on today's market to make decisions based on accurate fundamentals? Could the answer be in careful, unemotional, accurate charting?

General Cable (GK)

You should now compare the six-year action of Thor Power Tool ending in 1964, with the six-year action of General Cable ending in 1962 (see p. 36). The novice probably would not notice any meaningful difference, but there are some important differences. The main difference is that TPT had a perfect support level while GK had a very noticeable resistance level during its high level consolidation, both levels intended to give a false impression of the internal or technical condition of the stock. Fundamentalists who would never concede that there is any value to be gained by trying to predict a move by chart action are the very ones who give value to the study of a chart, because they are responding to the influences of the price action of a stock. You can only guess as to how many comments similar to this have been made by them: "Thor Power Tool has a very strong support level." An experienced chartist would change the word strong, to false.

Before General Cable turned upward from its perfect consolidation, many fundamentalists, without realizing that they are thinking in technical terms, would remark that there was "too much stock for sale around 18." When GK is topping out at above 100 in the future on extremely heavy volume, these people will not recognize that there is "too much stock for sale."

While the difference in the percentage of the price swings of these two stocks during the six years did not vary widely, there was a considerable difference in their actions during these swings. Each had four tops, but there was dullness and far less activity during the GK tops. An observation that should have been noted was that in April, 1962 the price of TPT had violent upward action (O) when the general market was already slipping before the bad break. This isolated strength must have attracted considerable attention — and buying.

Now that TPT has since dropped to below the 13 level it may have entered its accumulation cycle. By 1967 or 68, it may present a very sound appearing base, during which its action could be very discouraging to the general public. But if there should be some sharp rallies during this low range, with only short periods of quietness previous to the rallies, this would indicate that public confidence is being intentionally maintained and that lower prices can be expected. This is not the method used to discourage people into selling at a loss. That will come at a lower level.

Trend Lines:
Your Buy and Sell Signals

As an investolator using long range charts, you must realize the importance of *trend lines*. The long term broken trend lines cannot be ignored. They are not infallible, but ignoring them is not the way to success. When they are occasionally wrong, it usually is not too serious.

There are traders who keep daily charts, whose primary interest is in trend lines. They are apt to "play" the short trend lines too often and may be badly whipsawed (a word that is used to describe a trader who has been influenced into changing his mind and trading too often—usually at a loss). They try too hard to "beat" the market, and find themselves beaten instead.

Trend lines may be clearly defined by drawing a line along the high points of a downtrend, or along the ascending lows of an uptrend. At times these points will be so even that they may create a perfect trend line. Other times there will be some extreme high or low points, especially in a downtrend, that will give an imperfect appearance. These may be classified as sort of "thrust" moves and can be ignored when drawing a trend line. At these times you can draw a line through these thrusts, more or less averaging them out. Draw a line only after there is a definite trend and draw it to fit the picture best. Study the trend lines I have drawn, and you will get the "feel" of drawing them yourself.

Trend lines can be invaluable to an investolator. Following a certain long range trend to its conclusion can give you the perfect buy or sell signal. Depending on the type of trend line when "broken," you may make a fair estimate as to how far the new trend will carry.

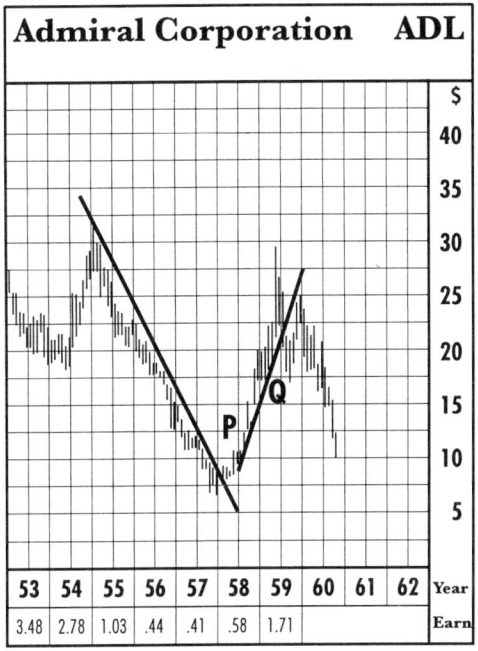

Admiral Corporation (ADL), and Lionel Corporation (LIO)

DOWNTRENDS. The primary purpose of a downtrend line is to let you know "when not to buy." How many bought during the steep downtrends of Admiral Corp. (ADL) from 1955 to 1957 and Lionel Corp. (LIO) 1961-62? A purchase at 9 (P) when ADL broke its trend proved to be perfect and with the benefit of not really having to form an opinion. A sale at about 19-1/2 could have also been made on the sell signal when the uptrend was broken (Q).

A purchase of LIO at about 6-1/2 (R) when its steep downtrend was broken did not turn out so well. A long period of uncertainty and lower prices lay ahead. While buy signals are not infallible, do you know of a better way

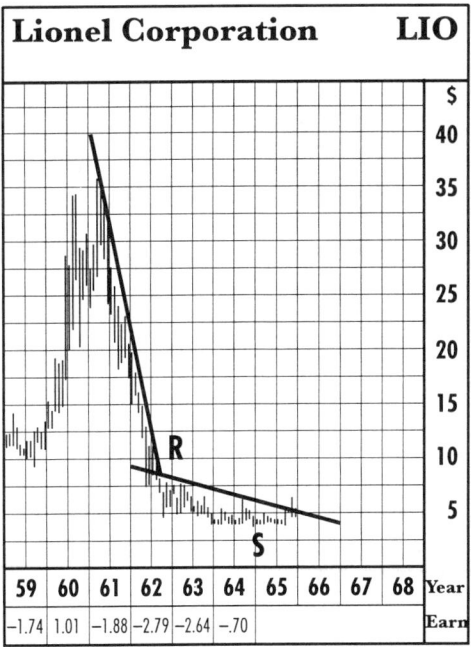

of having the odds in your favor? There are a wide variety of downtrend lines, distinguished by their steepness and the time involved.

The steep downtrend lines, when they are broken by an upswing are the lines of least value. There is such a short period of possible accumulation, that it must be assumed the shorter the "base," the smaller the rise. It may have a 200% rise, but you would be very lucky if it generates a 100% rise. It is also common for a stock to have a minor rally, then fall back into new low ground and spend as many as sixteen years before completing its base. You would then have bought too high and far too soon.

The perfect purchase of LIO would have been at 4 during that final long quiet period (S). The signal of a change of trend came when it broke the downtrend line in 1965.

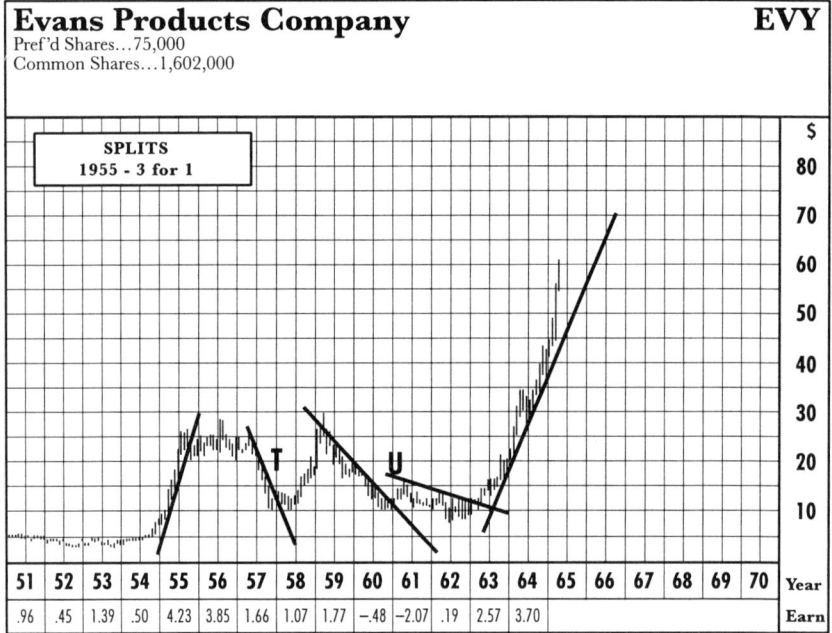

Evans Products Company (EVY)

Had you bought Evans Products at about 13 when its steep downtrend of 1957 (T) was broken, it would have been a nearly perfect purchase. Your only reason for buying would have been the broken trend line. Free from any emotional influences, you accepted this cue and transferred your thought to an act. Your next thought was to wait with patience. This began to pay off within seven months. With this short base of about ten months you were lucky to get a rise of over 100%. The fast rise of $8.00 in one month was the bait meant to attract the speculators, but should have been your cue to sell.

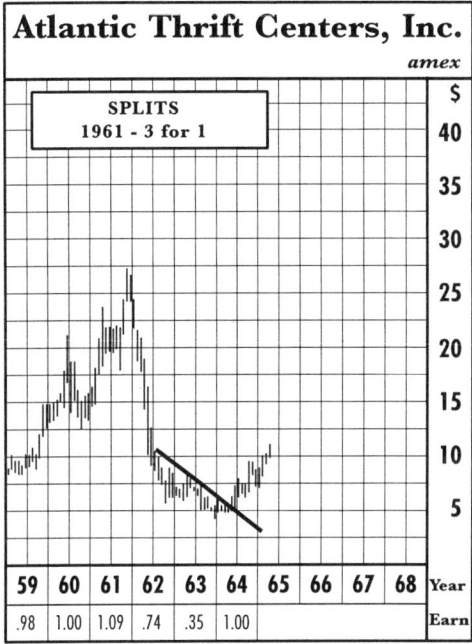

Again had you bought EVY in January, 1961, also at about 13, when it broke its less steeply inclined downtrend line (U), you would have been burdened with a worrisome loss for two years — and without dividends. But the forced wait would have been extremely worthwhile. A perfect trend line developed in this rise, which, when broken, was your cue to sell.

During your long wait in 1961-62, a new downtrend line formed at a much slower pace. The breaking of this trend line ended what is a long proven accumulation action. This gave you the perfect timing of a purchase with a stop-buy order, again at about 13. The broken downtrend of this type is one of the most valuable to be seen. These give an almost 100% assurance of a large rise to follow.

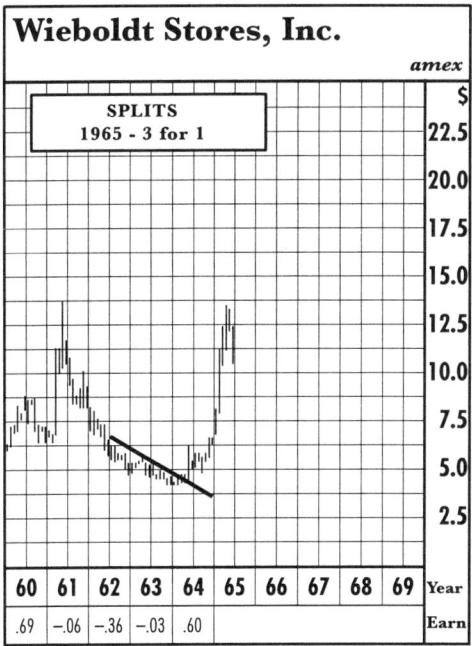

It is far more difficult for the average person to hold a stock over a trying period such as during the

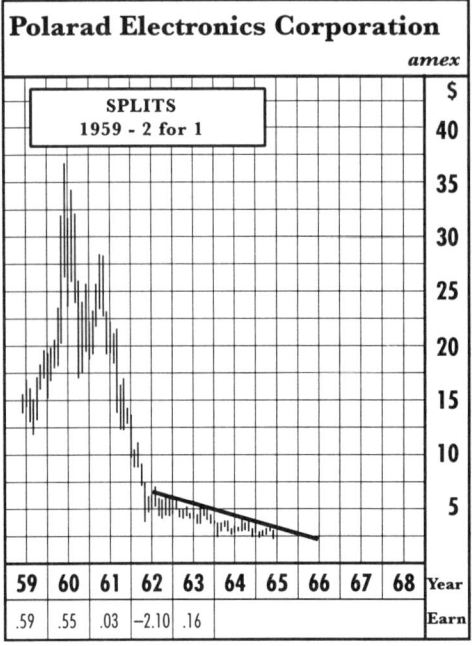

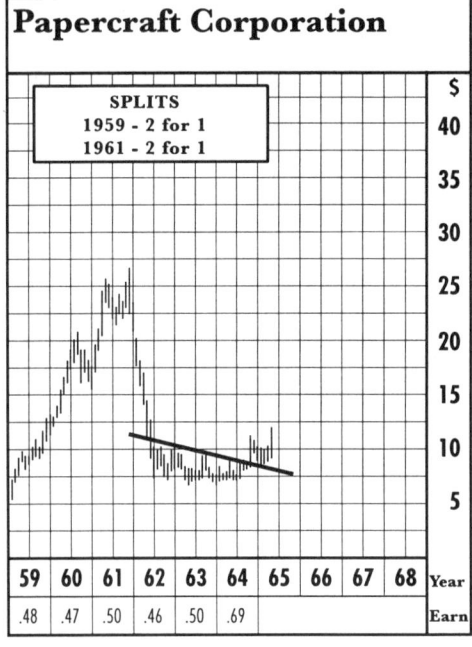

1961-62 action in the low price range, with its deficits and passed dividends, than it would have been to hold it during the previous two-year high level action around 25. EVY then had a lot of appeal. Its shareholders were elated by its recent rise and high earnings. At this time it was so easy for them to contemplate it moving higher, while during the low range it was easy to expect it to drop further. The discouraging action and the large drop in earnings creates such bearishness that this is where the high level investors sell. Isn't that the smart thing to do, sell when a stock is not acting very well? This is almost standard advice from brokers and advisory services. This is why people discover that they sold in a bottom range.

The gradual downtrend line of at least two years' duration, that forms after a stock has had a very large drop, and ends with extreme quietness, gives a near perfect buy signal when broken. The records show that a stock can be bought with confidence after the line is broken. A very common action following the breakthrough is a year or more of delaying tactics. This action gives more strength to an already fairly sound base, but appears to the public as a lack of strength.

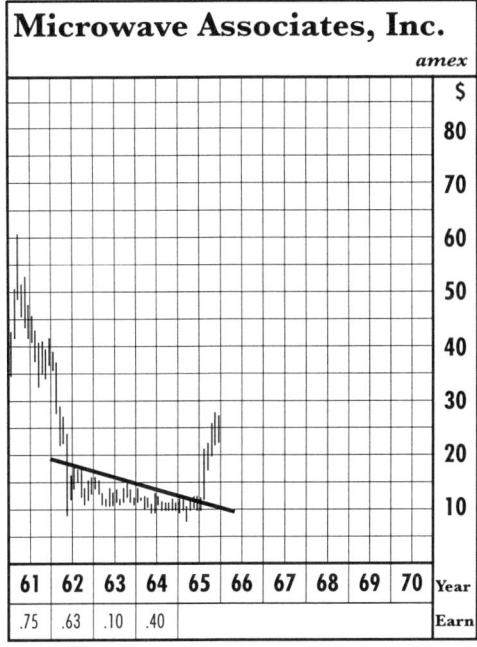

Study the varied examples as shown by Atlantic Thrift Centers, Wieboldt Stores, Inc., Polarad Electronics Corp., Papercraft Corp., Microwave Associates, Inc., and Hotel Corp. with its longer downtrend line.

The advantage of getting on board after actions like these is that most of the accumulation period is behind you, whereas if you bought a stock that had recently broken a steeper downtrend line, you may be getting on board at the *beginning* of its accumulative phase, and you would be in for a long period of waiting that would be a severe test of your patience. These broken downtrends give you an element of timing that has not been known to the average shareholder. These are the ones in which you should stake your claim for your share of the pot of gold at the end of the trend line.

The period of accumulation during these actions is not long enough to give assurance of a several hundred percent rise, but they do have an almost positive safety factor and almost a certainty of a 100-200% increase.

Hindsight regarding the past actions of these stocks should give you the foresight and confidence to buy on a similar action in the future, especially after a review of the charts on Boston and Maine Railroad.

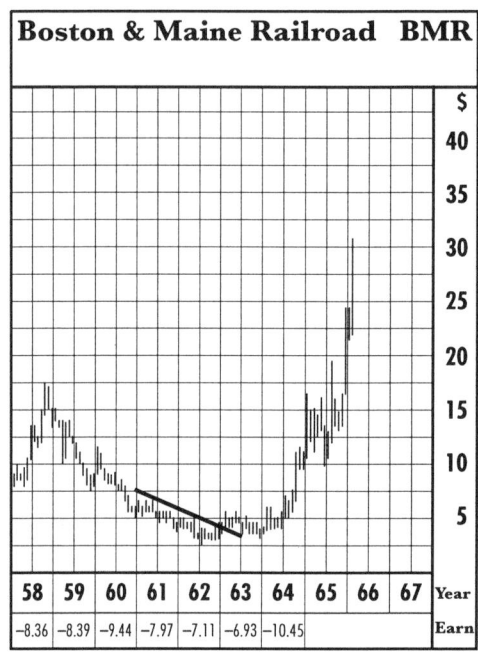

Boston and Maine Railroad (BMR)

In the face of a $35.20 per share deficit in the previous five years, would you have had the nerve to buy Boston & Maine at 3 in 1962, especially after the scare caused by the market break in that year? At that time I recognized that during the two-year downtrend it was under accumulation. Someone was obviously buying it, and for a reason that was not apparent to the public. At times an interpretation of a chart action is nearly as valuable as having a seat at a directors meeting. You can see that a reason is developing for a rise, but you have yet to learn the reason. That will come out at a later date, AFTER the rise is well under way. Was there any reason for you to believe it could rise over 900% in a little over three years after it had chalked up another $24.00 deficit during 1962-63-64? The huge loss over the years and the discouraging action would have warned you to stay clear of a railroad that was headed for bankruptcy. Your reasoning was obviously valid. That's what you thought.

Notice that during the two years while the price drop followed a perfect downtrend, the price rallies were extremely weak. To those who have no understanding of how market action influences the public, this does appear to indicate weakness in a stock. But what few understand is that during a prolonged action of this type, someone (don't ask me who) saw to it that this stock did not show strength. A

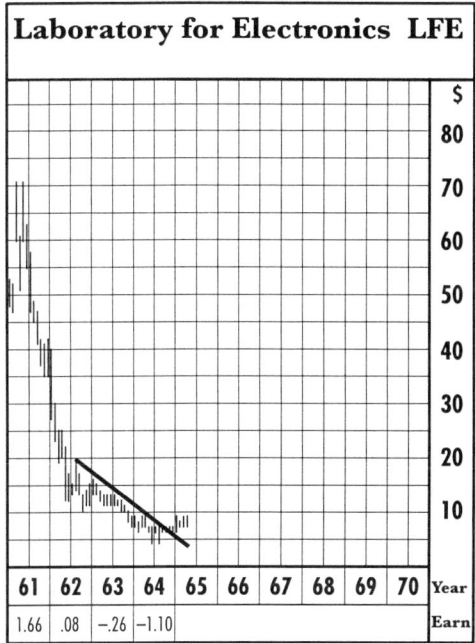

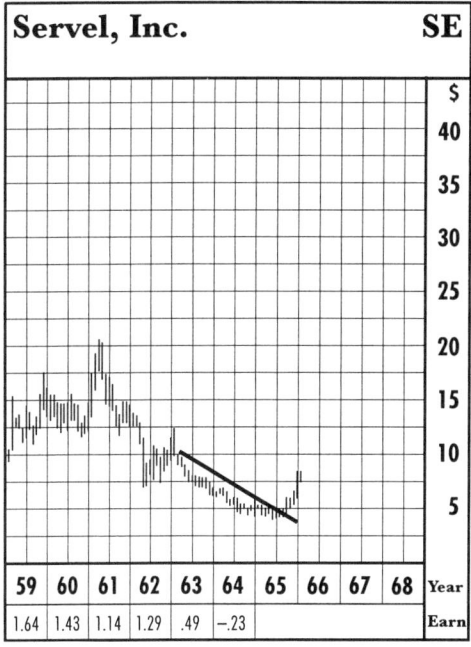

show of strength would encourage buying by the public and might encourage the present shareholders to hold on.

If this company had been headed for bankruptcy, you can be sure there would have been some very sharp and impressive rallies after a period of quietness, similar to the one in January, 1960. This is designed for the purpose of keeping the shareholders interested — and in the market.

Note in particular the chart actions of Laboratory for Electronics, Seeman Bros. (see Page 145) and Servel. Two of the best known stock market advisory services, Standard & Poor's and Dow Theory Forecasts, in 1965 advised selling these three in their bottom range. Standard & Poor's specifically said sell LFE at 7, Seeman at 4 and Servel at 5. Many people pay for this kind of advice. Would you?

General Cigar Co. (GCR)

The chart of General Cigar shows an especially sound base. I would interpret nearly 2-1/2 of its three-year downtrend as being accumulation. The next 3-1/2 years were very discouraging to the shareholders. The total result was a six-year base. In 1964 it sold at 235 based on the pre-split 3-for-1 price.

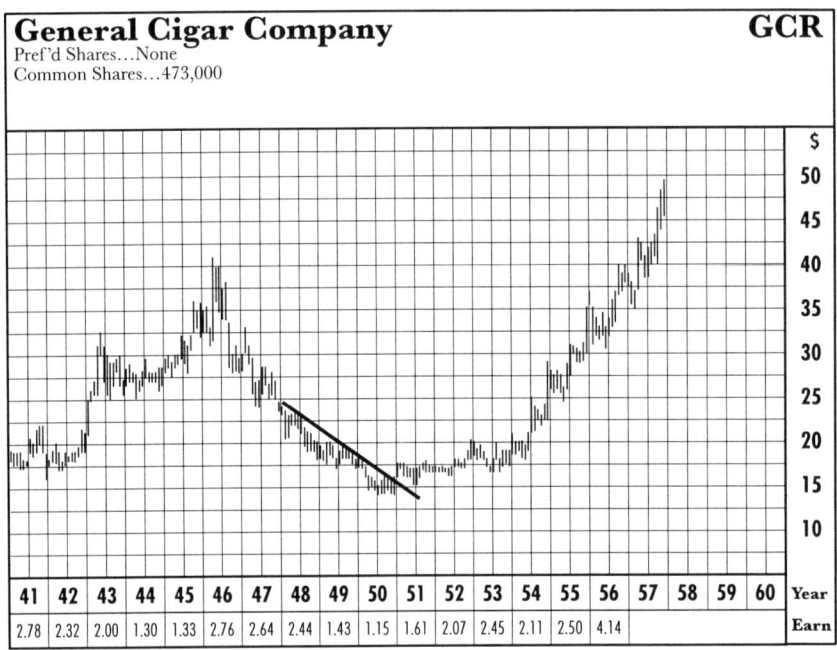

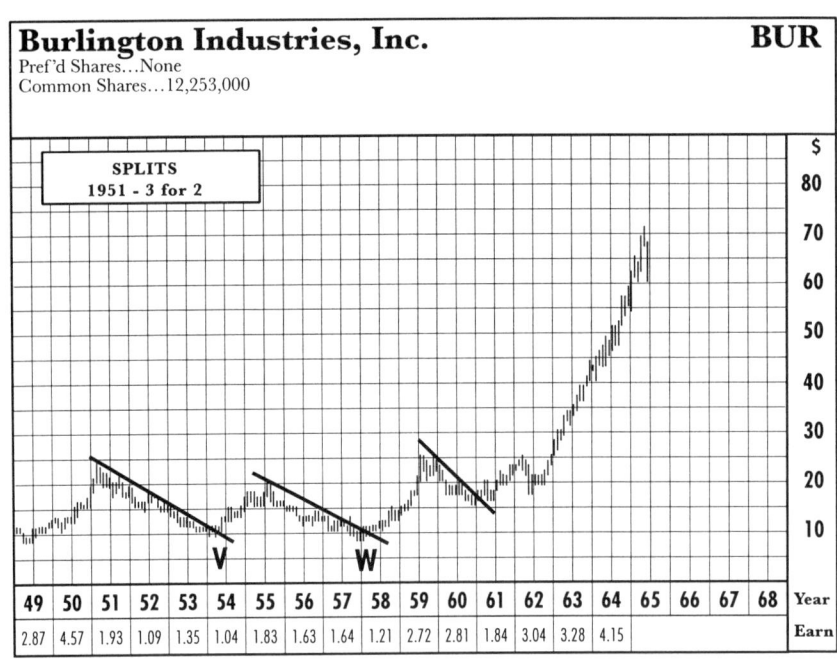

Burlington Industries, Inc. (BUR)

The downtrend of Burlington Industries, Inc. (BUR) ending with extreme quietness in 1954 (V) is action proven to be good accumulation action. Repeating this action (W) at even lower prices in spite of higher earnings indicated that the sponsors wanted more stock than what the first depressed period produced.

The secret to success is to recognize the underlying technical strength in a stock at the proper time rather than to be enticed into buying it when it is showing its strength during its fast rise when its strength is being dissipated, or in other words, when the purchasing power of the public is being used up. Obviously, the timing of a purchase is more important than the price. How else can the proper time be seen except by the use and understanding of a chart? If the timing is right, the price is bound to be right. The breaking of a gradual downtrend is the key to good timing of a purchase.

UPTRENDS. If you bought a stock on a sound base, you should seldom consider selling as long as the rise is small or merely slow, no matter how high it has moved. Slow uptrends when broken, should be ignored. Usually they are only an interruption during the markup. The rise is too slow to be considered distribution.

Crescent Corporation (CRC)

A rare exception and a very disappointing one that topped during a slow rise was Crescent Corp. (CRC). During the last three years of its uptrend it had above normal activity which apparently drew in the speculators for a distribution top. Unless it had an exceptionally heavy rate of trading to attract your attention and a suspicion that public buying was abnormally heavy, you no doubt would have failed to sell it. You would have found yourself in the role of an investor, collecting only cash and stock dividends. If you had bought at 5 in 1950 (X), or at 9 when the downtrend was broken (Y), a failure to sell would have only been disappointing. There was far more to be gained during this period of time than meets the eye. CRC has paid eight stock dividends since 1953. This would amount to at least 25 shares on a 100 share purchase. Remember, stock dividends are all profit. If you bought at 5, you would have 100% profit from these shares at 20, plus cash dividends on them.

There are two prerequisites to be met before you should consider

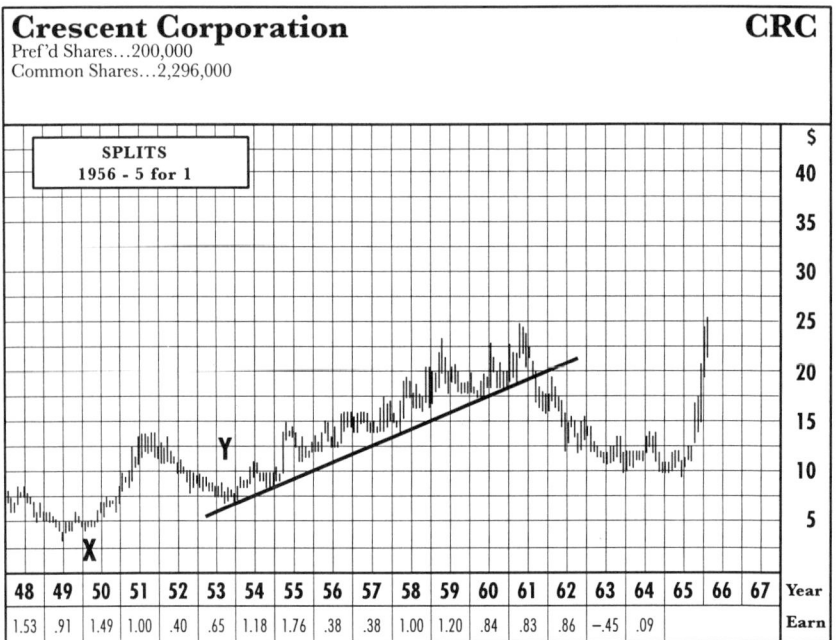

selling a stock: *a fast rate of climb and the percentage of rise from its base.* Distribution can seldom take place unless the public are excitedly (insanely excited would be more descriptive at times), buying at a pace far above that at which they are selling. This excitement can be generated by the mere rising of prices. With proper assistance by the manipulators, when (in their opinion) the time is ripe, a rise will be accelerated and publicized to a degree that will give confidence to the most timid Mr. Milquetoast. It is then that distribution takes place.

There are a wide variety of distribution tops, both in periods of time and range of price. During these tops there are heavy buying waves by the public. It is quite possible for the insiders to sell in six months what it took them sixteen years to accumulate.

Another prerequisite is: has the stock risen to the heights you were justified in believing it should go, according to the length of time and type of action during its previous base? In other words, the sounder the foundation, the higher the rise to be expected. From a base of four years you should expect a minimum rise of over 200% from its average base price. A longer base would indicate more. If, as the early slow markup proceeded, it spent years at one or two price levels consolidating, this would be a positive buildup of more internal strength and you can expect another 100 to 300% rise based on the original price.

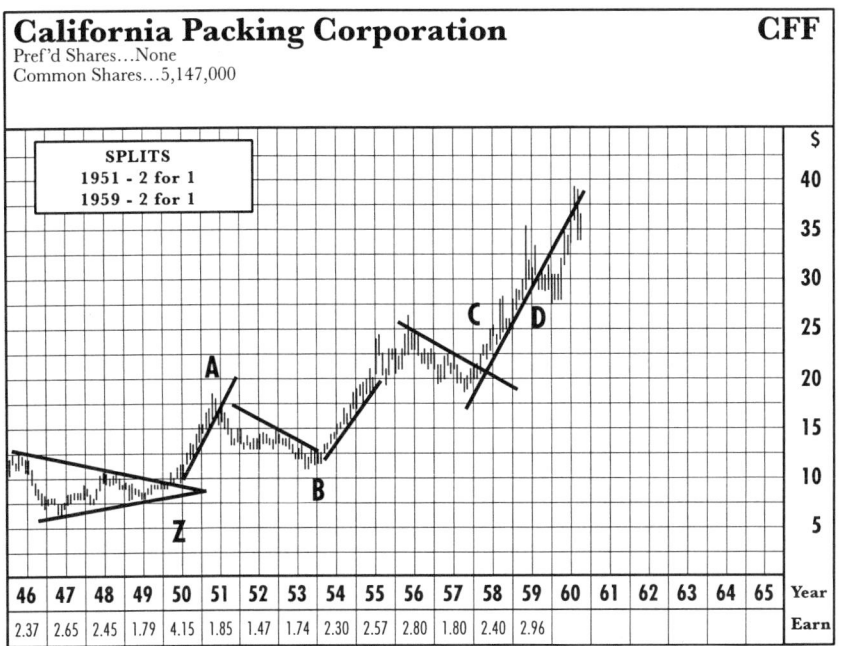

California Packing Corporation (CFF)

California Packing Corp. (CFF) broke through a downtrend which formed the upper half of a perfect triangle completing a four-year base in 1950 (Z). A perfect uptrend line developed that was broken after a moderate rise (A), but more was to be expected from this base. The action following the three-year downtrend consisted of over two more years of accumulation action, ending in 1954 (B), adding more technical strength to an already sound base. A higher rise can now be expected.

When the following uptrend was reversed, a sale here was not justified if you wished to benefit from the full rise of CFF. The percentage of rise from the base price of 8 or 9 was not enough. After a two-year downtrend which brought out profit taking (and of course losses were taken by the disappointed speculators who had previously bid a little too high), the uptrend was again resumed (C). Again the uptrend was broken in 1959 (D) but not for long. Here again a sale was not justified when the trend was broken, because the last downtrend period at least recovered the strength that was dissipated on the rise above 25. On the following rise, a perfect uptrend developed and CFF topped violently at 73. The price dropped back so quickly that it is doubtful that you would have sold voluntarily. A stop sell would have been executed at about 59.

It is interesting to note that of these three reactions, there was considerably less time spent on each succeeding one. A speeding up process is normally to be expected as the price rises. Perfect buy signals came at 10, 13 and at 22. It could be said that it should also have been bought at 31, but I could not recommend it. I could recommend hold but not buy. This would be too high to risk a purchase. There were other stocks available at bargain prices at this time with far less risk.

Steep trend lines when broken are invaluable to an investolator. While the proper type of downtrend line is the signal to get on board, the signal to abandon ship comes when the proper uptrend is broken. Picking this broken uptrend is more difficult than when buying. A selling decision must be made at times after certain actions of only a few months, while your buying decisions follow the action of years. There will be more uncertainty, and there will be errors, by far the most common of which will be selling too soon.

You must sell when an uptrend line of over 45 degrees has been positively broken, providing that the percentage of rise has been at or above the minimum reasonably expected according to its base.

It is nearly impossible for the public to become excited enough at a slower rate of rise to buy in large enough quantities for an important distribution top. It then stands to reason that an uptrend of less steepness when broken, should be ignored. Normally it would then pay to hold during whatever type of setback that follows. You must consider this reaction as being only temporary. Also do not sell if a steep uptrend line is broken when the line has formed for only a period of a few months during the early part of its markup.

A further discussion on the rule of selling when an uptrend line is of over 45 degrees is in order. Because of certain limitations within the boundaries of charts, at times two different stocks within the same price range will have different price spreads in their horizontal lines. Because one is charted with its horizontal lines on a $1.00 basis, its uptrend would easily have been OVER 45 degrees. Breaking it would have been the sell signal.

The uptrend line of the other stock charted on a basis of $2.00 per horizontal line would have been LESS than 45 degrees, thus giving no selling signal. This would result in getting two interpretations from similar actions, and a failure to sell the latter when it should have been sold.

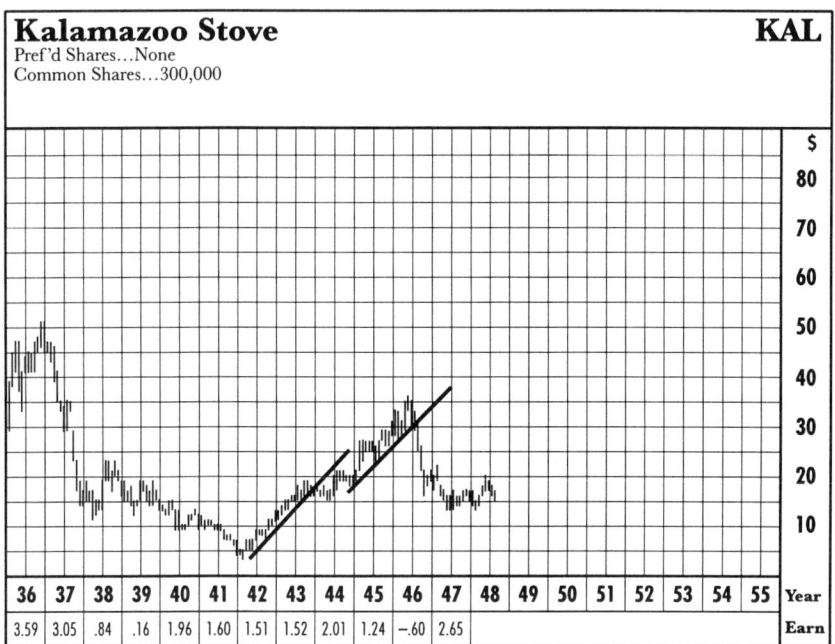

Kalamazoo Stove (KAL)

The chart of Kalamazoo Stove (KAL) on a $5.00 per line basis, shows a perfect uptrend during 1942-43 that was broken. Its rise was at the rate of less than 45 degrees, but had the horizontal lines been at the $2.00 rate, the trend would have mattered little because the previous base indicated a higher percentage of rise from its base price of about 10.

The following uptrend as shown on this chart was also under 45 degrees in steepness. On the basis of my selling rule, no sell signal was recognized when this trend line was broken. If the chart had been on a $2.00 basis, a perfect sell signal would have been given at 31, because at this price the expected minimum rise of 200% had been realized.

Keeping these horizontal lines priced about right, becomes almost automatic, as seen in the charts. As the price of a stock rises above the upper edge of its chart, the price rate of the horizontal lines is increased in the chart of a later issue, so as to keep the stock's range within the chart's allotted frame.

Because of the wide range of prices among stocks it is impossible to set a price ratio of the horizontal lines to fit the various stocks within their price ranges. Judging when an uptrend line is rising at an angle more or less than 45 degrees is a problem which must be left up to you. Only by studying the charts for a time and comparing older charts to newer ones and adding a measure of common sense can you develop this "feel" for the proper relationship between stock price and chart grid. But it is important to learn—and the sooner the better—whether or not the price scale of the horizontal lines has distorted the price action of your stock.

There are bound to be some borderline cases where you would have to use some judgment in deciding whether the rise was merely in the markup stage or was fast enough to be distribution. If the daily rate of trading has not increased to an extremely heavy pace compared to previous volume you can be sure the stock is not yet in the top range, and you may be justified in ignoring the broken uptrend line even though it may be steeper than 45 degrees.

Goodrich (B.F.) Company (GR)

You should carefully study all past actions and familiarize yourself with the various trend lines. Notice the long uptrend of Goodrich Co. (GR) ending in 1946. Because of the 3-for-1 split and far higher prices at a later date, chart "B" was condensed. This trend does not show the steepness of about 55 degrees it really had at that time when it topped at 89, also on a $5.00 scale. While studying these actions of the past, you must make allowance for these changed conditions. On this scale there would not have been a sell signal as in chart "A" because the trend was less than 45 degrees.

This perfect uptrend was marred by a shakeout (I am surprised there weren't more) in July, 1945 (E). This just before the speeded up action that culminated in a top. This shakeout may have induced you to sell, believing it to be a change in trend. In the more recent chart this shakeout did not appear to be much but at that time GR sold four points below the trend line.

This is where an investolator should learn to use some judgment on a selling decision. During most of the previous five months before this shakeout took place, the price range was within five points. You should consider this action too quiet for a top on a $60 stock and should have ignored this break. The following nine months had a 33 point range. This is the increase in activity you should watch for in a top—a turbulence which followed a steady rise of over 3-1/2 years. It will pay

TREND LINES: YOUR BUY AND SELL SIGNALS 89

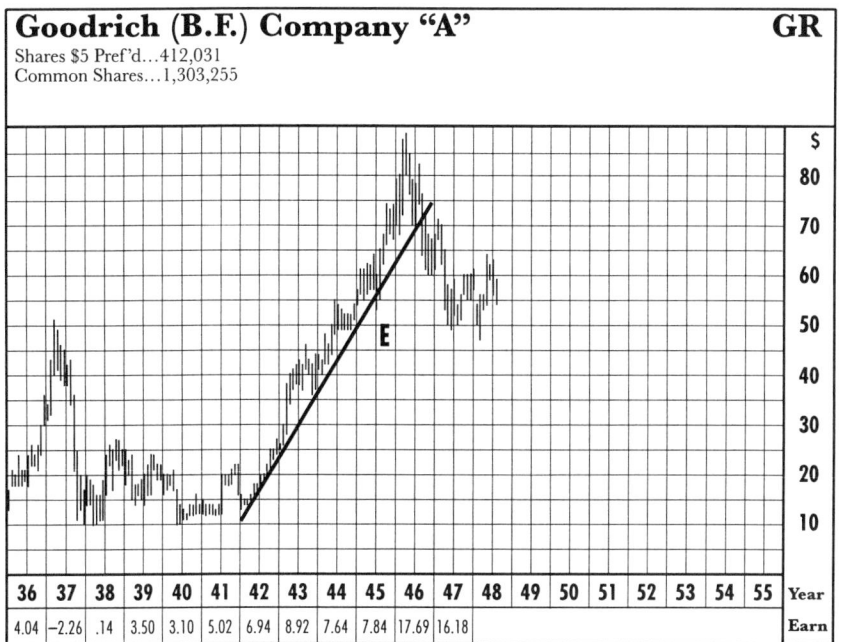

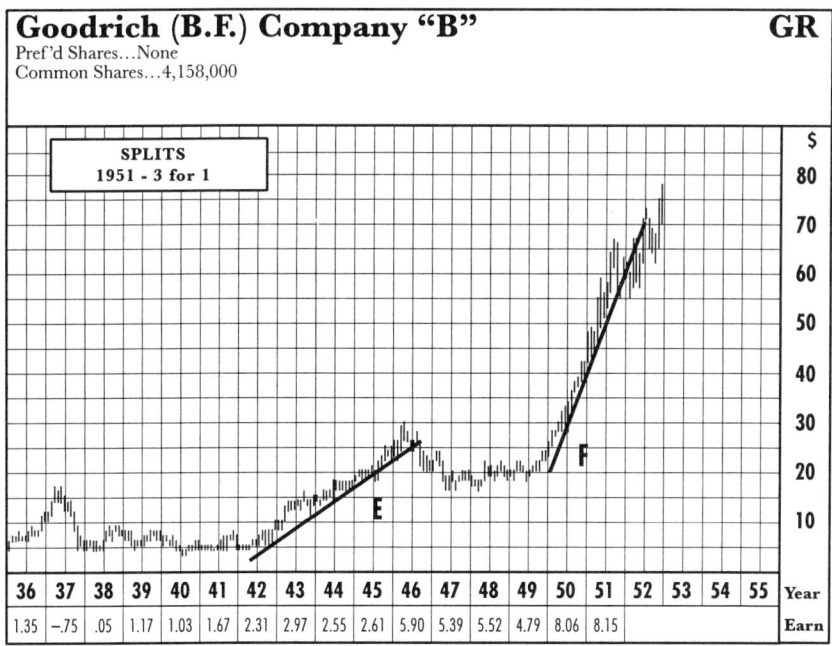

you to sell voluntarily when the price changes become quite active, on
the upside, after the rise has reached the high range in which a top may

be expected. This can often be far above the broken trend—perhaps six months later.

After a three-year base, Goodrich formed another perfect uptrend (F) which when broken may have tricked you as a novice into selling too soon. If you had noticed that the rate of daily trading had not increased to an unusual degree you may have carried it over. That would have been a great break for you as it rose to over 700% above its base price, breaking a perfect uptrend with its sell signal. If you had sold too soon, which is a mistake you MUST make at times to protect yourself against far worse mistakes, you would have seen at that time, many of the soundest foundations for future rises ever charted. A new position in the market could easily have been taken.

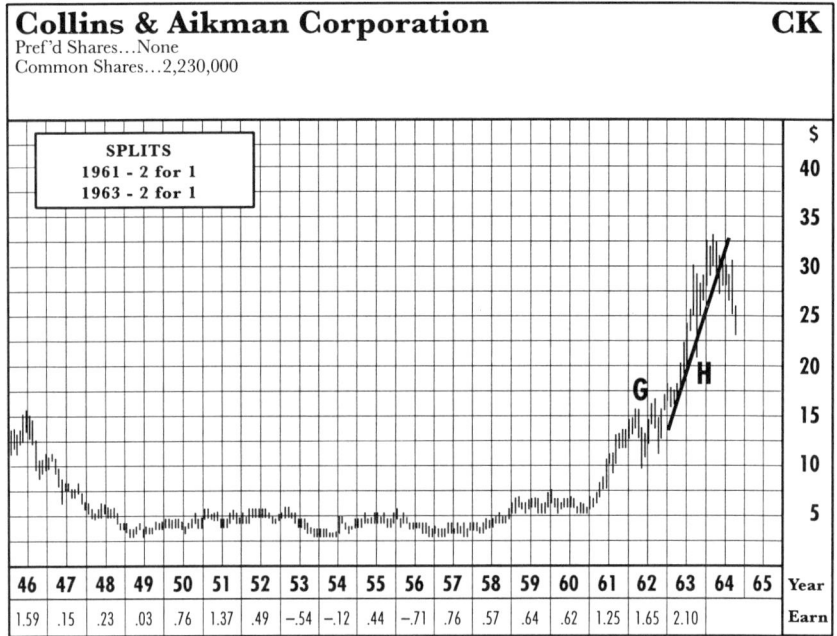

Collins & Aikman Corporation (CK)

The thirteen-year base of Collins & Aikman (CK) was an unusually sound foundation. When the uptrend of over 45 degrees was broken in 1962 (G), you would have ignored this as a sell signal, because this base indicated a far larger rise. The records show that when a trend line is broken at this early stage of a markup, the price usually does not recover so quickly. Obviously the manipulators of CK preferred to keep it on the move. After all, accumulation had begun fourteen years previously. Perhaps even the manipulators became impatient for their profits.

CK broke another trend line in November, 1963 (H). You should not have allowed yourself to have been influenced by this because the selloff was caused by the panic selling when President Kennedy was assassinated. An unpredictable disaster never actually changes the basic trend of the stock market. If you did not "cash in" with a voluntary sale around 30, you should have been sold out at about 28, below the broken trend line.

Study the long rises of past charts and draw trend lines along the ascending bottoms and compare them closely. Pore over them until you can see there is quite a distinct difference. The long uptrend line when broken is the key to unlocking your profits before they are lost. Many of them can be called borderline situations, very difficult to decide, and at times you are bound to be wrong when you sell. If you are, then forget it: don't consider buying it back in the near future. Look for another "deadbeat." They have a habit of coming to life after a great many shareholders have given up.

Every chartist knows the value of trend lines when they are broken, especially the importance of waiting *until the trend line is broken*. Buying when the recommended downtrend line is broken will seldom be a mistake. Selling when the recommended uptrend line is broken may be a mistake 20% of the time, but it will always be a mistake with a profit. This method is meant to protect you against the probability of carrying a stock down into the next accumulation period of many years' duration. Selling too soon is good insurance against holding a stock too long. If there is a more reliable method of picking a selling point, I wish someone would teach it to me.

Taking a profit too soon, as proven at a later date, can leave one in an unhappy mood. But it should be considered in a different light. You should feel fortunate at having had the opportunity to make this error. A large profit was realized. You should feel fortunate that you are not among those who bought in these high price areas and since have taken billions of losses. Many have become destitute because of their high-level investing.

Selling Short

Selling a stock "short" is commonly done by speculators who believe a stock is selling too high and who anticipate a drop in price. Selling short is selling a stock that you "do not own." The first thing that the average person asks upon learning this is, "How can you sell something you do not own?" It is difficult for him to understand that a "bear," as the short seller is called, initiates a trade by selling a number of shares and completes it at an undetermined price and date when he buys it back, or "covers" it, as it is often termed.

A person who unknowingly buys shares that were a short sale is entitled to take possession of his stock, but the seller in this case, has no stock from which to make delivery. In order to make delivery of this stock (which is compulsory), the seller's broker borrows the stock from some other client. This borrowing is made possible by margin accounts. When a person opens a margin account, his broker asks him to sign an agreement giving the broker permission to lend his margined stocks to other traders. These shares will be returned when the short seller completes his trade, and more often than not, he has chalked up another loss.

There is nothing wrong in being pessimistic at times about the future price of a stock. But there are plenty of reasons why it is wrong for a novice to sell short. He is then a speculator betting his money on the market, and is then subject to all the adverse influences that afflict the speculators.

"Shorting" a stock too soon in a bull market is a bear's most common mistake. Selling too late in a bear market comes second.

The odds are so much greater against the bear than they are with the bull, or one who is "long" in the market. Because of growth potential the average stock over a period of time will rise more than it will drop.

While short, a bear is obligated to pay dividends to the one from whom the stock is borrowed. The lender is entitled to the dividends, but he is not now a registered owner with the company, because his stock is held by the broker and his stock is listed as being under "street names only." The dividends on these stocks are paid by the corporations to the brokers, who immediately credit these to the accounts of the shareholders. But one who has had his stock loaned out, will not be receiving these.

In other words, when a speculator sells a stock short, there is at that time more stock owned than has been actually issued by the corporation. So the short seller must pay the lender any dividends, warrants or stock dividends declared during the period this stock has been borrowed.

A bear can lose money more than twice as easily as he can make it. Example: A. sold short 100 ABC @ 40. On a 100% rise to 80, he would have lost $4000, or 100%, *plus* declared dividends and commission. If B., also with $4000 sold short 50 XYZ @ 80 and "covered" or bought it back @ 40, his profit would have been only 50% or $2000, *less* declared dividends and commission.

Conversely, a bull can make money nearly twice as easily as he can lose it. A $4000 purchase @ 40, and sold @ 80, would be a 100% gain or $4000 plus dividends, but minus commissions. A $4000 purchase @ 80 and sold @ 40 would result in a 50% loss or $2000 and commissions, but he would have received the dividends. Only half as many shares would have been bought at 80.

Many high-level investors have held their shares long enough to recover a 50% loss, but it is doubtful if many bears have carried their stock over a 100% rise and regained their loss. In the first place the bear would have had to put up much more money in order to have held his loss at 100%.

A bear may be right when he thinks a stock is selling above its true value, but he does not realize that others may not think so. His logical reasoning is worthless and illogical when mass psychology is guided by market manipulation. Important tops (those that hold for many years) always take place far above a stock's true value.

Too many shorts in a stock may help defeat their own purpose. These bears are potential buyers and when there is a heavy short interest in a stock, there is also a very strong impetus for it to move into new high ground when they "run for cover," buying at a loss.

Every thirty days the New York Stock Exchange reports a list of companies in which the short interest is 20,000 shares or more. Some of them have an extremely heavy short interest, but usually these are stocks that have millions of shares outstanding and are actively traded.

On October 15, 1965 I noticed that there was a short interest of 23,300 shares in Dr. Pepper. The close on that date was $37\text{-}1/8$. The majority of these bears are in trouble and don't know it—yet. This stock, compared to its low of 4 in 1957, is extremely high, and apparently these bears think it is too high. The volume on DOC for months averaged only a few hundred shares per day. This stock is in strong hands. It is merely consolidating its gains. A base for a large fast rise is building up. There may be a shakeout first and these bears would have an opportunity to take a profit, but usually a weak appearance will only attract more of them. *NEVER sell a stock short when trading is extremely light.* Dr. Pepper is a bear trap that will close on these people some time in the future.

Previous to 1934 short selling was an important tool in the hands of pool managers as they were openly spoken of in those days. They would initiate a downtrend with a "bear raid" by driving down the price of a stock by short selling. The public, frightened by this show of weakness, would sell heavily. The pool would cover their short sales at a profit and buy long for the inevitable rally.

This practice was partially blocked by a ruling that a short sale could only be made at a price higher than the last sale. It now takes a little more finesse to drive a stock down by short selling—and it takes more time. In order to create a heavier supply than demand, the sponsor now can sell short only as often as it is possible to do so on an "uptick."

There were enough traders throughout the country during 1930-31 who were bearish enough to sell Case Threshing Machine short (now J. I. Case), that at times a premium was being charged for borrowing the shares for delivery by those who sold short. There were less than

200,000 shares outstanding at that time and probably some of this stock was loaned several times. There could have been a terrible squeeze if all longs had suddenly refused to sell and refused to allow their shares to be loaned. It is certainly the height of something or other when traders buy stocks, and the brokers loan them to pools and other bears, so they can drive the value of a stock down to where a margin trader would get a margin call and have to sell out. That makes about as much sense as if someone carried insurance on your home and you loaned them matches and gasoline so they could burn it down.

The following quote is from literature sent me by an advisory service: "Don't be afraid to short stocks that are down considerably from their highs. Remember that no matter how much a stock is down already, the maximum downside potential profit from shorting at any level is the same, 100%." The writer's ignorance is showing badly in this statement. It is impossible for this potential profit to be realized unless the company goes broke. I don't think anyone could figure out a more positive method of losing money in the market than by this type of thinking. It is possible to make a profit shorting a stock after it is down 50%, but anyone who tries it is just plain reckless.

There are books advising how to make money selling short. I wonder, not how often, but how seldom, did the authors pay income tax on their short sales? I can tell you in one short, simple sentence how to make money selling short. Sell high and buy low. But doing so is not so simple. You may sell high, but invariably not high enough. My advice is, don't try it.

Compare this type of risk with a well purchased stock that can and often does move up several hundred percent. Which would you rather have going for you?

Why You Should Consider Buying On Margin

Buying stocks on margin primarily is like buying anything else on credit, but in some respects there are vast differences. It is not necessary to have a credit rating. You are required to make a very heavy down payment because of the wide range of price fluctuations. You are under no obligation to make future payments at any future date. Your only obligation is to keep your equity in the stock above a minimum margin requirement. The stock remains in the hands of your broker as collateral.

The initial margin rates of 50% to 90% are set by the Federal Reserve Board and are subject to change without notice.

If the price of your stock has dropped to where your equity is below 25%, you will get a "margin call." (Some brokers have set this rule at 30%.) You either deposit enough money to bring your equity to 25% or better, or sell a portion of your holdings in order to protect the remaining shares. If your margin dropped to 23%, $23 out of each $100 worth sold, will be applied to your unsold stock. If you sold out entirely you would lose your position with a heavy loss.

As an investolator, I suggest that you always buy your stocks through a margin account even though you pay for them in full. Certainly if you buy securities when they appear to be in a sound base or consolidation on a minimum of 70% margin, you are taking little

WHY YOU SHOULD CONSIDER BUYING ON MARGIN

risk. You will pay interest on the debit balance, but you will receive dividends from the extra shares you were able to buy. Your margin account can take the place of a savings account.

There is probably no easier way to borrow money than from a margin account. Suppose you bought securities that cost you $10,000. You deposited $9,500 or 95% margin. Months later you bought a new car. Let's say with your trade-in and some cash you would still be owing $1000 on it. Instead of paying high interest rates and making regular monthly payments, you merely phone your broker for a check for $1000, and pay for the car in full. It is as simple as that. Your margin account will then have a debit of $1500 instead of $500. In fact, if the minimum margin requirement at this time was 70%, you could draw up to $2500 without any questions asked, providing your stock is at or above its purchase price. There is no deadline on paying it off as on your car payments. Instead of sending in your normal car payments at regular intervals you may make deposits in varying amounts and dates. Interest charges are stopped at once on the amount of each deposit. Within the margin limitations you can borrow without all the bother of filling out application forms for credit rating, etc. And you will have saved yourself the cost and nuisance of changing the registration after paying the car off through the installment plan.

If you were to have an emergency at a time when you were low on cash, you could draw money immediately from your margin account, providing it was available. If there was not enough available, you could sell a few shares and draw the proceeds at once. If your stock was in a "cash" account, normally you would have to wait four trading days until the "settlement" date before you could make a withdrawal after selling it. This would take a week if this took place over a three-day holiday. If your emergency took place when you were a thousand miles from home where your stock was laid away, or in a safe deposit box, there could be many more days' delay before you could get your signature on the certificate and delivered.

Another advantage is that your stock will be held by the broker; its safety is assured, and it will be there when you want to sell it.

If you deal with a nation-wide broker you can walk into a branch office in Miami or Seattle and draw a check within thirty minutes from a margin account. They merely wire your account number to their head office asking if the amount you ask for is available. You endorse the check and have them verify your signature. The bank where you can cash it is usually nearby. I have done this in both cities.

Branch offices are handy also if you want to buy or sell. One time from a distant town in Florida I phoned the Miami branch collect, and sold 40,000 bushels of rye. They did not know me from Adam, but did not hesitate to take my order. They only required my account number and branch office where it was located.

Another advantage with a margin account is that you can withdraw part of your paper profits on your securities without selling them. Suppose you had a paper profit of $1000 on your stock based on a 70% margin. You could draw $300 of this. The $700 remaining paper profit of course covers the increase value of the stock by 70%. $300 would then be added to your debit balance. But do not overdo this privilege as the price rises. You can find yourself on a 70% margin at too high a price.

There are circumstances under which you can draw money from a margin account when your margin or equity has dropped below 70%, but only if there is *new* money in the account, such as dividends or deposits. You can do this as long as your equity is above 25% of the previous day's close. But of course it would be foolhardy to lower your margin to this extreme.

Your broker keeps a record of this new money in what is called a Miscellaneous Account.

If you buy on a minimum margin you must realize the importance of buying right. It is far safer to buy a stock in the proper price range on a 50% margin than it is to buy high on a 70% margin. I do not mean to minimize the importance of buying "right" even though you pay for it outright. There is little comfort in holding a stock far below its cost, even though it is paid for and is in a safety deposit box.

There are those who think that when you buy on margin, and the price of your stock drops a dollar, you are called on to make up this amount. This is not the case. The fact is that if you bought a $20 stock on a 70% margin, you would not get a margin call until it dropped below 8, when your equity would be below 25%, or less than $2.00 per share.

During the 1928-29 stock market boom margin rates were set by the whims of the brokers themselves. It is doubtful if they were influenced by any concern for the safety of the public, but most probably by their own desire for more commissions. In those days of no restrictions, I can't imagine the average broker trying to convince a client to pay for a purchase in full, when an order on a 15% margin would give him a commission of nearly six times more than a cash order—especially when most brokers at that time were just as gullible as the public on that historic rise.

The disastrous break which resulted from this speculative binge is what really made history—and broke thousands. Margin calls and distress selling were synonymous. Traders had little time to meet margin calls with cash. It was sell, sell, sell. During the worst of the crash, traders could buy on the opening of the market and be sold out by the margin clerk before the close. Small margins literally meant sudden death to an account, and at times to its owner.

In two days during the 1929 crash, American International broke 50%, from 60 to 30, Eastman Kodak from 222 to 164, General Electric 296 to 210, Radio Corp. 57 to 26 and General Motors 53 to 33-3/4. There were 971,000 shares of General Motors traded on that second day. GM at that time had only a fraction of the shares that it has today. This was before stock splits had become popular.

The 1929 crash was not the end of margin calls. During the two years following the Dow Jones Industrial high of 296 in 1930, to its low of 42 in 1932, the attrition of margin traders was almost steady. The pace of the margin clerks was now more routine. Those days of spending half the night making margin calls by phone and telegram and the other half sleeping on cots in downtown offices were over.

The reasons of the Federal Reserve Board for deciding to change the margin requirements are not always consistent with the market moves as indicated by the Dow Jones Averages. If these rates were set for the purpose of helping to prevent the public from overbuying in the upper price ranges, they have failed badly since the 1946 top when 100% on purchases was required. Compare this with the DJI 1956-57 top of 521, nearly 150% higher, when the margin was only 70%. No doubt this contributed to much heavier losses for margin traders during the 1957 break. The margin was set at 90% during the 1959-60 top, but had been lowered to 70%, with the DJI 50 points higher, long before the 1961 top was toppled by the 1962 panic selling. You can be certain that this break was aggravated by margined accounts. Doesn't it seem incongruous that the margin rate was less during a period of distribution above 700 than it was during accumulation for a two-year period in the late forties, when the DJI averaged 175 and the margin rate was 75%?

The Federal Reserve Board did give the margin traders a break by dropping the margin requirements to 50% before the moderate final shakeout in 1949, during its three-year bottom. Again it was lowered to 50% before the final mild shakeout in 1953, during what I call a consolidation period. The previous two years it had been 75%. After the severe shakeouts of 1957 and 1962 the rate was lowered to 50% from a 70% rate.

This seemingly generous gesture toward giving the public a break was of little benefit, because during most of these four periods at the 50% rate, the vast majority were sellers. During these periods, the public attitude ranged from nervousness to being badly shaken up.

No agency can protect the greedy and gullible from themselves, but it seems that the FRB could use some rule for increasing margin rates, such as when the DJ averages have had a 50% rise above the last shakeout and volume has increased heavily on a rising market, they could raise the rate to 90% or 100%. There is no rule that would work out perfectly but it would certainly give better protection to the public than a 70% rate, after the market rose over 100% as it did from 1953 to 1956. The inexperienced do consistently buy in the higher range. So the fewer shares they can buy, the less they will be hurt.

Public confidence should be given a boost when margin rates are lowered to 50%, but in a mixed market, when during a given period some stocks will be under distribution while others are being accumulated, confidence should only be directed to those stocks which are undergoing an accumulation or consolidation action, or to those that have not yet topped out.

When Mueller Brass sold at 22 in May, 1960, the minimum margin requirement was 90%, but during its top above 40 in 1963, you could have bought it on a 50% minimum rate. Anyone taking advantage of the 50% rate then would have lost money twice as fast on the following break, for the simple reason that they had bought twice as many shares. The moral is: At all times you must remain selective in your purchases, irrespective of what the margin requirements may be.

Many a trader has sold a stock short, with a full cash coverage, only to discover that when it rose against him, he was on a margin basis. For instance, if he had sold Chrysler short at 45, over 350%

above its previous low (many sold short previous to this), he would have had a paper loss of 50% when it sold at its high of 67-1/2 in 1964. His margin would have shrunk from 100% to 33%, not including the dividends he would have had to pay. Would he have had the courage to hold his short position over the top to where he could have covered his sale at a gain the following year? This is doubtful. If he had sold short at 45 on a 70% margin, at 67-1/2 he would have had only $9.00 of his original left. Before this price was reached, he would have put up more money or been forced to close out his trade because of failure to meet a margin call.

The mere thought of buying stocks on margin is as frightening to the average person as parachute jumping. They immediately visualize being sold out with a heavy loss. This can easily become true when stocks are bought haphazardly in the higher price range. Those who bought in the upper levels of 1961-62 on a 70% margin were lucky if they escaped close attention from the margin clerk.

The margin trader, as a speculator, is very prone to buying too high. Generally, he uses stop-loss orders to keep himself out of serious trouble, cutting his losses short. Normally this only gives him a longer span of activity in the market, which means more experience for his money, so to speak. A stop-loss order may be either a buy or sell depending on whether the trader was long or short in the market. Using the phrase "stop-loss" is quite appropriate, because when used by traders, they often mean just that.

I do favor buying on margin, if you buy in the proper range as can be determined by a study of long range charts. If you buy on a 50% margin, it is more important than ever that you do it only after a proper period of accumulation or consolidation action has appeared. When you do this you are buying in a comparatively safe range and should never entertain the thought of taking a loss.

Bond Stores, Inc. (BND)

Let us use Bond Stores as a hypothetical case in which you first bought 200 shares on a 50% margin at 13-3/4 in February, 1954 (I), after what appeared to be a substantial bottom. Against the actual cost of $2750, you deposited $1400 which more than covered the commission. You then have a debit balance of roughly $1400. You let your dividends be credited to your account as they pay off your interest

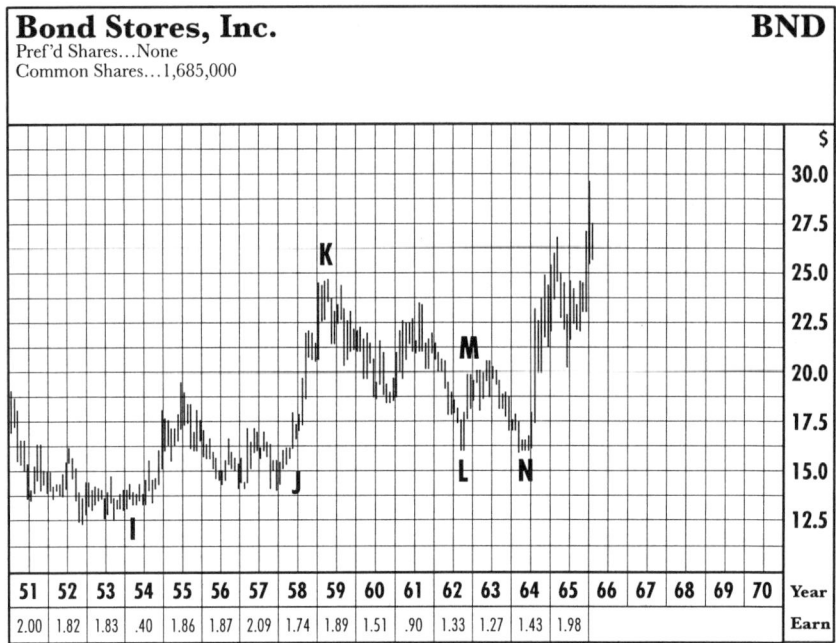

charges and decrease your debit balance, which in turn, lowers your interest charges. In 1955 the stock appeared to be beginning its rise, but it turned down for a two and one-half-year setback, a period that proved to be very discouraging. You considered it a late mover when you bought it compared to other stocks, but now it had become a late, late mover.

Now after BND had extended its base to nine years, you had the confidence to buy another 100 shares at 18 in August, 1958 (J) as it sold above the previous highs of 17-1/2. You were able to make this purchase without any additional money. At 18 you had a paper profit of $800. Because the margin requirements had again been reduced to 50% from 70%, you would be permitted to use half of your profit to purchase more stock. The other half covers the increase in the value of your stock at 50%. This $400 has a purchasing power of $800 on a 50% margin rate. You have $600 in accrued dividends after interest charges. This gives you an additional $1200 in purchasing power, for a total of $2000. After this purchase you now had a debit balance of $2600.

This rise continued into 1959 (K) and BND appeared to have begun its markup phase. But it was not planned that way. During the 1962 market break it sold as low as 16 (L). The 1959 top had not carried high enough nor fast enough to be a distribution top. So this action must be an extension of the accumulation phase. Someone, it would appear, wanted more shares of BND.

When the downtrend line was broken in November, 1962, you again sharpened your pencil. You found that since your purchase in 1958 you had been credited with $1150 in dividends above your interest charges. The minimum margin rate had again been reduced to 50%. With this new purchasing power of $2300 you bought another 100 shares when it crossed the 18 level (M) after the downtrend was apparently reversed. This purchase added another $650 plus commission to your debit balance, which is now over $3300.

This rally fizzled at 20-1/2. The next down turn ended at 15-7/8 in 1964 (N), after the directors cut the dividend rate from $1.25 to $1.00. At this time I mentioned to friends that I considered this to be a final drastic attempt to discourage the public into selling out in this low range.

You were never in any danger of being crowded for margin during this long wait, but for a person having bought with expectations of a large capital gain, within a reasonable time, your patience was thoroughly tested. You withstood the natural tendency to sell out in disgust and instead bought more with paper profits and dividends.

My confidence in BND during your hypothetical case never wavered. I backed up my own opinion from time to time by buying more as I made a profit on other stocks or commodities, until I acquired 17,500 shares.

On Wednesday, December 29, 1965, the financial page quoted the volume on BND at 72,100. Because in recent days only a few hundred shares had been traded I believed this could be an error in wire transmission. I checked with my broker and he told me that a block of 68,100 shares had been sold at 23. This was 3-3/8 below the recent high. I said to my broker, "This probably clears the deck now for Bond Stores to start its rise." Three days later it rose to 29-1/2. The sponsors of BND probably knew this block was overhanging the market and one can only guess how long they had been waiting for it.

I received a notice from my broker dated March 17, 1966, that Bond Stores was offering to buy up to 500,000 shares of their common stock at $30. The expiration date to accept this offer was March 29, just five days before an ex-dividend date. The company thereby saved $125,000 in dividends.

Sad to say, I did not accept this offer to sell and I advised my numerous friends to hold. On March 29, BND closed at 28. With an assist of a weak general market BND dropped. It was not selling pressure that forced it down, but lack of purchase orders. Some days there were only one or two hundred shares traded. There was just no incentive for the public to buy.

If my friends and I had offered our stock to Bond Stores, they would have taken close to 20,000 shares. If we had attempted to buy these back later, this demand would have held the price up, and little stock would have been sold by the public. It is doubtful that we would have been able to repurchase this amount below 28.

In my opinion there were powerful psychological forces at play. This was proven by the fact that almost all of those who bought BND on my recommendation (whom I promised to notify when I thought it was time to sell) called me on the phone and asked if they should sell at 30. This proves the power of suggestion, because previously as the price of BND moved up through 24, 27 and as high as 29-1/2, no one questioned me as to whether they should sell or hold.

For instance from 16 to 29-1/2, BND required little purchasing power to move it up because there was not much for sale. On volume of less than 15,000 shares the price rose from 23-1/2 to 29-1/2 on January 3, 1966. Certainly there was not much of an urge to sell by the public in this price range. If BND had had a normal, quiet consolidation of several months below 30, and then moved up through 30, it would have done so with ease. A volume of less than 20,000 could easily have moved it up from about 29-1/2 to 31-1/2 in one day. But because of this tender to buy 500,000 shares at 30, the public offered nearly 700,000 shares.

In my opinion, this purchase of nearly one-third of the total shares of BND increases its technical strength, tremendously. This huge amount is not now overhanging the market. When the markup phase is under way, BND should move up with little resistance because of less profit taking.

Now that the directors put a large portion of the company's cash surplus into the purchase of its own shares, an interesting viewpoint is created. If the price of BND reaches 80, it will have a paper profit of $25,000,000 or an increase of nearly $15 to its actual basic value. Also nearly one-third of its dividends will revert back into its cash account, which theoretically will give leverage towards increasing the dividend which will then automatically draw more attention from the public. In 1964, long before this interesting situation developed, I said that when BND sells above 70, it will be far more attractive to the public than when it was selling below 17. Now the price rise will have a tendency to lift itself by its own bootstraps. Certainly it will help to heat up the speculative urge to the boiling point.

Since this purchase of 500,000 shares, the price drifted lower. I believe much of this selling is by persons who offered their stock for sale at 30 and are now selling those shares that were not taken by the company because they were bought on a proration basis. An exception was a case where 10 shares or less were returned to the stockholder.

There is just no incentive, from the public viewpoint, to buy. The public seldom recognizes a bargain. I believe the directors knew that BND was a bargain at 30, but did the general public think it was an unwise purchase? They must because as proven by its action since then, few are buying it back below at even lower prices.

The selloff in 1966 may prove to be the last opportunity to buy it below 30. Following the 1966 general market shakeout, it may be among the first ones to begin its markup phase.

Now let us pick up your theoretical example from where you last bought 100 shares BND at 18 in November, 1962 on a 50% margin. Since then the margin requirements have been raised to 70%, at the time of this writing in May, 1966. When BND moves up to 30 you will have enough paper profits and accrued dividends above interest charges to enable you to buy another 100 shares at 30.

This prediction of the future price of BND is based entirely on the supposition that I understand the theory of market manipulation and the psychology of the public.

The reader must realize that this is the way I learned to think when I received chart reading lessons in 1931. Always, when I study past actions of any chart, I think in terms of how the public are being influenced by this or that action. If this thinking is wrong as some would have me believe, can you tell me any other endeavor in which a fortune can be made by wrong thinking?

Volume:
The Important Messages Behind the Figures

The number of shares traded daily (either bought or sold) of a stock is spoken of as the stock's volume. This total is shown in the financial pages of newspapers under a column (sales in 100's) ahead of the stock prices. For instance the figure 11 will mean 1100 shares, or 1293 will represent 129,300 shares.

The large newspapers list the price of all stocks in four columns: *open:* the price at which the first trade was made; *high:* the highest price for the day; *low:* the lowest price; and *close:* the last price traded. The smaller papers usually list only a portion of the stocks, usually the best known companies and the most actively traded, and they usually list only the closing price.

The large dailies usually group a list of the most active 10 or 15 stocks for the day. During a period of panic selling, the volume on these can run very high. But the volume is usually even greater during the fast markup of a stock or during its distribution when trading on some will exceed 100,000 shares and a few will exceed one-quarter million. The high volume on these has a powerful appeal to speculators. Their reasoning is (if they reason at all) that a stock must be an extremely good one and going higher to attract such heavy demand.

They seem to overlook the fact that for every million shares bought at these usually exorbitantly high prices, there were also a million sold.

The total volume of daily trading in the market as a whole is also listed in financial pages and is watched closely by speculators.

Volume of daily trading can be an important subject, but I do not intend for the investolator to go into this too deeply. There are times when it can be very misleading.

Volume is always comparatively light when a stock is under accumulation, the "wearing out" process of inducing the shareholders to sell out. The public selling is light but their buying is even less. Volume is nearly always light on reactions during a rise and during the rallies in a bear market. An investolator who attemped to interpret this too closely, would only find himself in a state of confusion. Leave this for the speculators.

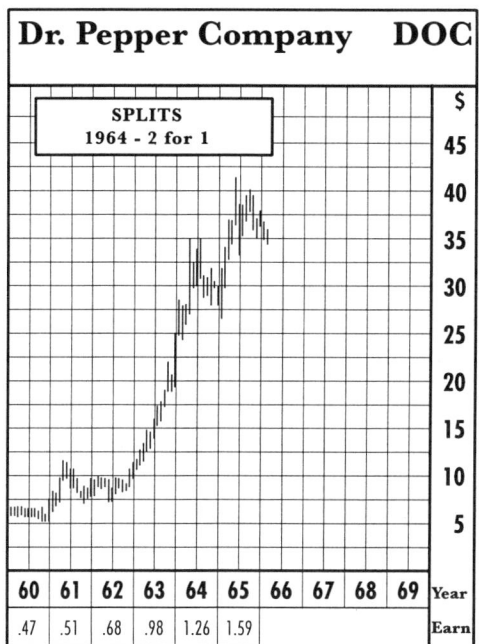

Dr. Pepper Company (DOC) and Royal Crown Cola (RCC)

Dr. Pepper (DOC) and Royal Crown Cola (RCC) were marked up by several hundred percent and both broke steep trend lines after the previous monthly action did appear to be toppy. *But if you were aware of the light volume during that time you would have realized it was not heavy enough for distribution.* Both rose to new highs in 1965, again on comparatively light volume. This can be the perfect cue that the top has not been made.

Volume MUST be heavy during distribution.

As I happened to be charting these daily, I recognized that they must have another rise that will take them far above their 1965 highs. When? I can only guess. The speculators have not yet been enticed into buying these stocks. Both of them had very sound bases, and someone bought a lot of shares during these bases which have not yet been sold.

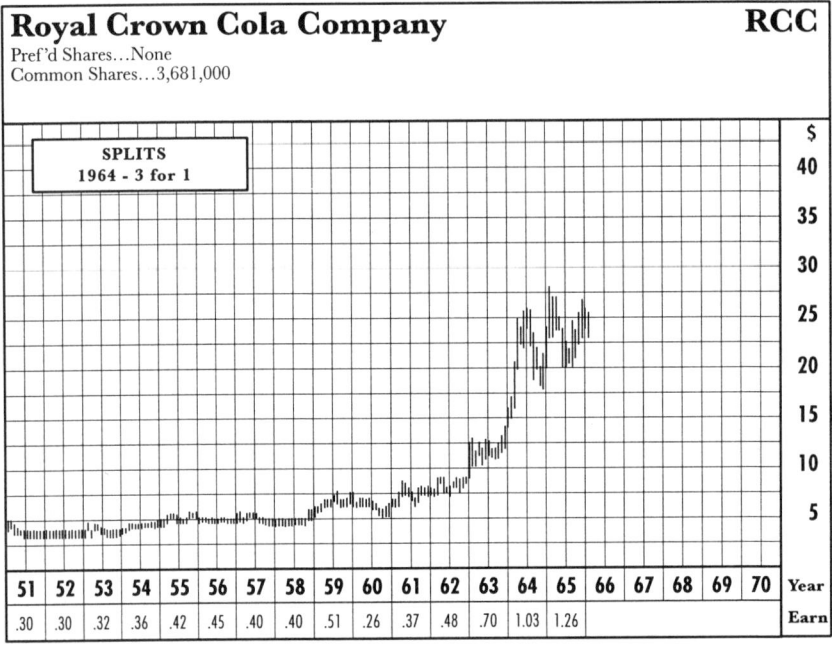

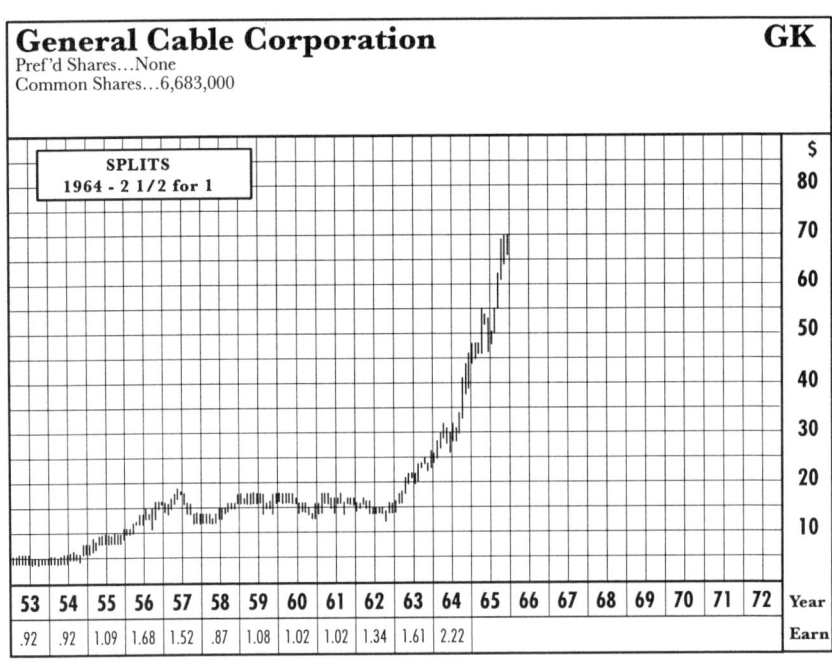

General Cable Corporation (GK)

General Cable (GK) is another that rose as high as 75 on light volume in 1966. It will go higher. One wonders from the record of these three how many others in the past had light volume previous to breaking a steep uptrend and would have been sold because of this, an action which later would have proven to be a mistake. Obviously then, if the volume has not increased heavily, you would be justified in holding for higher prices in spite of a broken steep trend line.

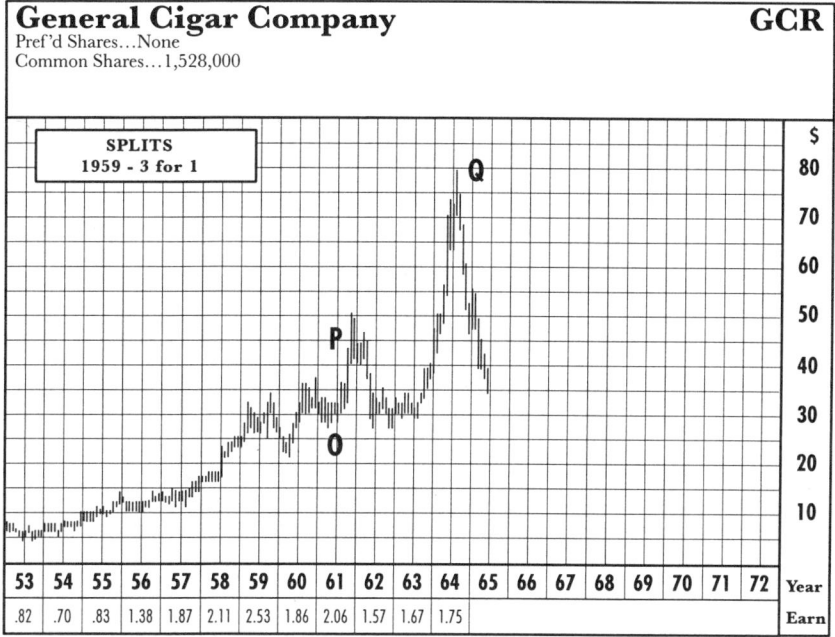

General Cigar Company (GCR) and American Snuff Company (SNU)

Because of a sealed prediction that I made in January, 1965, that the hindsight on General Cigar (GCR) gave the foresight on American Snuff (SNU), I checked on its action occasionally. As I was not charting it daily, I made this statement based on the similarity of their monthly charts. Its action did not surprise me, but its small volume during the action did. SNU made a new high on February 25, 1965, at 30-3/8 on only 300 shares. March 25, one month later, it made a new high at 30-1/2 on 500. The next day it required the demand of 1000 shares to push it up to 31. The following day it rose two points to 33 on only 1200 shares, then fell back to 32 on 400 shares.

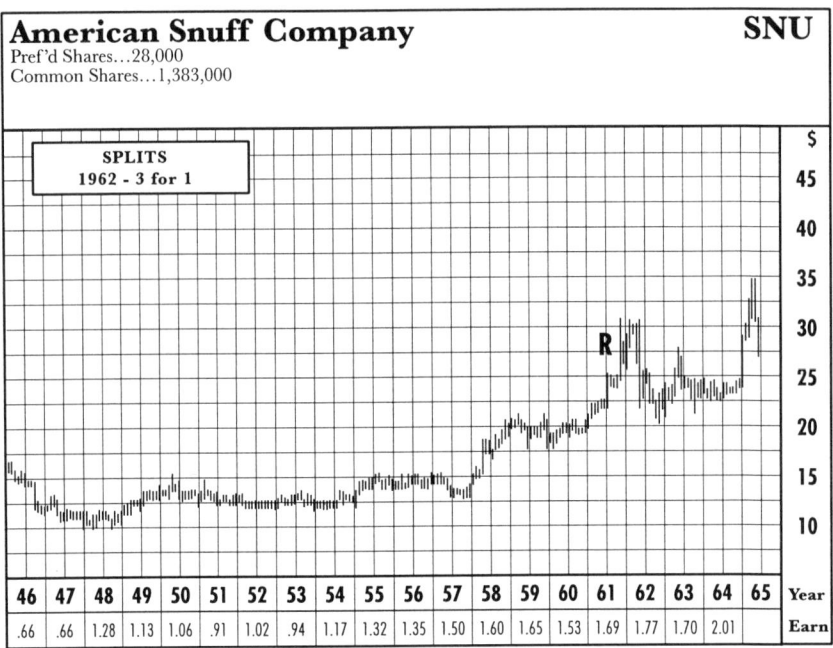

This is an extreme situation in *showing technical strength by the lightness of its volume*. SNU was in such strong hands that there was little for sale. The public that luckily had not sold out at lower prices were holding with confidence. There was little for sale, but there was enough demand to move it up. So few shares passed over the tape at that time that the speculators did not notice them. When the public eventually does, they may create a demand of possibly 50,000 or more shares a day above 60. The public still holding it will do so with more confidence than ever. This is where the smart money will gladly offer the buyers all the stock they want. Instead of profits, the speculators may only get a sneeze out of snuff. SNU has an extremely sound combination of a base and series of consolidations behind it. What more proof do you need?

When you see new highs made on extremely low volume you must realize that any setbacks will be temporary. A serious break and prolonged setback can only happen when the stock is in weak hands, namely those of the public.

While on the subject of American Snuff and General Cigar, take particular notice of the similarity in their price actions. Both dropped from temporary tops in 1961. GCR spent only sixteen months in the

30 range building up technical strength (O). Five months later its rise hesitated for two months just below its November, 1961 high (P). It was then "baited" with a fast rise, and the public took the bait. The volume on this top must have been tremendous for the manipulators to have sold out so quickly what it had taken them many years to buy. It topped at 79 (Q) with smaller earning than in 1957, when the high was only 17. You have to admit this represents good manipulation.

SNU spent fifteen months longer than GCR building up its strength after its temporary top in 1961 (R). It spent one month instead of two just under its previous high. When it started up from this point it appeared that it was going to duplicate the rise of GCR. The rise was stopped at 35 and the wearing out process was again instituted, during which volume was extremely light. So light in fact, that there was no sale at all on December 13, 1965.

Falling back from 35 proves to me that the insiders are anxious to pick up more shares.

Checking over the quotations of May 20, 1965 on the N.Y. Stock Exchange, I noticed numerous stocks that had very light trading that day. This is an important item for an investolator to watch. These common stocks with such light trading indicate that they are in strong hands; they have not recently been under distribution. They are all subject to a moderate setback at any time, but there is little risk in holding them for a fast rise which will precede a distribution top. The minimum rise that you can expect on some of them may be about 75% where they have already moved up considerably from their base. Some may move up over 300% from their prices on this date.

What figure represents the kind of volume which undoubtedly means distribution is underway? A 50,000 share day on a stock like Belding Hemingway would be comparable to 500,000 on General Motors. Bear in mind that as long as a common stock is idling along with daily average volume of less than 1000 shares, sometime in the not too distant future it will have a fast rise above its present price, whether its price is 8 or 80. A question is often asked of me when I make a positive statement similar to this. "Why," people want to know, "do you feel so certain that these stocks will go up?" From my experience in the market and the study of manipulation through the use of long range charts, the answer is simple: The insiders do not buy stocks for mere dividends; they are after capital gains. When they are ready, the stock will be marked up in a way that will attract and excite the public.

The following list of ten stocks had sales of only one to two hundred shares on May 20, 1965 when the DJI closed at 922.01, down 5.26. These stocks are subject to further setbacks, but their light volume is proof that they have not yet topped out.

Allen Industries	30-3/4	Barber Oil	82
American Brake Shoe	66-7/8	Belding Hemingway	19-3/4
American Consumers Ind.	18-1/2	Book-of-the-Month Club	22-3/4
American Snuff	32-1/2	Broadway Hale	42
Armstrong Rubber	42-1/4	Brown Shoe	60-3/4

Because of these, and so many others trading with very light volume, I can only form a positive opinion that the vast majority of our stocks are going to sell at far higher prices, always subject of course, to further setbacks for the purpose of frightening weak holders.

It is not necessary for volume to be so extremely light as those above to indicate that they are in strong hands. But the less volume, the more positive the indication. Six months or a year later these stocks may go through gyrations at the same approximate price level that may bring out an average of 1000 shares a day for a while. This would be just more of the wearing out process.

It is admittedly difficult to judge tops solely by heavy volume. Too often heavy volume will be seen on a price rise, only to increase suddenly and heavily at a higher price many months later after a reaction. Almost always the last new highs to be seen during a top will be on decreasing volume, as the speculative purchasing power is drying up. The reason for this is that the "pool managers" place the stock on the market at a slower pace, allowing the price to continue its rise with the idea of holding buying enthusiasm. Trying to time your selling price by studying *only* the vagaries of heavy volume may only complicate your selling decisions.

There is one positive rule to keep in mind while on the subject of heavy volume: You will seldom see heavy volume on a sound base. Heavy volume may appear on a shakeout during a rise, sometimes because of adverse news. But only a rally of varying degrees and time will follow heavy volume on a selling climax during a bear market. The final lows are yet to be made.

For instance, the bottom of the 1962 break was not made on the day when over 14,000,000 shares were traded. The low point was made some time later on far less volume when selling by weak and frightened holders was drying up. At a time like this, the price is allowed to drop in order to give a final weak appearance.

Daniel Seligman stated in *Fortune* that, "A two point rise on only 200 shares is presumably just a temporary aberration in the market; but if the rise was on 20,000 shares, the investor might legitimately wonder whether the big 'insiders' know something that has not reached the public, and are beginning to accumulate."

Now let's analyze this gem of enlightenment. Some experienced traders might say his ignorance of the market was showing. One wonders if the arrangement or the combination of the words in the latter half of this sentence is a deliberate attempt to plant a seed of thought into the novice's mind, misleading him into buying at the wrong time. The implication is that the 20,000 shares was an increase in volume which attracted attention. The words, "might legitimately wonder" gives the reader the impression that he could be correct in thinking the insiders were "beginning to accumulate." If the price rises two points because the insiders are BEGINNING to accumulate, the reader will wonder how high it will go before the insiders END their accumulation. So he may feel quite safe in climbing aboard. Everyone takes for granted that "insiders" know what they are doing and why. If the reader would be influenced to believe that accumulation is taking place when the volume on a stock increases to 20,000, what will he think when he sees volumes above 500,000 on a single stock. The natural instinct of the inexperienced when he sees heavy volume on a rising market is that the majority must be right. And for a limited time they are.

The fact is that many times it would be proper to quickly buy a stock when it shows strength with an increase in volume, but it is also a fact that too many times it would be a serious mistake. Ask any experienced trader and he will verify this. How many times has someone remarked "Every time I buy a stock, it goes down"? Buying when a stock is "showing strength" is the main reason.

As to the first part of Seligman's statement—has any reader ever seen a common stock with such a thin market that it went up two points on a volume of only 200 shares? I never have. I assume he is still referring to the same stock when he speaks of the 20,000 share volume.

I also assume that the price rise was also two points. How could the "insiders" or anyone else buy 20,000 shares on a two point market rise when there were only 200 for sale in that range? If anyone wanted to buy that many shares in one day and were willing to bid for it, the price would have easily gone up over 20 points unless organized selling by the insiders came out. In the first place the insiders just do not buy that way. If they did, it would be positive proof of manipulative activities to the SEC. They accumulate by buying heavily on a falling market when the public is frightened, or buying lightly when the public is selling nervously. Seldom do they buy during a rising market except on dips during that rise. If Seligman is comparing one stock with a 200 share day with another one that had a 20,000 share day, it is a senseless comparison, because Studebaker, for instance, had some 20,000 share days during quiet periods before its 1-for-5 reverse split.

Belding Hemingway is an example of an extremely thin market. One week, in April, 1964, the price of this stock rose 1-1/8 to 19-5/8 on only 900 shares. It reacted quickly and the next week only 500 shares were traded at 19. This stock can be said to be in very strong hands from an analysis of its action. There have been days with no trades. It is technically strong, but it is not in the area where it shows its strength. That will show up when it rises to a far higher level. It is now in an over-sold condition, but still in the bottom range. You may wonder that if this is so then why isn't it moving up? For the simple reason that it is not acting "well." It is a dog. It has no "appeal" when only 500 shares are traded in one week, but when you see 20,000 share days on it above 60, it will take on the rosy hue of a blue chip. Outside of company officials I am one of its largest shareholders.

Stock Splits

Stock splitting by corporations is an innovation widely adopted since the roaring twenties. Many stocks were sold at prices of multiples of $100 in those days. Today, those common stocks selling above 100 are very scattered among financial quotations, and they are candidates for being split in the near future.

With our booming economy of the past few years, stock splitting has become common among our growth stocks. Very seldom is a split proposed by a corporation when its stock is selling below 50.

When the directors of a company decide to split its shares, commonly at the rate of 2-for-1, this automatically cuts the values of its shares in half, but doubles the amount. The usual reason given is that the sponsors want the stock to sell at a price range where it will be more within reach of the public and will then be more widely held. They explain that shareholders of a company are more likely to patronize its products. This may be true in companies such as soft drink or auto manufacturers, but the excuse sounds rather feeble when you realize there are dozens of companies that the average person could seldom, if ever, patronize if he wanted to in his lifetime. They just don't sell a product that he can use or a service that he needs.

I have a different viewpoint as to why most stocks are split. It is my opinion that the real reason is not to have the shares more widely held; it is to make them easier to be widely "distributed" at the top.

I will use the soft drink industry as a hypothetical example. Sometime in the future, near the end of our present economic boom, the shares of these companies will be run up in prices far higher than they are today (February, 1966). There will be some very real competition then toward inducing the public to buy the shares of the various companies. Distribution may take place about the same time in all of them. There will be rosy reports, and hints, touting their company from various sources.

Now suppose all of them except one were topping out around the $200 range. The exception was topping out in the $50 range. Now providing that all other conditions were about equal, and they all had moved up about the same from a percentage standpoint, don't you think the lower priced one would have far more public appeal? It would be far easier to unload 200,000 shares of the lower priced stock than it would be to unload 50,000 shares of one of the others in the higher range.

This form of competition, not suspected by the public, I believe is the basic motive for the stock splits.

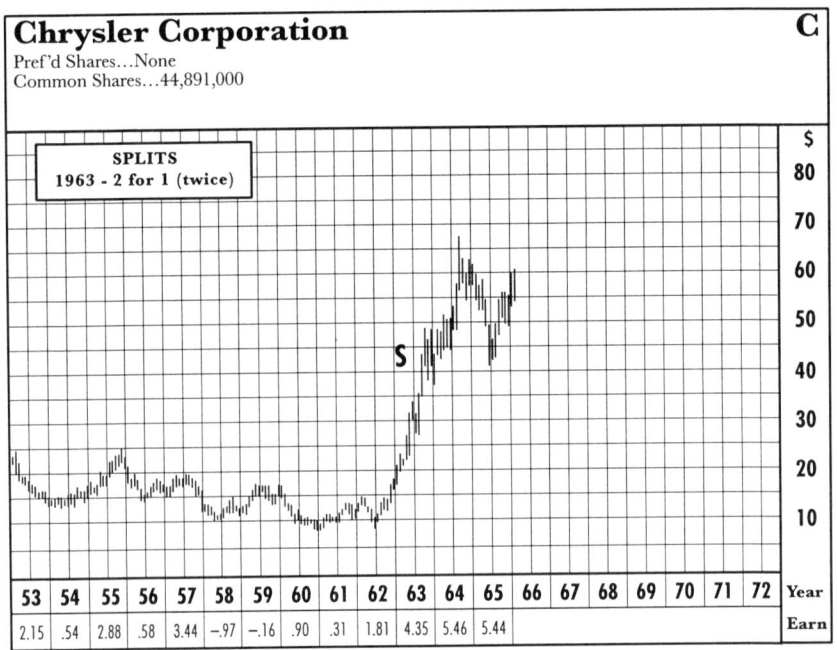

Chrysler Corporation (C)

Let's study the chart for Chrysler Corp. (C). It had two 2-for-1 splits in 1963. An owner of 100 shares in 1962 now owns 400 shares. The majority, human nature being what it is, prefer owning 400 shares instead of 100, even though the value is the same.

Much distribution took place from 43 to 49 (S). Before the two splits these prices would equal 172 to 196. Psychologically it stands to reason that a person who might very well hesitate to buy 100 shares at the latter high prices, may enthusiastically buy 400 around the lower prices of 46. People also prefer to buy round lots, rather than odd lots—(odd lots are any number of shares under 100). They are far more apt to buy 100 shares at 46 than 25 shares at 184. And if you consider those in the lower financial bracket, few of them would buy 5 shares at 184 but may not hesitate to buy 20 shares at 46. There would be far more reluctance to buy on the latter part of its rise from 225 to 270, based on the pre-split price.

People are greatly impressed by stock splits. They associate them with growth and higher earnings, and rightly so. With the psychological effect of the fast 400% rise from the 1961 and 1962 lows, they invariably have fallen in love with Chrysler and few would consider selling such a wonderful stock. But anyone holding this stock should check the long term chart and note the steep trend line that followed the price rise. When broken, any emotional or fundamental reason for holding on should have been discarded, and "Fact, the Dictator" should have become the guide. Usually when a trend line such as this is broken, no amount of wishful thinking, fundamental reasons or emotionalism will hold it up.

Perhaps people may argue that the sponsors, in the case of Chrysler, would have four times as many shares to sell because of the two stock splits, and that it would be difficult to sell that many more shares. They do have a point. But I maintain my theory that it is far easier to unload 4,000,000 shares to the public at the average price of 50 than 1,000,000 at 200. In either case the same amount of money is involved. It is a far better selling gimmick than is pricing a product at $4.95 instead of $5.00.

When Chrysler was on the final run to 67-$1/2$, many people who bought were probably not aware of its recent stock splits, but may recall that it was selling above 60 in 1959, when it was operating in the red. Now that its earnings are high it must be a bargain at this price . . . or so they believe.

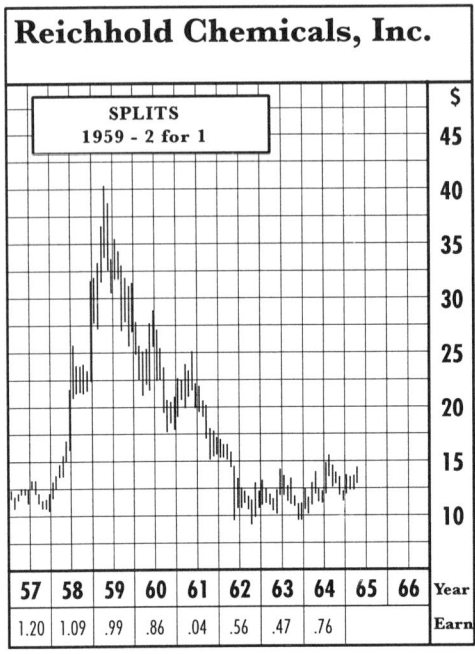

There is one slight advantage that can benefit the public when a company splits its stock. A lower priced stock usually will have a larger percentage rise than a high priced one. It is impossible to say how much. But a check of the long range charts will prove that a $10 stock can rise 300% far easier than a $50 stock. But this benefit is only for those who owned the stock and sold on the rise. Certainly it held no advantage for those who failed to sell or those who bought in the top range.

Reichhold Chemicals, Inc. and Tractor Supply Company "A"

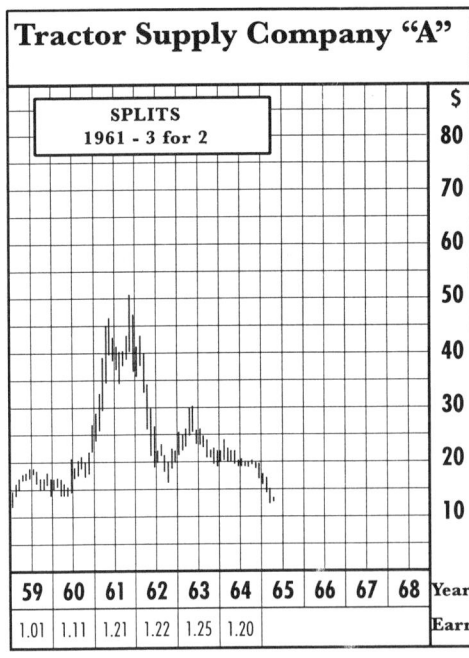

If you will check the charts, you will note that there are many stocks that from their past records, can hardly be classified as growth stocks, but did have stock splits, and this almost always took place in their top range. The timing of these splits facilitated distribution. Reichhold Chemicals, Inc. and Tractor Supply Co. "A"

were perfect examples. You can be certain that these splits helped the cause of distribution.

There are people who really believe they are getting something for nothing when they exchange their shares for the double amount. Recently a widow told me with a good deal of enthusiasm that the company in which she held shares that her late husband had bought, had given her two shares for one. No doubt she was not in the habit of checking its quotations. I found it difficult explaining to her that she had received nothing of value, that the price of the stock became half of what it had been previously. I almost felt like a heel afterwards for divulging this disappointing bit of enlightenment.

Usually there is a rush to buy when a split is rumored, but too often these buyers do not gain a profit. Check the charts and you will see that a very large percentage of splits took place near the top prices. Most of the remainder, at lower levels, were followed by shakeouts of varying sizes, because heavy selling sets in by disappointed shareholders when the price fails to develop a sustained rise immediately.

When Chrysler surprised Wall Street in October, 1963 with their announcement of the second 2-for-1 split in one year, a tremendous buying wave appeared the next day. The stock's price moved up 9-3/4 to 99-3/4. It never sold at the magic number of 100 at that time. No doubt too many people had sell orders at 100, so the smart money sold out at lower prices. A month later it sold $20 lower.

Perhaps the record for stock splits is held by Christiana Securities Company. Previous to being split 80-to-1 in 1961, it had sold above $18,000 per share. At that price, it was probably traded only by millionaires!

STOCK DIVIDENDS. At times a company will declare stock dividends in lieu of a cash dividend, or in addition to a cash dividend. A stock dividend is similar to a stock split in that it gives you nothing of intrinsic value. You gain a few shares but the price of the shares drops this equivalent in price. However, if you are not in need of cash, a stock dividend is preferable. You do not have to pay income tax on a stock dividend until you sell the stock, whereas a cash dividend which is not reinvested is taxable as income. Your tax on the stock dividend will not be calculated until you sell and will be considered a short or long term capital gain, depending upon when you bought the original shares.

The Dow Jones Trends

The Dow Jones Averages, which have been thought of as an important barometer of the stock market for many years, made their debut in 1896 with a total of only twelve stocks. Today the Dow Jones Industrials consist of thirty important companies which are supposed to be representative of our varied industries. This latter is debatable when it is found to consist of three oils, three chemicals, two steels, two automobiles, and two electric equipments. Not included are office equipment, electronics, publishing, broadcasting, drugs, grocery or beverages. Believe it or not, American Tel & Tel is included in the Industrial average. Over the years a number of companies like International Shoe, Famous Players-Lasky, Nash, Postum and others have fallen by the wayside, and more popular ones have taken their place.

Originally, the prices of these stocks were totaled and divided by the simple divisor of 12, but complications in this simple arithmetic set in when companies began splitting their stocks and paying stock dividends. When a stock is split 3-for-1, its price is multiplied by 3. The divisor is then reduced by a few decimals to give a true average. While the figure as represented today by the Dow Jones seems distorted it actually represents the true price of the average stock if there had been no splits. As this is written the divisor for the DJIA is nearing 2.50.

A good question: In time will the divisor become less than zero?

The Dow Jones Rail Averages are based on twenty railroad stocks and the Dow Jones Utilities include fifteen stocks.

The Dow Theory, formulated by Charles H. Dow, who was editor and co-founder of the *The Wall Street Journal* before the turn of the century, has been called the tool of investors. This was valid years ago under certain circumstances. For example, a signal is given that the trend has changed from a bear to a bull market when both the Industrials and the Rails have risen enough to indicate that the downtrend is broken. This is a signal to buy stocks. In a reverse change of trend, the signal is to sell. Or if there has been a long congestion in the market completed by the breaking into new highs, a buy signal is given; should the averages break certain lows, a sell signal is given.

Years ago there was an advantage in following this theory, but in recent years there have been too many false signals for this "tool" to be profitable, especially since too many stocks are moving counter to the DJ.

In June, 1965 when the DJI sold below 857,000, the Dow Theorists claimed that this confirmed the railroad average signal that a downtrend was under way. This after the DJI was down 80 points. The market turned right around and rose to 995. Leave this tool to the Dow Theorists; it is too expensive for you.

An investolator is not immune to this same type of error when selling his stock when an uptrend line is broken, but he has the know-how to recognize another bargain and has not really lost his position. In fact, he may have vastly improved it.

You cannot buy or sell the Dow Jones Averages as such, but the public watches them and is influenced by DJ actions. And because of this a chartist should watch the DJ closely, and try to understand how the public thinking is affected. You must remember that to the average watcher it is like the shell game. Often, what seems to be obvious . . . just is not so.

When one person asks another, "What did the market do today?" the answer will almost always refer to whether the Dow Jones Industrials closed high or low. Many years ago that could be a fairly true reference to the market as a whole, but since the 1946 top, the DJ Averages have ceased to give a true representation of the market except for short periods of time such as during a violent market break. Many shareholders have been painfully aware for some years now that while the DJI have been in a strong uptrend, their favorites have been dropping or stalling.

I, among others, have watched my late movers, become late, late movers. Dr. Pepper, Belding Hemingway and Bond Stores for instance.

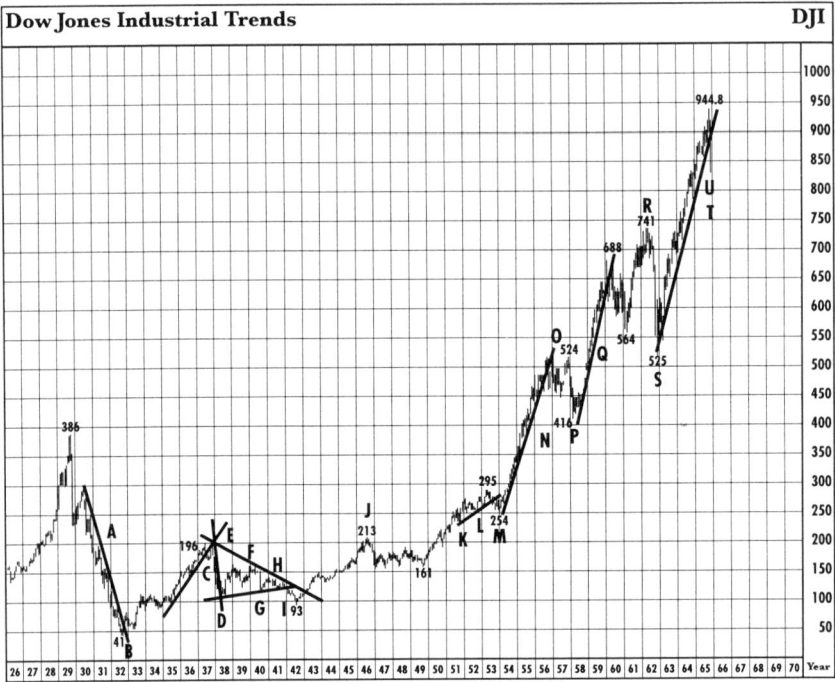

During a period when the DJ averages are extremely weak, as in 1957 and 1962 when the public panicked, even those stocks that are technically strong will be sold by a few remaining weak holders — those who lack confidence and determination to hold on.

The DJI have had some very important trend lines in the past. The 1929-32 downtrend line (A) up to the present was certainly the most important and distinctive of all. An experienced chartist or one who observed trend lines could have remained bearish right to the bottom. It is a known fact that some traders who became bearish in that bear market became indoctrinated so bearishly that they fought the trend when it turned up. Becoming a perennial pessimist caused them to lose many of their previous gains. If they had paid attention to that simple and at times positive indicator, the broken trend line, they could have saved themselves some costly errors. Selling short had become a way of life with them. We had entered a bull market but they did not recognize it.

The bear market of 1929-32 took a deadly toll among the investors and traders. A tremendous number of investors sold their stocks while trying to bolster their failing business or to keep up the payments on their homes, and in some cases, in order to eat. Those who were able to hold on to their stocks through 1932 were extremely lucky. Few of those who had cash had the courage to buy.

We know now that it was the beginning of the greatest economic advance in our history when the Dow Jones Averages broke the 1929-32 (B) downtrend. Optimism then was a scarce commodity. Few would have conceded that we had a great future ahead of us.

When the perfect uptrend was broken in April, 1937 (C) nearly all stocks should have been sold. All but a few were following the general pattern of the DJI. At this time it was a good policy to let the trend of the averages be your guide.

The downturn in 1937 (D) developed a trend line that was almost straight down. The crossing of one like this is suspect. It may be only temporary, as this one proved to be. There were few actions at that time that gave a satisfactory picture. About the only reason for buying a stock then was that it was selling much lower than previously. That is not reason enough. It is safer to wait for an action that you can have confidence in. More time was needed for a sound appearing base.

At this time most stocks were acting similarly to the DJI pattern. The 1938 (E) rally proved to be just that. Only a rally. After a sharp reaction in 1939 the averages rallied to the 1938 high, followed by seven months of quietness. This is one of the rare times in market history that it did not rise from a quiet period (F). This was during the winter of the "great stalemate" of World War II when the French were confidently entrenched in their heavily fortified Maginot Line and the Germans were busily preparing their Panzer Divisions for their spring invasion through the low countries, making worthless a tremendous investment in concrete and steel that the French had touted as being impregnable.

For once the public were NOT selling stocks during a period of quietness. They were holding with confidence because obviously with the rising war economy, they had visions of great prosperity. But when the Germans invaded France and drove the British off the mainland with such ease, these visions were shattered, replaced by a grave fear, resulting in the sharp break in May, 1939 (G), and the beginning of perhaps the best accumulation period of all time.

By mid-1941 I was predicting to anyone who would listen to me that the DJI was forming what I considered to be an accumulation triangle (H), with the probability of a false move or shakeout before the rise would start. By this time I had picked up a type of thinking that I had not been taught. I was trying to anticipate how the manipulating managers would plan action that would best mislead the public. I was well aware of the false moves for the benefit of those who operate in the biggest casino in the world. It came as I predicted, but from a most unexpected reason—Pearl Harbor.

Obviously Wall Street was in a good position to absorb the shocking event. Most stocks were already being traded in the bargain basement.

The market at the time of Pearl Harbor had already broken through the lower line of the triangle (I). Obviously someone knew what was coming and was prepared to pick up bargains by the millions of shares. The market timing could not have been planned better. To the public the future looked dark and they were discouraged sellers during the following year. With my ability as a chartist I was quite confident in my long position in Pepsi Cola which I had taken at this time. I formed my opinion from the action of my daily charts, as I had not yet learned of the advantages in long range charts.

When the war ended the public went on a buying spree and found themselves holding the bag as usual by mid-1946 (J). The DJI did not have a really distinct uptrend line on this final rise; but most stocks were breaking perfect ones. These gave the perfect selling signals. Few recovered from this break in less than four years, and some had not recovered in fourteen.

This 1946 break was the beginning of an entirely different market from the past. Stock movements began to follow an independent course that has developed to where at the time of this writing, in 1966 you can see every type of action that you can imagine. Bull and bear trends are to be seen all through the charts. Some stocks have gone into sound-appearing accumulation periods and others have about completed theirs. Others appear dangerously high but may go higher.

What caused this extreme change? Did the public concept of our markets change almost overnight to where they became very selective in their buying and selling? Does anyone believe that this change came as a natural phenomenon? In my opinion the Master Plan of our markets was changed. No one can logically deny that price movements influence public opinion. Instead of a bullish and bearish opinion being controlled collectively, it is now controlled by individual stock price movements. During a period when Chrysler was under distribution during 1964-65, there were hundreds of other stocks that were under accumulation, or consolidation.

Many stocks developed sound bases following the 1946 break that could be readily recognized by an investolator. There was a wide variety in time and action. They all consisted of actions that would influence and worry the public into selling at a loss.

There were comparatively few stocks that had spectacular advances during the 1949-52 (K) rise on the averages. There were practically no situations when a stock should have been sold when it broke an uptrend. Most uptrends during this period were slow and you should not consider selling when a slow rising trend is broken. Remember, distribution can seldom take place on a slow rise.

If you had been tempted into selling a stock during this time, justified or not, it mattered little, because there were many exceptionally sound bases and consolidations taking place. As an investolator, you would have soon taken a good position in one of them, and settled down to wait for the big rise that was due to follow.

At the time, I could see nothing that indicated a top in this three-year action during 1951-53. It was too quiet and taking too much time for a top. The DJI cannot top out that quietly in a narrow range. On a top there must be more violent action to keep the public excited, and buying. More shares can be distributed in six months in an active, rising market than can be sold in three years of slow action. Wild, unreasoned buying seldom can be stimulated that long. Far too many people without the incentive of fast rising prices and new highs would be turning bearish and would sell out long before the three years were over. When the two-year, slow uptrend line (L) was broken in 1953 (M) this was interpreted by chartists as signaling a change of trend. The vast majority of speculating chartists are too apt to have blind faith in broken trend lines. Few understand that this was a well executed, mild shakeout that served the purpose of turning them bearish. Fundamentalists who normally are not interested in such gobbledygook (from their viewpoint) as broken trend lines, you can be sure were indirectly influenced by this one. The broken trend line in the DJI had a very bearish influence throughout the brokers' boardrooms.

If you look at the charts of individual stocks during this 1951-53 period you will see that a large percentage of them were having a good consolidation action. The daily action of the stocks I charted showed very discouraging action from the public viewpoint, which had the effect of making a very positive bull out of me. During this time I know I was sounding ridiculous to brokers and other traders when I predicted that DJI would have to go to 450 or better to make a top. It is doubtful that they had ever heard anyone make a statement that the market HAD to go anywhere. That just did not make sense to them. My explanation was this: There were many long, quiet bottoms and consolidation periods among stocks which to me indicated a substantial rise ahead. I set a minimum of 450 on the DJI because I believed it would take at least that much of a move to get the public excited enough to buy during the distribution top.

At the time I expected this future top to hold for many years, with even a possible depression to follow.

But long before the uptrend was positively broken in 1956, I was certain that the final top action was not even close. By late 1955 many stocks were barely moving up from where they were when the DJI crossed the 300 level early in 1954. Many were having a quiet reaction and a few had not even risen out of their bottom range, all proof to me that this was not a final top.

A check of the hundreds of stocks proved how wrong it would have been if you depended on the breaking of the DJI trend line as your guide to when to sell your stocks. Each stock should have been judged by its own action. Beginning in early 1955 individual stocks broke steep uptrends during the 2-1/2-year rise (N). Many of these proved to have been perfect selling signals but for some of them this seemed doubtful for a time. You must adjust yourself to the fact that on numerous occasions, when you sold after a steep uptrend was broken, you could have sold later at a higher level, on a secondary or final rally. To take large profits you must be a doer. Don't think in terms of what you could do. It is so easy to miss a large profit by reaching for that dollar that often isn't there. This is one of the prime weaknesses of the speculators. Let the broken steep uptrend line be your guide.

That triple top in 1956-57 (O) and the '57 (P) shakeout, combined to make this one of the most ideal formations for baffling the traders ever devised. I could never prove that this action was under guidance, but I could never be convinced that this action merely "happened."

As I have said before, the public is greatly influenced by the actions of the DJI, so these actions must be studied.

The object of analyzing this formation and how it influences the average trader is not merely to review it as you would an item of history. There is something to be learned from it. It is meant to impress upon you that until you have trained yourself to adopt a "contrary opinion" type of thinking, your opinions in the market will be guided largely and wrongly by market actions.

The DJI double top in 1956 alerted the public into thinking the market was in possible trouble. When new lows were made in early 1957, chartists and non-chartists alike saw this as a selling signal, and normally they would have been right. The shakeout could very well have begun at this time, but it was not planned that way; a more effective one was in the works. The market was supported and these alert, early sellers were whipsawed. The bears and sold-out bulls were largely induced to buy on the rally that stopped cold at the double top. The turning down from what was eventually a triple top, was proof to most observers that the market was really in trouble. Didn't it fail to go through the double top? You can be sure that this was an important topic of conversation around the brokers' offices at this time. Nervous selling turned to panic when the recent DJI low was broken. Many were convinced during the 1957 shakeout that we were headed for a depression. Morale was shattered.

That triple top was further proof to me that the market was going far higher. That resistance level was false.

You will *never* see a DJI top, except a temporary one, that will appear like this. Distribution cannot take place on a broad scale in this kind of action. Too many people become cautious, which was the intended purpose of this triple top.

Before the 1957 bottom was complete the margin rate was dropped to 50%. This action should have given confidence to the public that the market action was not as serious as it appeared. But did it? When the public is frightened it takes more than a favorable margin ruling to allay their fears. Only when the stocks were again in strong hands and the DJI rose through the triple top with ease, did their emotions get back on an even keel. I had remained steadfast throughout the break.

It is a common understanding among traders that weak rallies denote weakness. But that is often not true. The weak rallies in early 1958 gradually strengthened into a steady rise far into 1959.

Again during the strong uptrend of the DJI in 1958-59, individual stocks moved according to the phase they were in. Many did have a strong rise and an investolator would have sold out when they had broken their trend, or before, but not because the DJI trend was broken.

The DJI (R) top was another repetition of the last three. Again stocks were having all kinds of actions. Many gave perfect selling signals when their uptrends were broken. But if you had sold others merely because of the general change to a downtrend, you could very well have lost your position. Again you should not have been influenced by the change in trend of the DJI alone.

The 1962 (S) break was extremely severe and nerve shattering to the vast majority. As in 1957 I was holding stocks that had not yet been given their "run." Again I was a steadfast bull. Hindsight clearly shows that a large percentage of stocks were toppy during the 1961 top. But it also showed that many had had only a moderate rise and a few were still in their bottom or consolidation base range. This was a clear cue that our market had much higher to go. And again the margin requirement was cut back to 50%, a good omen from observations of the past.

The 1962-65 uptrend in the DJI (T) was broken sharply in 1965 (U). Again, this should have been ignored. Only pay attention to the broken uptrends of individual stocks. This broken uptrend proved to be just a shakeout.

According to the Dow Theory, the Industrial and Rail averages confirmed one another during the June, 1965 break that the main mar-/ket trend had changed from a bull to a bear market. The Dow Theorists who should have given up long ago, were whipsawed again. In 1966, a bear market was again confirmed, and again they will be wrong. Like a stopped clock, only at times will they be right. Let's hope the Dow Theorists will fully accept the verdict when the final end of the bull market will be confirmed.

From the understanding of the market that I have gained from the study of individual stocks in relation to the DJI, as long as there are numerous stocks still in the accumulation phase, and others that are obviously going through a consolidation period, or slow markup action, no matter what kind of a nose dive the averages may go into, I know that the DJI will rally and have another run far higher than the previous top. These are sound bases. In other words, the sponsors of these stocks are not spending years accumulating only to be left holding them when a depression falls in their lap. With the exception of an odd situation, all stocks will be moved to a high level and distributed before a depression develops. It is as simple as that.

The climax of the 1962 break came while my wife and I were camped by ourselves on an uninhabited Northwest Island on the Barrier Reef out from Gladstone, Australia. We were enjoying four of our hobbies: seashell collecting, camping, skin diving, and taking natural history movies, in this case mostly of small sea life that we found on the coral reef at low tide. We had been dropped off on this island by a commercial fisherman and when he picked us up a week later on his way in with his catch he told me that he had heard over the wireless that the New York Stock Market had had the worst one day break in its history. He had learned previously that I was a speculator on the New York market. I was shocked, but I doubt that he realized the full effect it had on me. My first thought was, could there be more severe, one day breaks? Before we arrived at Gladstone seven hours later my nerves had simmered down. I convinced myself that because there were so many stocks that certainly had not had what I call a distribution top, this could not be the break that would signal the beginning of another great depression. It could only be an unusually severe shakeout.

I made arrangements at the post office which operates the Government-owned telephone service for a collect call to my broker at 1:20 a.m.; 7:20 a.m. in Los Angeles. The operator at Sydney told me that no business office would be open that early. I had to explain that the New York market opened at ten, and the L.A. broker's office would be open at seven because of the three hour time differential.

My call went through nicely and I found the market was in a rally. I sold some Chadbourne Gotham and a few hundred Bond Stores and Dr. Pepper as a little insurance against a margin call in case the market had more panic days. This proved to have been unnecessary.

This 1962 break was about 50% worse than I could have anticipated. After it was all over I came to the conclusion that the severity of this break was encouraged and allowed to drop to this extent for another reason besides shaking out the public. Perhaps the insiders wanted to teach President Kennedy a lesson in the law of economics, after the hassle he had previously with the steel companies over their attempt at raising steel prices. Many blamed this for the market break. Whether it was intentional or not, obviously it worked. From then on there was a big improvement in his attitude toward big business.

During this fifteen-month, 31,000 mile tour with a four-wheel drive pickup and camper, my broker each week would airmail five pages of market quotations from *The Wall Street Journal* to addresses which I would try to predetermine. At times this did not work out very well. Sometimes we would remain longer in an area because we found more interests than we expected or we found less and our mail would arrive after we passed our pickup point. I received the quotes a month late one time while in the outback.

I doubt that any tourists ever saw Australia as we did. We skin dived in most of the coastal areas and prowled the woods and desert looking for specimens and any kind of nature study to film, varying from small sea life to insects of which we found plenty. We stumbled onto a most interesting new hobby, taming praying mantes and grasshoppers. One large grasshopper became spoiled. While sitting on a finger he would eat only the most tender shoots of grass which we would hand him. A four-inch praying mantis while traveling with us for nearly three months, even by plane, laid six batches of eggs. Confidently she would ride on my wife's shoulder, never flying away. Can you imagine anyone becoming attached to an insect? We did.

From the understanding of the market that I have gained from the study of individual stocks in relation to the DJI, I can state that as long as there are numerous stocks still in the accumulation phase, and others that are obviously going through a consolidation period, or slow markup action, no matter what kind of a nose dive the averages may go into, I know that the DJI will rally and have another run far higher than the previous top. There are sound bases. In other words the sponsors of these stocks are not spending years accumulating only to be left holding them when a depression falls in their lap. With the exception of an odd situation, all stocks will be moved to a high level and distributed *before* a depression develops. It is as simple as that.

Where You Can Obtain Long Range Charts[1]

When I submitted the manuscript of this book in person to one of the editors of Sherbourne Press I was fully aware of the fact that I was neither a writer nor a salesman. I knew my writing was so substandard that I decided to concentrate on selling my idea, then my manuscript was bound to be accepted.

I had with me a late issue of a stock chart book. After an hour of pointing out the various chart patterns and explaining why stock prices acted the way they did, I knew that I had the editor sold. Lady Luck was on my side in this interview. This editor admittedly knew little about the stock market, but was young enough that he was able to quickly "grasp" this concept of the market. If he had been a man of sixty, with preset ideas of the importance of fundamentals or believed that there was no manipulation in our markets today, I may have found myself looking for another publisher.

This young editor was disturbed by the fact that my readers would be almost forced to buy a copy of a chart book. I had already given much thought to this subject. It was a fact we had to face.

---

[1] Here at The Ted Warren Corporation and The Ken Roberts Company we use The U.S. Chart Company for both stock and commodity charts. They were created especially to include everything Ted Warren wanted in a charting service. Call or write for information to: U.S. Chart Company, 333 S.W. 5th Street, Grants Pass, OR 97526, (541) 955-2885, FAX (541) 955-2889.

I explained that the average investor spends far more every year for the purpose of getting financial information than the cost of one issue of a chart book. The average speculator subscribes to at least two of the following: *The Wall Street Journal, Barron's Business Week, Financial World, Forbes, Magazine of Wall Street, Survey of Current Business* and *U.S. News and World Report*. He believes it is necessary to keep up-to-date on business events. He will enjoy reading the news items and market comments and opinions, and will feel closer to the market. But if all he knows is what he reads in the periodicals, he is apt to follow the crowd and may soon find himself in trouble. If he hangs around the broker's office and absorbs all that comes off the Dow Jones' News Ticker he may choose the choice items that will apply to his wishful thinking.

And how much money have people poured down the drain seeking financial advice, much of which has proven to be faulty?

I pointed out to this editor that there were over 25,000 people who bought stock charts at least once a year, some, six copies. I am sure these people recognize that these books are well worth their cost. But I am teaching insight into these charts. I do not believe that I need to apologize because the reader will be required to buy stock charts, any more than any teacher should have to apologize because his students are required to buy textbooks.

Once you have made a commitment in the market you do not really need another copy of your stock charts until it appears that your stock is nearing a selling point. In the meantime you can add for yourself the monthly range of your stock, or any others that you may be interested in watching.

If you were to keep up-to-date on all the sources of information that other authors advise you to, your cost would be far greater than an occasional copy of a stock chart book. It would also be time consuming—and far less profitable.

If you do continue to buy some of these periodicals, which many of you will by force of habit, I must warn you that just one discouraging item you read, especially if it is followed by heavy public selling and lower prices, can put you in a dither. You may find yourself derailed by selling your stock when you should be buying, or rosy reports may cause you to ignore that broken uptrend line. Another safeguard is to instruct your broker to never call you up concerning any news item. This habit of calling up clients and excitedly announcing the latest rumors or reports generates many extra commissions for the broker. After all, commissions are their bread and butter. From experience I know that hasty decisions are far more apt to be wrong. You must hold fast to this new concept by being an "investolator."

If you cannot immunize yourself against the influence of financial news items, it is better that you not read them. Your time can be better spent in familiarizing yourself with the proven chart patterns of the past in order to recognize them in the future. This is comparable to training military pilots to recognize all aircraft by their silhouettes.

For anyone who really wants to make a thorough study of past actions for the purpose of recognizing sound formations in the future, I highly recommend that they review stock charts going back ten to twenty years. This beyond all doubt will prove the value of using the charts. You will see how sound these base patterns have proven to be.

All but a very few diehards of those to whom I have had an opportunity to really point out and explain WHY stocks act the way they do, are enthusiastic about stock charts. Many of those who are accepting gratuitous advice from me occasionally buy a copy.

An acquaintance who had bought copies of stock charts previous to having several explanatory sessions with me said, "I found the charts interesting, but until you explained them, those price movements had little more meaning to me than a bunch of hieroglyphics." His, and his broker's opinions in the past, had proven unprofitable. Now he is capable of picking his own bargains.

A friend who has a long list of accomplishments, including time spent as an investment banker and in special service for the Allies in Russia during World War One and the Bolshevik Revolution, listened to my explanation of why a study of the stock charts can be so valuable. He told me that I had changed his whole concept of the stock market.

You need not buy stock charts. Ask your broker if he has a copy of a stock chart book. If he doesn't, he can probably borrow one from another account executive. If you do not have a broker, go to one of the larger, nationally known firms and inquire among the account executives to see the latest edition of their stock chart book. When you locate one who uses this book of charts, he will be glad to discuss it with you. Do not expect him to be an expert on charts, but he no doubt sees the value in using them.

The right kind of stock chart shows every type of action taking place that you can imagine, and if you look back at recent actions you will see a large percentage of stocks going through very similar actions—bottoms, consolidations and tops, as other stocks have done in the past.

If you send for a stock chart subscription, use a fine pencil to keep it up-to-date on those stocks that you prefer to watch. A visit to your broker and a glance through his latest copy is not very satisfactory, as checking and double checking the present patterns with those of the past can be time-consuming. You are not yet expert enough to pick out a sound base by a mere glance. Above all, at this time, again read the important highlights of this book. When you have picked what you think is a bargain, do not check up on its fundamental aspects, for they may pull the rug of sound reasoning right out from under you.

If you are living in a rural community where you are nearly forced to send for a stock chart subscription, you must realize that the price is a very small investment, both from a financial and emotional viewpoint. You will feel secure in the knowledge that you bought your stock in the proper range. When you buy by the hit or miss method, unless you are lucky, you will experience plenty of anxiety and even periods of panic. If you buy as an investolator, a review of your stock's "picture" will bolster your confidence.

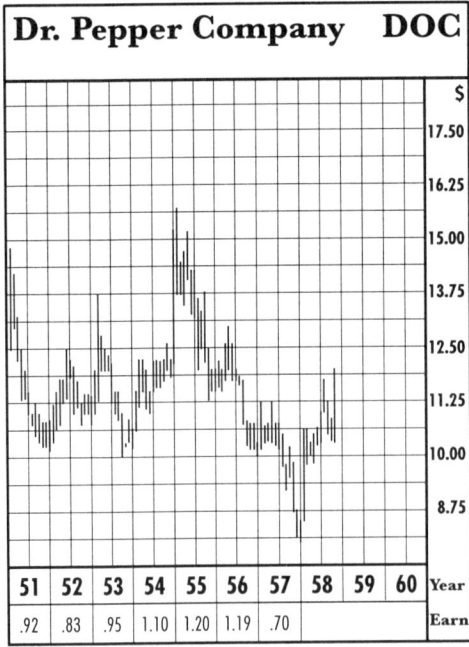

Check the charts of the glamour stocks of the past years and see where they are today. You will see that someone took a bad beating because they bought too high. You should view these large drops in prices with the same attitude that a motorist should view the picture of a bad car accident. Let it be a warning to the reckless.

There are many publications of stock charts with both a weekly and monthly range. There may be reasons to prefer one chart

book over another. Choose a publication which suits your perspective and is well proportioned in time and price. One could easily prefer those charts which show volume of trading, but it is my belief that too close attention to volume can only help to mislead the average person.

A long range stock chart must have a contrast of action, such as the previous top, to have any real value. Also, it should be on a scale that does not distort a quiet action to an extent that it appears to be highly active. When a stock is undergoing a quiet accumulation period, it should appear that way. Note the contrast in the two charts of Dr. Pepper. The stock was undergoing a twelve-year accumulation period which could be seen in the chart with the one dollar scale, but the novice investolator would never guess it by viewing the chart on a 25 cent scale. The latter chart is practically worthless. Also, when a base takes as much time as Dr. Pepper did, the chart should be extended to show the past high point and the long decline.

Think of these charts as you would a jigsaw puzzle. Look for the pieces that resemble those that have proven themselves in the past, especially the bases and consolidations. From these formations you will initiate your commitments. By this simple method you need not be a genius or to have a "flair" for the market. Just cool common sense is sufficient.

Making the Market Make Money for You

By now you should be ready to use the techniques I have explained to make money on the market. You know how to find a bargain stock . . . preferably one that is ready to move . . . how to buy it on margin, how to calculate its potential with reasonable accuracy and ways of telling when the sell-out time has come in order to take a sizable percentage of profit.

The hypothetical case of your dragged-out experience with Bond Stores (Why You Should Consider Buying on Margin) is about the worst that can happen to you by buying on margin, providing you buy during an established bottom, a bottom that has proven its worth because it compares to similar ones in the past. Though disappointing, BND will prove very profitable.

Now let me outline the other extreme of a hypothetical case, also beginning with an outlay of $1400 on the same date as the Bond Store purchase.

Curtiss Wright Corporation (CW)

You noticed in 1954 that Curtiss Wright Corp. (CW) since 1939 had a series of tops at about 12. This gave the appearance of being an extremely long false resistance level, or false ceiling, followed by two years of quietness below 10 (T). This quietness appeared to complete

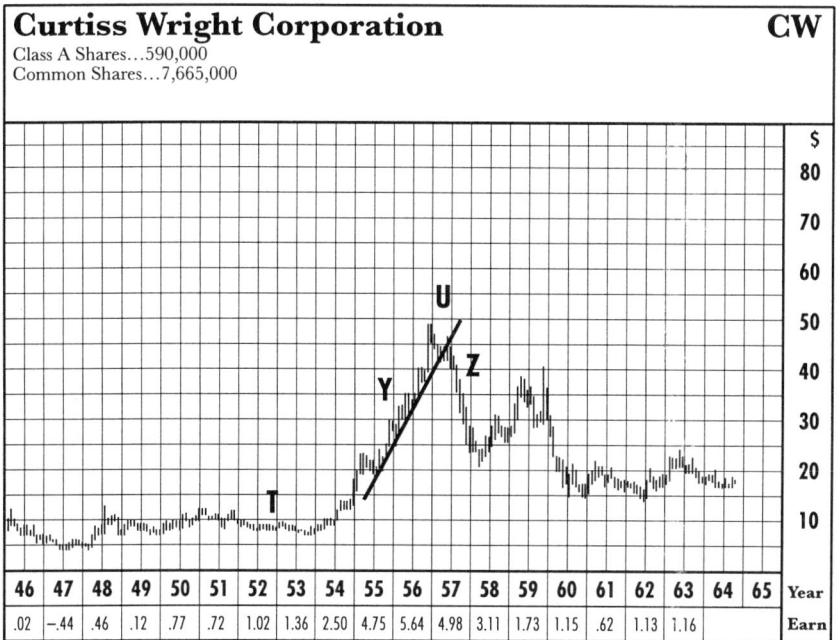

a sound base that you had been watching for. In February, 1954 you bought 300 shares at 9, opening a margin account of $1400 with your broker which covered your purchase on a 50% margin. Your debit balance would then be about $1400.

CW moved up to 10 and stalled quietly for over three months. You bought another 100 shares at 13, also on a 50% margin basis, as it sold above the thirteen-year highs, using paper profits of $1200 and nearly $125 in dividends above interest charges. The next four months' quiet action in the $13 range encouraged profit taking, as it appeared to lack the buying power to push it higher. This is the sluggish action you want to see as it leaves a strong base.

From here, it gathered momentum as the public became attracted by the rise into new high ground. In 1956, a perfect uptrend line of over 45 degrees developed. This is just what you had hoped to see. It was now a case of merely watching and waiting for either an extremely fast rise above the trend line, where you would voluntarily take a profit, or the point when it broke through the line on the down side, indicating a change of trend.

You failed to sell on the speeded up rise to 49-1/2 late in 1956. You expected the five point rise in one month to carry higher. Instead you sold in June, 1957 (U) at 41 when this trend line was broken. An unsophisticated shareholder, finding himself with a large profit after several times having decided against selling, could again have decided against selling, which now would be a bad decision. A common mistake is to decide against selling just ONCE TOO OFTEN. There is a temptation to follow the line of least resistance by sitting tight. Such a person may have acquired a feeling of false confidence. Hasn't it proven to be a good stock? Why sell it?

You realized a profit of $12,100 on your CW and received $2,300 in dividends after interest charges. You used $400 of this to pay income taxes up to 1957. From your original $1400, you now had a cash balance of $15,400 or a purchasing power of $22,000 on a 70% margin basis which was now in force.

You may wonder at how the figure of $22,000 was arrived at. This seems to be a mathematical problem that few of us have met with. Divide 15,400 by 70. Your answer is 220. Because 70 is a percentage figure, you add two zeros.

When you anticipated a possible breaking of the CW uptrend, you sent for a recent issue of a stock chart book and began searching for new bargains. You found very few stocks that appeared sound. Most stocks had moved too high for a safe purchase.

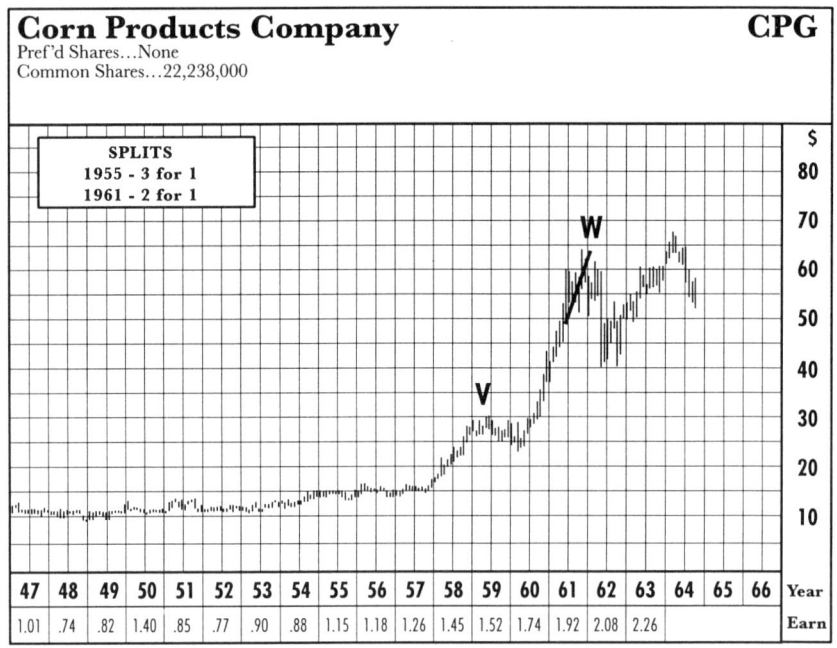

Corn Products Company (CPG)

However, Corn Products Co. (CPG) had an outstanding base and was now in a slightly higher consolidation. It was obviously a late mover.

You bought 700 shares at 30-$1/2$ as soon as you sold your CW which left your account with a debit balance of almost $6,300. This debit was increased by about $1,400 by April 15, 1958, as you paid your income taxes. This amount was available because of a surplus above your 70% requirement at the time of purchase, credited dividends and the 30% that you may use on accrued paper profits.

Early in 1958, the Federal Reserve Board lowered the margin requirements to 50%. This ruling had the effect of increasing your purchasing power by nearly $10,000. You immediately bought 200 shares of CPG at 36. This increased your debit balance by over $7200. You bought another 100 at 38 as it continued its rise, by using half of your paper profits, and also adding this to your debit balance, which is now about $18,700.

Your dividends over and above your interest charges are whittling away at the debit balance. But you are also drawing part of this to pay income taxes on the dividends.

Even though the minimum margin rate was raised to 70% late in 1958, you may draw out all of the dividends as this is new money. The new rate is not retroactive; it applies only to new purchases.

You ignored the breaking of the first uptrend line in 1959 (V) because the sound base and consolidation of CPG indicated a larger move.

The next upturn developed a steeper trend line and you were alerted into watching for a selling point and also checking the latest charts for another bargain.

Because of the 2-for-1 split in 1961 you now had 2000 shares, but at half the former price.

In October, 1961, the trend line was broken and you quickly sold at an average price of 52 (W), which was equivalent to 104 before the split. You found you were a little hasty in selling as it turned up again. The next selling point was at 56. Losing out on an $8,000 profit should not be allowed to influence you in any way. Thinking in terms of what you missed on this move may defeat your purpose of selling another time when you should. There is no more positive way of outsmarting yourself than trying to sell for that highest dollar.

Corn Products was one of a few that made a new high that same year. Learn to recognize these when they resist the downside and have a sound base behind them. These strong formations spell "jackpot" to anyone who can spot them. This jackpot totaled over $75,000, including nearly $5,000 in dividends after interest charges. Taxes paid on previous dividends and to be withdrawn very soon on capital gains would be about $14,000. Your taxes happened to be the same amount as your principal when you bought CPG, so your cash balance remains $75,000 after taxes. You actually had a cash balance of $15,400 when you bought CPG, but remember you paid out $1,400 of this for income tax on your Curtiss Wright profit. You now had a purchasing power of $107,000 on a 70% margin basis.

In October, 1961, there were few stocks that appeared to be a safe purchase. Too many were too high. Those in a downtrend did not give any indication that the trend was about to change. Those in a reasonably sound appearing uptrend were subject to a substantial setback at any time. An investolator should never reach for those in an extended uptrend nor feel for a bottom among those in a downtrend.

You decided to diversify and picked three that showed sound pictures. Dr. Pepper (DOC) (see Page 63) was having a reaction after what appeared to be a false start from a twelve-year bottom. General Cable

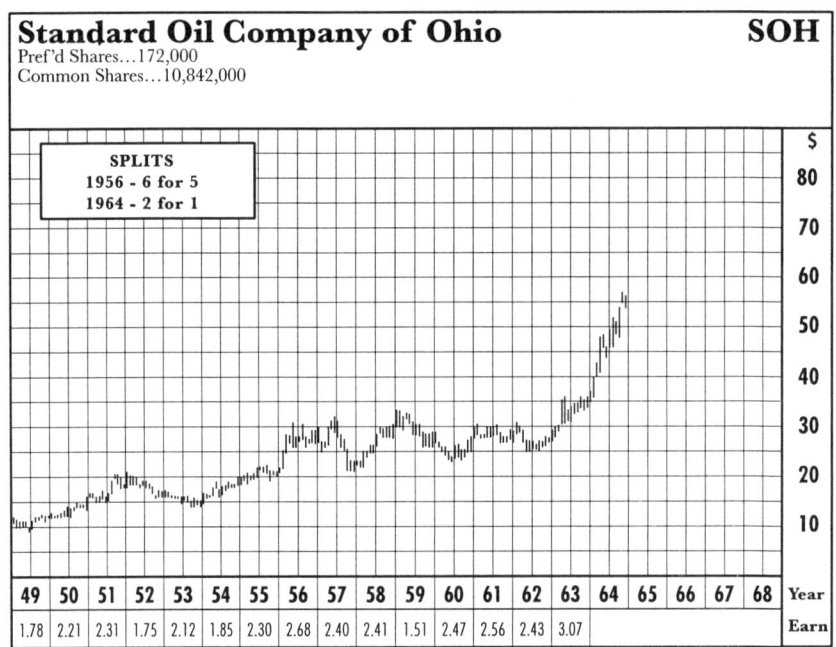

(GK) (see Page 36) and Standard Oil of Ohio (SOH) were each in a five-year high-level consolidation period that appeared to be nearing an end.

With your purchasing power of $107,000, you bought 600 shares SOH at 54, 1000 GK at 41 and 2,000 DOC at 16.

Next year (1962) came the severe shakeout and panic. All three held up well, especially DOC. If you had the confidence of an investolator, you weathered the shakeout with little concern. You had another sound reason to bolster your confidence. As long as so many stocks had obviously not been under distribution recently, you knew that a general market reaction, though severe, would be only temporary.

Shortly after the Dow Jones Averages made their lows, the minimum margin rate was again lowered to 50%. This was the fourth time since 1946 that it had been lowered to this rate. The market as a whole, each time previously, proved to be in the bargain range and large rises followed in the majority of stocks. But did the unsophisticated public accept this as a clue to the future trend of the market? Of course not. They were too frightened to reason this out.

As an investolator, you did not need this as a clue, but it did give you more confidence in your opinion as to the future trend of your latest commitments.

This drop in margin requirements again gave you an increase in purchasing power. In September, 1962 you decided to take advantage of this ruling. At this time, GK, selling at 33, represented a loss of $8,000, SOH at 52, a loss of $1,200, and DOC with a profit of $4,000 at 18 left you with a total loss of $5,200.

To figure your purchasing power on the new 50% margin basis, you deduct your $5,200 paper loss from your original cash balance of $75,000 which leaves $69,800. You double this to $139,600. Then total the present value of your holding which comes to $100,200. Deduct this from $139,600 and you then have $39,400 additional purchasing power.

You immediately bought 200 more SOH at 52, 400 GK at 33 and 800 DOC at 18. This totaled more than your purchasing power based on your principal and was not sufficient, but the deficiency was more than covered by accumulated dividends.

In December, 1962, your added paper profits allowed you to buy another 700 shares DOC at 21, and in January, 1963 you added another 500 DOC at 23, giving you a total of 4000 shares.

In April, 1963 when General Cable sold above its 1961 false ceiling of 45-1/2, you bought 600 at 46, giving you a total of 2000. Standard Oil of Ohio also broke through its false ceiling of 59-1/2 during 1961-62, and you bought 200 more for a total of 1000 shares.

In April, 1964, when DOC neared the 70 level with a burst of speed, you sold your 4000 shares at 64 with a profit of over $180,000. During 1962-63 you received $8,300 in dividends above interest charges on which you paid $1800 in taxes. You now earmarked $55,000 for income taxes on your DOC profit and 1964 dividends.

Part of the reason you sold DOC was that you had already picked three candidates for a future rise. Bond Stores (BND) (see Page 102) appeared to have a fifteen-year base. The directors had recently cut the dividend from $1.25 to $1.00. Selling was very light on this depressing news which to you indicated the stock was in strong hands. Also you had a strong suspicion that this action was induced by a desire to frighten shareholders into selling. Someone seems anxious to acquire a lot of these shares and obviously they must have a good reason. This is reason enough for you.

Borg-Warner (BOR) (see Page 33) was in its tenth year of high level consolidation and appeared, in this final quietness, to be acting as if it could not rise above 50. A healthy sign.

Woodward Iron (WOD) (see Page 42) was slowly moving up from its eight-year triangle. All had a different type of base, all appeared safe, subject only to further minor setbacks or delaying actions.

Your problem now was to figure your new purchasing power. You can figure it on the total value of your account on a 70% margin basis or on a dollar for dollar exchange on the sale of your DOC because it was bought on a 50% basis. You find that it works out that you can buy the most on the exchange method. You do not dare to use the full amount of $254,000 (sale price after commissions) on a purchase because of the danger of not being able to draw the $55,000 for taxes when due. This leaves you a purchasing power of $199,000. To insure the availability of this, you instruct your broker to enter the $55,000 in your miscellaneous account. It is not really transferred; it is only a method of bookkeeping. In spite of a possible, even probable, paper loss during the year, this will be available to you. Otherwise you would have had to have a very large paper profit in order to draw this amount. This large profit would be most unlikely in the near future. This is something the successful investolator must adjust himself to;

unless his timing of a purchase is nearly perfect, he must realize that he will most likely have a waiting period at a possible loss BEFORE the big rise begins.

You exchanged your DOC for 100 Borg-Warner (BOR) at 47, 2500 Woodward Iron (WOD) at 28-1/4 and 500 Bond Stores (BND) at 16-3/8. This totaled $201,900, $2,900 more than your allotted purchasing power. This small difference is of no concern. Your broker merely debits your miscellaneous account by this amount. This will be more than replenished by dividends credited before your final tax payment.

In May, 1965, when General Cable sold at 55, equivalent to 137-1/2 before the 2-1/2-for-1 split, and with the Dow Jones Industrials having had a steady advance of over 400 points since the 1962 break, you reasoned that the market could be due for a change. After this much of a rise GK could easily go into a consolidation period. You realized that GK had definitely not topped as the volume had been too light.

The first week in June when General Cable dropped below 52 you sold your 5000 shares at 51 when its uptrend line was broken. Your 2000 shares had been increased to 5000 because of the 2-1/2-for-1 split. This sale proved to be far too soon. On an error of this type you must console yourself with the thought that not many people have the opportunity to make an error with $170,000 profit!

After earmarking $50,000 for income taxes on this profit and $8,400 in dividends above interest charges, you had an exchange value or purchasing power of $202,000.

Because of considerable profits credited to your account, both paper and real, you sharpened your pencil and did some more figuring. You deducted the $50,000 tax money from your present cash balance of $129,000, leaving you $79,000. The present value of your 5000 Bond Stores at 22, 1000 Borg-Warner at 51, 2500 Woodward Iron at 31 and 2000 Standard Oil at 53, totaled $344,500. 30% of this, $103,350, plus your credit balance of $79,000 gives you a total of $182,350, which you could actually draw from your account. But you are only interested in the purchasing power this will give you on a 70% margin basis. Dividing this by 70 and adding 2 zeros gives you your answer, $260,500.

When you sold GK, you had already noticed that in spite of the market being near an all-time high, as measured by the averages, there

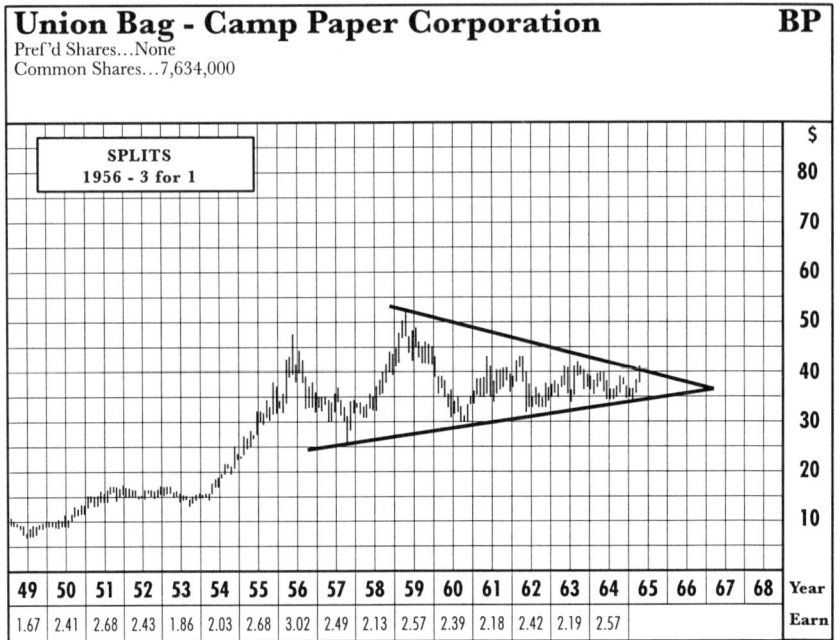

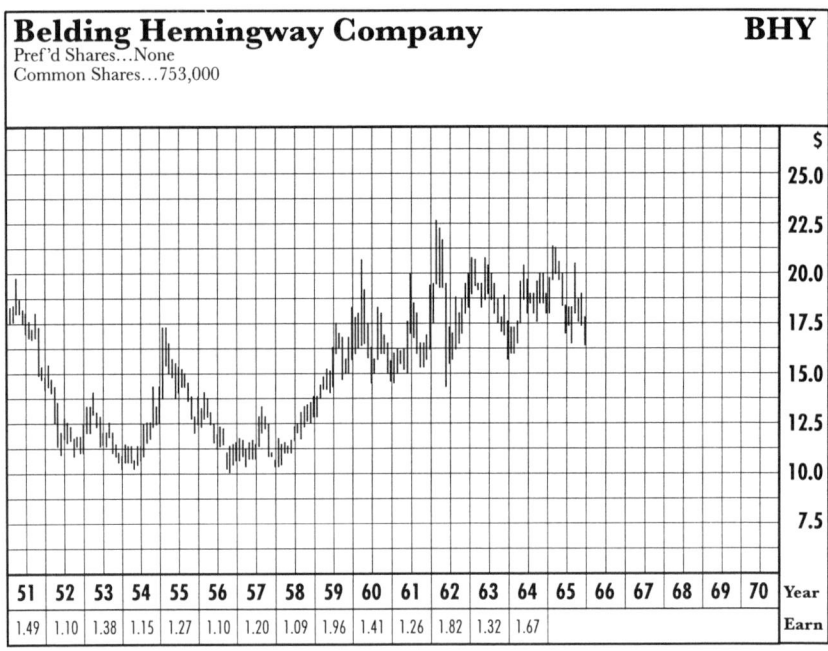

were numerous bases, both high-level and low-level, that appeared to be near completion.

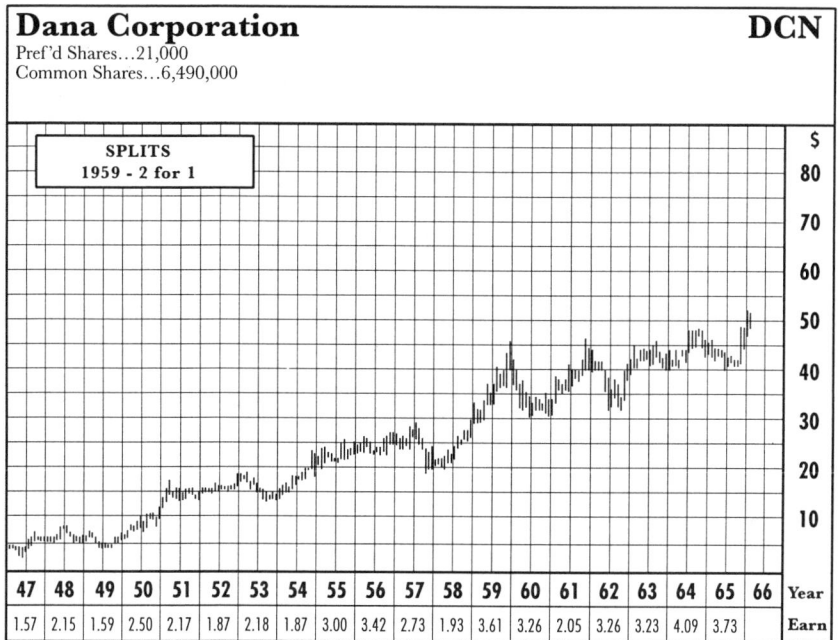

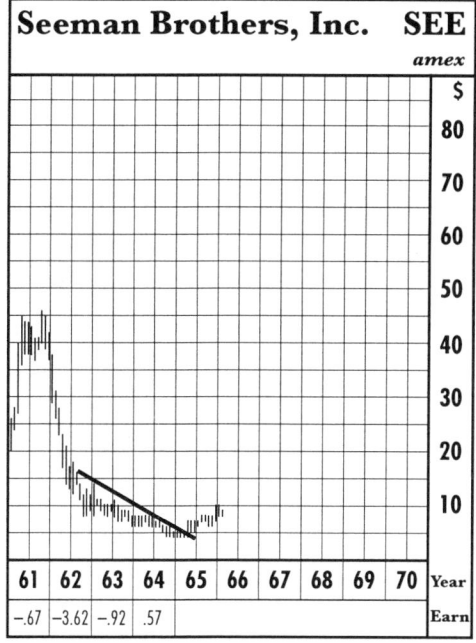

After considerable calculating and pencil pushing you bought 1000 Dana Corp. (DCN) at 44, 2000 Union Bag-Camp Paper (BP) at 41-1/2, 5000 Belding Hemingway Co. (BHY) at 18-1/2, 4000 Seeman Bros., Inc. (SEE) at 6, and 5000 Polarad Electronics Corp. (POD) at 2-1/2 (see Page 78).

You liked the picture of DCN because of its obvious false resistance level at 46-1/2. The upside breakthrough had the appearance of a false start, with the price having dropped back into the consolidation range and again turning quiet.

BP had recently broken upward through the downtrend line of a long triangle which had "filled out" to near perfection. A terrific base.

BHY had what you consider an eighteen-year base. This could not be distribution. It was also public knowledge that its officers owned 33% of its shares. This should be a guarantee that the price of BHY has a great future ahead.

SEE, you noticed, had one of the smoothest bear markets ever seen. In over three years the rallies were extremely feeble. The extreme six-month quietness above 4 was the dying gasp of this bear market. This appeared to you to be one of the most perfect bases of this type. POD appeared to be in that final quiet period or dying bear market that SEE passed at 4. Another perfect base.

POD is traded on the American Exchange. Because the minimum price at which a stock can be bought on margin is $7 on the American Exchange (the minimum is $5.00 on the New York Exchange). The POD purchase was based on cash. This cut down your purchasing power by nearly $4000 from $260,500 to $256,500. Your recent purchases totaled $256,000. Including commissions, your cost was more than your purchasing power. The money earmarked for taxes will cover this shortage, and dividends will then more than cover this before your final tax payment.

A brief discussion of the crazy rules on which the price of a marginable stock is set is now in order. I am at a loss for words almost in giving my opinion on these rules. According to these regulations, Polarad, at prices from 7 to 36-1/2 was not considered too risky on a 70% margin, but automatically becomes a risk below 7 and must be paid for in cash. Surprisingly, this seems to be a trait in financial circles. When a stock becomes low priced, it is commonly looked upon as being a risky purchase. Brokers, being prone to recommending a high rising stock, probably touted Polarad above 20, but would not have the nerve to recommend it below 5 during the 1963-65 period.

If margin requirements were again reduced to 50% in the near future following a market selloff panic as happened in 1957 and 1962, do not hesitate to use the windfall of purchasing power that this ruling would give you. Bases that are in the making would probably be completed during this period. I am sure that many would show underlying strength by resisting the selloff and having quick recovery, perhaps making new highs.

These hypothetical examples are definitely possible, if you follow the rules strictly as I advise you to do. Your problem will be staying with the rules. It is too easy for you to start "thinking." In spite of my advice to ignore your friends' and broker's opinions, and the general thought prevailing during heavy selling and buying periods, you will find it difficult to prevent yourself from going along with the crowd. To avoid this, do not talk about the market, nor read the financial pages. Discovering stocks that are soaring while yours seem unable to make headway, may derail your train of thought. If you bought right, do not let a "panic" market influence you into selling. If you had a large profit on your stock, you would have sold before the panic selling set in, assuming there was a broken steep trend line.

With the experience I have today, I can do just what has been done in this hypothetical case, as long as the price actions continue as mixed as they have since 1946, and providing that I don't outsmart myself by "thinking," thinking that I could do better and switch too soon.

You can very well say that I made this hypothetical case so profitable by picking stocks that I knew had gone up. Anyone can do that. True. I did have the advantage of this foresight on the first four stocks that were bought and partly on that of the fifth. But these were bought following actions that indicated either accumulation or consolidation which have proven to be sound bases by very similar actions in the past.

My opinion in choosing the final seven was based entirely on hindsight and these should move to where at least a 200% profit should be taken if sold when a steep trend line has been broken or after an extra fast rise has taken place. Taking a loss should not be considered at any time.

The fifth stock bought, Standard Oil of Ohio, should be held for that minimum profit of 200%. At the time of purchasing the last four stocks, it was up nearly 100% already.

The remainder of this book is just as important as the techniques you have learned so far. It is here that we shall underscore basic techniques with past experience and future predictions and give numerous hints that will speed you on your way to success.

PART TWO

Fundamentalists vs. Chartists

Almost everyone who ever bought shares of a company is a fundamentalist. Millions of shareholders do not know that there is any other method by which to form an opinion about the soundness of a company or to make a forecast of the price movements of its stock. To them it seems most illogical, in fact impossible, to try to forecast a move without knowing anything about the fundamentals of a company. A fundamentalist believes it is the height of stupidity not to inquire into all the facts about a company. It is amusing to notice the reactions of people when I explain that it is a waste of time and effort to study all the data pertaining to a company. When I make positive long range predictions, they obviously think that I am under self-delusion and to be merely tolerated, rather than taken seriously.

If fundamentalists could correctly analyze the worth or future prospects of a stock, why then would a stock spend many years in a low range, begging to be bought, before rising several hundred percent? Would this not prove that it had been undervalued and unrecognized by the fundamentalists?

The fundamentalists themselves prove that they are not on a very sound footing when the vast majority of them buy high and sell low.

If you are a fundamentalist, you probably know exactly what products a company is manufacturing, you have been pondering whether demand will continue to be as good for these products next year as they were last; you are listening for rumors, watching the tape, occasionally sending a dollar to an advisory service for a sample of their advice and reading *The Wall Street Journal* regularly, hoping to see that little item that might tip you off to something really good. Yes, you could be called a fundamentalist. But, if you will stop and analyze yourself closely, you will probably discover that you are more of an emotionalist. You will find that many of your decisions have been made emotionally. Is this true? If so, then it is time for a change. Forget all you ever knew about the fundamentals of the various companies, and knuckle down to the study of long range charts. After you have spent a few evenings checking and rechecking these charts, and picked a likely looking candidate for a rise from a bottom or a consolidation period, take notice of its name; you will need this when you order your broker to buy it. And buy it now. Be a "doer," not a "should have done it." Act with confidence even though you never heard of it before, and follow through with patience.

To most people, the viewing of a stock chart is meaningless. It is only a record of its past action. To them there is no other reason for viewing a chart. But there is an old saying, "There must be a reason for everything." By now you will realize that I have explained the reason why prices fluctuate the way they do, and why certain actions can be expected to follow a previous type of action.

If a close investigation of fundamentals during a period of accumulation weighs heavily in a stock's favor, the average fundamentalist still may not buy it, because the stock is not "acting right." While most fundamentalists disclaim any interest in charts, they do watch the actions of a stock, and without being aware of it, they are influenced by these actions—to their sorrow. Having learned how some of these actions influence the majority, the investolator forms a contrary opinion. As proven by a study of charts over the past, the most discouraging action of a stock is the "right" action for a base.

If you have been active in the stock market and have had enough experience to believe that you should now be showing better results in the profit column, you should now take stock of yourself:

- Have you been taking small profits because you got tired of waiting?
- Have you taken losses because you bought too high?

- Have you lacked the nerve to buy when a stock was low and later bought it with enthusiasm when it was much higher?
- Did you sell when Eisenhower had a heart attack or when Kennedy was assassinated?
- Were you panicked into selling during the 1962 break?

If so, you are a speculator and have been making the mistakes that come naturally.

The temperament of most people is just not suitable for the role of a speculator. But unless a person is unusually flighty he should be able to fit himself into the role of an investolator in the method I have outlined. Various sources of information have been said to be the tools for use by speculators and investors. Can this information be translated into showing what phase of its market cycle a stock may be in? Of course not.

Are you capable of weighing all the known fundamentals against one another? After all, some may be bullish, some bearish. It is the unknown factors that are important, because they are unknown to you until it is too late. The groundwork of plans for expanded business or a money-making product may take place years before you and I are aware of it. Those in the know, you can be assured, are also building the groundwork for a large rise in the share prices of their company by maneuvering their stock through an accumulation phase which may easily be detected by its price action.

The fundamentalist can visualize the future of many companies from the news media and statistics available, but this does not indicate what trend the price may take. A company's future gives no indication as to the technical condition of a stock. A fundamentalist may properly evaluate a stock at 35, but he has no way of knowing whether its next move will be to 17 or 70. If an action as shown on a chart is one that appears sound as proven by past actions of others, an investolator can feel fairly certain that something is "cooking." There may be a bullish fundamental reason coming up, or it may be merely manipulation. An investolator shouldn't care less. The price action of the stock indicates that the smart money is interested in buying it.

So, the fundamentalist allowed another bargain to pass by unseen, because the fundamentals and the price action did not combine to entice him into buying it. This combination comes at a higher price.

The average fundamentalist wants to own shares in something that he can be proud of mentioning to his friends. From a "sophisticated" viewpoint even a sound stock that has remained quiet for very long may be rated as a "dog." In order for the average fundamentalist to feel friendly toward it, it must have shown ability to rise in price over the past years, and the more the better. The fundamentalist must "like" a stock before he can put his money in it. And because of this, the majority of his purchases have been made far too high. He then finds that there is little consolation in holding a stock at a loss even though it is a "good" one. Actually, the long range chartist has the only practical viewpoint; an investolator can only "like" a stock when it appears to be a bargain. It makes little difference whether it is a dog or a blue chip.

The more people I have talked to on this subject, the more I find who admit that after all the data and dope sheets have been studied, their trading was not very successful. The available information seldom induced them to buy at a low price. I would like to suggest to the fundamentalist to throw all these tools that he has been using, including the average broker's opinion, into the wastebasket and use one of mankind's simplest inventions, a pin. I would tell him to spread the financial page on the table, shut his eyes and pinpoint three or more common stocks. Because stocks spend far more time in the lower range than they do in the upper, he will have a far better chance of picking them in the lower range. Another advantage of this method is that it is not so apt to cause ulcers and will give him more time for relaxation. Of course, if he should really want to buy stocks low, he should become an investolator, learn to use the long range charts, and above all, learn to use patience with them.

You may be a little skeptical about accepting this long range chart reading advice, perhaps on the theory that if it is so good, why has it not been described before? A good question. It is a question I would like to have answered.

I have met with skepticism during all the years of my market experience. I was a skeptic when I was first made aware of chart reading. And now, I am teaching it. I have not heard of anyone else who has been trying to teach stock market success by this simplified, long range chart method. There must be others who understand it as I do. But probably they are not interested in passing their knowledge on to the public.

There is no quackery or crystal ball gazing in forecasting by the use of long range charts. It is a matter of ascertaining when a stock is changing from weak to strong hands in a bottom range or when it is changing from strong to weak hands during top areas.

Forecasting a rise from a sound base need not be qualified by any "ifs, ands or buts," only by a "when."

Financial reporters commonly refer to "whether or not the public is in the market." Without saying so, they imply that there is someone besides the public in the market. Who are *they?* They can be referred to as the "smart money," or insiders. Those among the public who are sharp enough or lucky enough to sell in top areas or buy when stocks are unwanted, are in the minority, believe me. Obviously then, there is opposition, and these opposing forces are in the "know." Then is it not within reason that these forces will attempt to influence the public? Can you name any endeavor, reasonable or radical, honest or crooked, good or evil, selfish or unselfish, motivated by love or hate, that doesn't try to widen its influence for its own special interest? These interests vary over a wide range of monetary or power motive. Salesmen, businessmen, advertisers, lobbyists, politicians, religionists, communists, and so forth, could be included. Is it then inconceivable that stock market prices are controlled by inside forces for the purpose of influencing the public to buy and sell at the wrong time?

I will demonstrate the extreme difference in point of view between a fundamentalist and an investolator. An investolator would have recognized Chadbourne Gotham as a bargain in 1964, but certainly the high-level action of International Business Machines had no inducement for him to buy it. Yet the public, who are practically all fundamentalists, bet heavily on IBM. There were 2,033,100 shares traded in 1964 against 539,200 shares of CGI. In value, the difference in amount is tremendous. At an average price of $450.00, the value of IBM traded was $914,875,000 compared to the value of $1,482,800 of CGI at an average of $2.75 per share. While the public trading may have been "on balance" (they sold as many shares as they bought) in IBM, I am certain that because of the typical discouraging action as shown in the chart of CGI, the public bought far less than they sold. This tips the percentage of money used by the public to buy CGI in comparison to IBM at even less than it normally would appear.

So the betting odds made IBM an overwhelming favorite because everyone knows it is a good stock, while CGI was a long shot because it is a dog.

IBM could move right on up to 600 or 700, but in 1964 it appeared to be in a high-level consolidation. If so, then it may be a bargain at 500 in the future. It will be easier for CGI to move up 300% from 2-3/4 than it will for IBM to rise 100% from 450. Many fundamentalists who bought IBM during 1961 took heavy losses when it broke 50% in 1962. Certainly it was not dividends they were after. Its dividend in 1961 averaged less than one-half of 1%. CGI paid no dividends.

A friend bought me the June, 1964, issue of *Forbes* Magazine in which there was a list of "loaded laggards." What interested him was that it listed three stocks that I was highly recommending and in which my friend knew that I was heavily committed. These were Belding Hemingway at 20, Bond Stores at 16-1/8, and Chadbourne Gotham at 2-3/4. Bond Stores was listed as having a working capital of $23.21 per share and a book value of more than twice what it was selling for.

A few days later he asked me in a puzzled manner, "Why, with that kind of a factual item, didn't they move up?" He knew that trading was very light in all three of them and that a little demand should affect the price. I explained to him that the vast majority of investors and speculators are fundamentalists, and are constantly in search of some item that will give them a clue to making a good purchase. But these items are merely cold statistics. The fundamentalist reasons that if they are such bargains, then why are they on the bargain counter? There must be something wrong with them. He is not going to be dumb enough to buy something that has to be underpriced before people will buy it. That's the way they sell seconds at a towel factory. Cheap.

This item in a national magazine may induce a reverse psychology. In a week or two it may cause holders of these stocks to sell. Their reasoning is that if a stock can't move up on a bullish item like this, there is little hope. So they place more bargains on the bargain counter.

The fact is that a bullish item, if it does not influence the public emotionally, is practically worthless. If the price action of a stock has been moving up rapidly then a bullish statistic will merit his attention. The combination of rising prices plus bullish statistics will stimulate him into action.

The public are more susceptible to sudden, surprise news that will appeal to their imagination. For instance, when Texas Gulf Sulphur

(TG) announced their rich mineral strike in Canada, the public not only bought TG by millions of shares, but also Curtiss Publishing (CPC). The latter was bought only because they owned land near this strike. This type of news is exciting. It brought out the gambling spirit.

The extreme low of TG was made in 1962. It rose so fast after the strike was made public that few bought below 50. The speculators who survived the sharp shakeouts from 60 and 70 and held it for the next large rise, I can assure you were rare. Disappointed fundamentalists sold heavily on those three shakeouts.

The fundamentalists who bought CPC on the basis of this strike, took a bad beating. Anyway it was exciting while it lasted. Then came the losses.

This could not happen to an investolator.

Authors list a great many "tools" that you should use in order to form an opinion on the stock market. To use these tools profitably, skill and experience are necessary. What can happen to the novice while learning to use these tools? Plenty. Besides he may never learn to use them properly. The use of many of these tools would have to be applied to numerous stocks before one met with your approval. Using these tools can be very time-consuming.

Is there a fundamentalist with the ability to state within an hour of study, with any degree of success, what will be the next major move of any stock that would be picked at random from the financial pages? I can determine in one minute of studying its chart, whether or not a stock is in a bargain range, whether its action is uncertain, or its price is too high to consider buying even though I may recognize that it is in the markup stage.

When the chart "picture" of a stock indicates it is dangerously high, no doubt the "picture" as shown by the weighing of its fundamentals would appear very bright. And can anyone deny that when the earnings of a company are at their lowest, the price of its shares is usually around the lowest range? Doesn't this prove that a correct appraisal of fundamentals can lead you into having incorrect opinions? Isn't this the reason why so many may be right, but at the wrong time? Isn't this another reason for there being so many high-level investors? It is better to be a mere optimist.

If I had to depend on using the tools that fundamentalists advocate in forming a positive opinion I would be as hopelessly lost as if I was far off a trail in a tropical jungle without a compass, with the sun straight overhead.

Recently I examined some stock market literature brought to me by a long-time friend and school administrator. I found among his collection of texts and reading material a small booklet distributed by a large financial magazine in which the writer emphasized that the charts ". . . have some good features," but the author of the booklet regards the past highs and lows of a chart as being virtually useless for the investor in visualizing clearly where the market will go next. He did not give the reader the benefit of what these good features were. The author, who remained anonymous, probably wrote what his employer wanted him to write. No doubt a chart meant no more to him than this page of words would mean to an illiterate aborigine. I am sure he knew little about chart reading and probably cared less.

What does this writer expect of a chart? Does he think a chart should be equipped with flashing green and red lights indicating to the trader where the market will go next? While he used the word investor, I am sure he meant trader, because seldom is an investor ever seen using charts. Many times a speculating chartist will clearly visualize where the market will go next, but too often his vision is short-sighted. He overlooks the large profitable rises.

Financial magazines, etc., could not afford to show the value of chart reading. That would be against their own interests. The fundamentalist reads these thoroughly, hoping to pick a clue as to why or when a stock will have a move. But they are apt to find that the good news, even though it is true, too often seems to come out at the wrong time, and the discouraging news usually comes out long after a stock has topped or is in a low range.

How much of this news is just plain touting? It would be virtually impossible for magazines and newspapers to prevent the spreading of exaggerated and sometimes outright fictitious news items or "knowledgeable" opinions. It is beyond their ability to check the authenticity of all reports.

It is said that general economic indications play an important role in foretelling future trends. But, can the average person locate these indicators that will give him a cue as to the next trend of a stock? Where are they? These writers who belittle the general principles of chart reading, themselves admit that business trends and the general market trends may go counter to one another. So if a person could locate these economic indicators, and buy accordingly, he might find that these cues could turn out to be miscues.

Let's concede that a fundamentalist was able to forecast the general economic trend. How would he have fared in so many of the stocks that have had their own individual bull and bear markets off and on since 1946? A person who remained a perpetual bull all these years, refusing to sell under any circumstances, would be far better off than a fundamentalist who subjected himself to all the conflicting influences that he is exposed to, including the worst one of all, the emotional influences that his mentality is not capable of warding off.

I got the intimation from a spot item in literature I have read that I could fit the image of a person described as "a simple chap" because he believed in "studying the charts" before purchasing a stock. I suspect what was really meant was "simpleton."

This gem of bewildering jargon was found in a textbook on market analysis: "The classical conception of science, formulated in Greek antiquity and perpetuated in a powerful and respected intellectual tradition, was modeled upon the ideal of a completely demonstrable and absolutely indubitable science, such as Euclidean geometry was then believed to be. This view relegated the variable, the changing, the probable to the realm of mere belief and opinion . . . The man-in-the-street notion of science frequently follows this tradition even today."

This item said a mouthful—and in large words. I believe the author was more interested in showing off his mastery of English than in teaching the science of investing in the stock market. I guess I will never know what I have missed in life with my informal education!

Many prominent authors of the past have belittled the use of charts. Statements such as the following may be found: "The use of these 'patterns' for forecasting purposes seems dubious." The writer did not state that they were dubious, but only that they seemed dubious. Referring to what is commonly called a "box," he says: "The theory has it that a move on increased volume above or below this area forecasts a dependable further move in that direction. The chartist takes care of this latter by calling it a 'False Move.' This is very tidy terminology, but rather a hardship on your pocketbook."[1]

---

[1] *The Stock Market,* Joseph Mindell, American Book-Stratford Press Inc., New York.

Would the author suggest a more descriptive name for a false start, or quick reversal? My interpretation of the writer's portrayal of the chart action is that he is referring to short term "boxes" of only a few weeks' duration and as played by active speculators. These "breakout" moves by buying, or selling short, should also be followed by close "stops" by the speculators who try this. They are only protecting themselves by these stop-loss orders against taking larger losses at a later date, and it is not the "hardship on your pocketbook" that he implies. This is a form of insurance against taking larger losses. The chartist, no matter how inexperienced he may be, is well aware of "false moves" and is trying to keep his losses to a minimum. Would any financial writer suggest doing otherwise? Can they explain how a fundamentalist would do it?

These false moves in a stock are positive proof of manipulation. If the technical condition of a stock is strong enough in one of these "boxes" to be a base for a strong rise, then why should it be weak enough to break out of the box on the downside just before it turns up and breaks out on the upside for a large move? Someone is buying the stock in the box, but withholds his buying for a time, then the normal selling pressure drives the price down, breaking out of the box on the downside, bringing about a flood of selling by the speculators thinking this is the beginning of a downtrend. This is called the false move, or the shakeout. Many shares during this period change from weak holders to strong ones. Then the breakout on the upside from the box gives the appearance of strength, thereby reversing the boardroom sentiment and generating bullishness among traders. The strength that will develop on this buying wave will depend on the technical strength that was in the stock previous to this box. The literature studied was just another attempt to belittle the use of charts, an opinion often seen in books pertaining to speculating in our markets. The fact is, that these short term boxes can be played successfully by an experienced chartist. Nicolas Darvas, in his book *How I Made $2,000,000 In The Stock Market* claims to have made his fortune by this method.

If an investolator should notice one of these boxes, he is watching the market too closely. Also, the investolator should never consider using a stop-sell order except when he may be expecting a steep uptrend line to be broken, after an extended rise of at least 200%, from a sound base as shown on a chart.

The investolator should be interested only in the long term boxes or consolidation periods as I prefer to call them.

The reader may run across statements similar to this: "that some chartists are such purists that they are not interested in sales, earnings and dividends . . . [they] feel that this might influence their interpretation of their charts." This is only meant to put the chartist up for ridicule. But I would like to say that these so-called purists do use logic. At least they are not going to be carried away by the data to be seen in financial statements. I will defy the run of the mill public to get a clear picture out of some of these accepted systems of accounting. Ask any corporation auditor how misleading some of these annual financial reports can be.

The accounting methods of Yale Express System represent an extreme example. On May 24, 1965, the company announced that it would file in Federal Court for reorganization under Chapter 10 of the Bankruptcy Act. They had changed their accounting methods so that their financial statements showed large losses in 1963 and 1964 instead of profits. A profit of 81 cents in 1963 was changed to a deficit of 52 cents, and in 1964 from a profit to a loss of $1.51. The company paid dividends of 44 cents in 1963 and increased it to 60 cents in 1964, in spite of losses.

The chart of Yale Express shows that its shares rose $9 to a high of 17-1/4 in 1963, over $5.00 of it in one month. This baited the speculators into buying heavily. No doubt there was plenty of ballyhooing and touting of the company during this period. In less than two years the stock dropped to 2-1/8. You can be certain that the fast rise to 17-1/4 was instigated by someone that wanted "out." And they did it with a profit.

Would this combination of maneuvers, price rise and dividend increases in the face of hidden deficits (at least hidden in its earnings reports) withstand a close scrutiny by the SEC, which is supposed to protect the public from the "fast buck" artists?

Moral: Don't take too seriously what you read in a financial statement.

The public should largely ignore some of this reporting to the stockholders. As far as being influenced by profit and loss statements, I would like to impress upon my readers that *earnings can change as quickly as the seasons.*

At times you will see sharp changes in earnings, but no change in the major trend of the stock. This indicates that the price is being kept under control. Crown Central Petroleum is a good example. In 1948 the earnings were $3.90; in 1949 it had a 12 cent deficit; and in 1950 earned $1.90; but the average price range for the three years was nearly identical, about 6-1/2 per share.

A friend brought me an article from a large monthly financial magazine where the author presented little for the cause of charting and chart reading for the patrons of the stock market. This writer seems to have joined the ranks in the battle against this method of forecasting price moves. The article, after a lot of quoting of others asks: "What's the use of a pattern that works except when it doesn't work?" No doubt this refers to the many week-to-week and month-to-month formations that some chartists play too closely. The failure of the average chartist is the same as that of the average non-chartist. He is so afraid of missing a move, he watches the short term actions too closely and therefore loses sight of the long term possibilities.

If the short term chartist would confine himself to thinking only in terms of major moves, he would do so much better. If the fundamentalist would only do a little "crystal gazing" at charts, (prejudiced non-chartists often use this term), perhaps he could "see" enough so that this logic would prevent him from buying after a several hundred percent rise.

These short term configurations that are played mechanically can be unreliable. When quick trend reversals and so many false moves or false starts take place, the toll of losses, even though small, is apt to be taken too often and is hard to recoup. If one really understands chart reading and has learned to overcome his emotional aberrations he will have a fair chance of coming out ahead. I do maintain that the average short term chartist will be able to hold out longer in his battle of survival in Wall Street than the average fundamentalist. At least, no matter how inexperienced he is, he has something to study, from which he can form an opinion. He is not groping entirely in the dark. For short term speculative trades, what has the fundamentalist to go on? Would these writers who report so negatively about the value of using charts be a little positive about what value, for short term trading, there is in studying fundamentals and earning reports, or reading all the financial periodicals and newspapers? These news items, good or bad, no doubt are handed to the news media, usually when the time is "right." When these items are really "newsworthy" the market action of the stock has often discounted it beforehand. Others knew it before the public did.

I challenge any of these "judges" on the merits of using charts, to disprove the value of studying long-range charts as I am teaching it. I challenge them to disprove that what I have described as sound bases are not sound bases. I challenge them to disprove that when a stock has moved up several hundred percent on a trend line of over 45 degrees it is sound judgment to sell it when the trend is broken. I challenge them to prove there is a safer or better way for the average person to make money in our markets.

Earnings and Future Prospects vs. Stock Action

I read one time that the master of hindsight has no place in the stock market. I believe this refers to the kind of person who always points out that he *would* have bought here and *should* have sold there. If he is the type who is always berating himself for his mistakes, I agree. But certainly one should not treat these mistakes as something to forget. The mistakes you have made in the market are a part of your education. They certainly have been in mine. There are many elements of hindsight that the fundamentalists study before they make a decision. But the study of these is by no means indicative, and may often mislead in the forming of an opinion as to what the future price move of a stock will be.

The hindsight of earnings can only give a general impression of what future earnings will be and in the case of utilities this is usually correct. A general increase in earnings indicates higher share prices. Normal optimism can expect this. But normal optimism plus wild enthusiasm is what keeps people from taking large profits after prices have moved up sharply.

Shouldn't the hindsight of having seen a very large rise give you the foresight to expect a drop to follow?

After having seen your stock have a large rise it is time to shed your natural optimism and adopt a pessimistic attitude toward the future price trend. Don't wait until this attitude is forced on you by the persistent falling of prices, where invariably you may sell when you should be buying.

There may be reasons for poor earnings in the future that you cannot possibly see in the past history of a company. Sometimes if you are clever, you can foresee that a product which has been developed by a company may create higher earnings in the future, but by this time the price of the stock has probably discounted this. Others were aware of this before you were. Your foresight has now become hindsight to them. Throughout the stock list are hundreds whose year to year earnings could not possibly be determined by the closest study of their fundamentals. That is why the average person (who is nearly always a fundamentalist) winds up confused and makes up his mind emotionally. But he never realizes it. How many people in the past have failed to recognize, even refused to recognize, that a stock was any good until it sold at a price far above its recent lows? Why didn't they? Because there was no fundamental message for them to see that would indicate a big rise. The fundamentalist often refuses to believe that a big rise can develop without increased earnings.

Following are some extreme samplings of companies whose shares sold far higher while earnings were much lower than they were during previous years in a bottom range.

Company	Year	Earnings	Low	Year	Earnings	High
Columbia Pictures	1950	2.06	8-1/2	1961	D1.09	35-1/4
Consolidation Coal	1948	3.50	9	1956	2.39	50-1/4
Continental Baking	1948	5.84	11	1961	3.42	58
Esquire, Inc.	1950	.92	4-1/8	1961	D.72	23-1/2
General Time	1954	1.12	6-1/2	1960	D.36	34-1/2
Hall (C.M.) Lamp	1957	1.86	3-1/4	1959	D.93	20-1/2
Hydrometals	1958	D.19	7-1/2	1960	D1.38	43-1/2
Seaboard World Airlines	1962	.29	1	1959	D10.83	44-1/2

Seaboard World Airlines, Inc. (SBA)

In the Seaboard World Airlines (SBA) comparison, there were wide price swings above 30 which began in late 1958. That was a cleverly

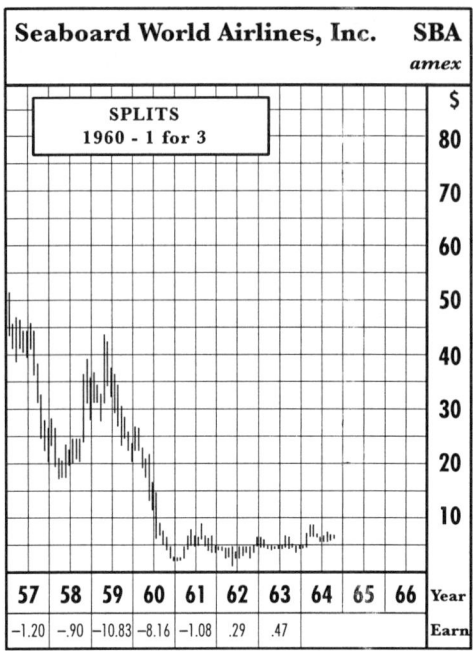

manipulated action that induced the public to buy at a time when the fundamental outlook was bad, very bad. But was this outlook really visible to anyone except the insiders? Did the fundamentalists during this top investigate before they invested? If they did, their investigation was faulty. Surely there were no fundamental reasons for thinking that the stock should go as high as it did, let alone higher. Many thousands of shares were bought by people who apparently thought it would. In 1962 and 1963 when SBA was back in the black, these high-level investors were selling out. I am sure that if someone clipped all the items that he could find that were favorably influencing the public to buy, from periodicals, newspapers, advisory services, the Dow Jones news service, etc., during the ten months that SBA traded above 30, he would have filled a small scrapbook.

It is so obvious that people buy stocks like this mostly because they were moving up, influenced by the speculative urge. Is this not convincing proof that an extremely large amount of buying and selling is purely emotional? Or did the fundamentalists decide, after a careful study of background history, management, competitive position and other data, that these stocks should be bought? If so, then there is something lacking in this type of hindsight.

The chartist, on the other hand, does not waste his time trying to forecast earnings, etc. He should only be interested in a stock when it indicates by its quiet bottom action that it is under accumulation by the insiders, for a number of years. If it develops a good base, he can be certain that it will be run up in due time, whether it will have increased earnings or go into the deficit column. He can rest assured that when the price is moved up properly, the public will become interested, and grab the bait. The insiders are not playing for peanuts. This is the type of hindsight for you to use as the basis for your foresight.

When I try to explain this line of reasoning to one who studies all the dope sheets and statistics available, like a bettor on the horses does his racing form, he comes back and talks glibly of a dozen aspects of his stock. He seldom understands me and cares less. Actually he has learned little, after all his studying, that will give him a real clue as to which way his stock will move. Oh, yes, he has formed an opinion all right, a very good one, too — that's what he thinks. But, there is something he does not realize: his mind was probably made up *before* he read all this information. He was probably influenced emotionally by market action, wishful thinking or was just a plain ordinary "Wall Street Bull" at the time. Often he is right, but too often he is wrong.

The novice who has taken a course, either free or paid for, is in the same category. He has learned things about the market that I have forgotten years ago, and am not the least concerned with. Either type comes up with about the same line of thinking. Neither one realizes that a little knowledge of the market is dangerous. A person that has never bought a share in his life is just as apt to pick a winner as one who believes he has all the answers. I don't care whether a company's product is beverages, brewing or broadcasting; all I want to know is whether the insiders are buying or not.

A question often asked is, "Do you think the earnings will increase?" My answer to that is, "I don't know and I don't care." They don't imply it, but I am sure they can't help but think I've made a foolish statement. They are so earnings conscious that they think a stock can't go up unless the earnings increase or there are at least some visible future prospects of increasing business. The long range charts contain plenty of proof that higher earnings are not necessary to stimulate a big rise.

Foster Wheeler Corporation (FWC)

If you had studied the past of Foster Wheeler Corp. (FWC) as a fundamentalist in 1949 when in February and June it sold below 10 while earning $6.62, could you believe that it would sell as high as 67 eight years later during which time it lost $1.39? Why would people sell a stock at a loss when it was earning 65%? Because they had bought it at higher prices and were fearful that it would go lower. Fear

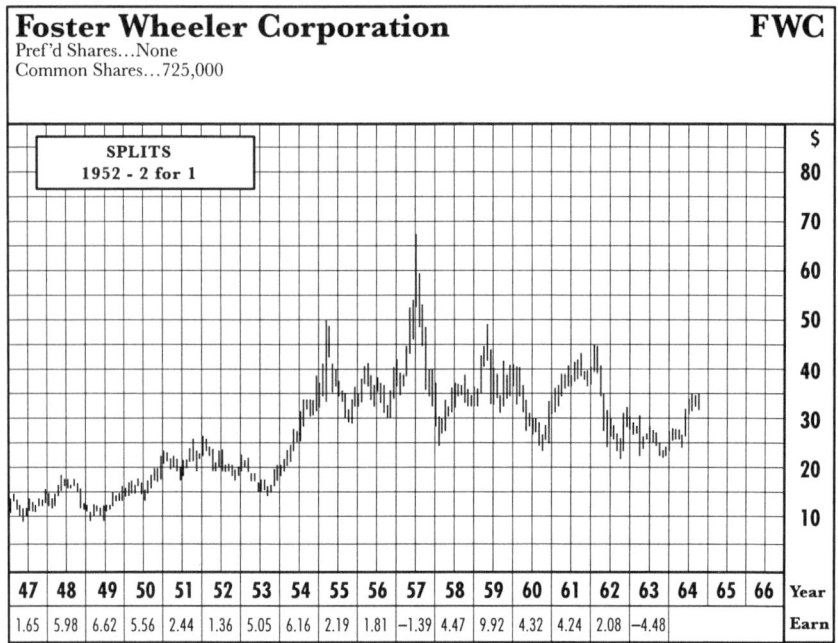

blinded them to the fact that it was foolish to sell at this price. The earnings of $6.62, as you will notice, were not a flash in the pan. The previous year they were $5.98 and in the following year $5.56. Knowing the general attitude of the speculative public, I can assure you that few of them were buyers at this time. FWC was selling too low. There must be something wrong with the company. That's what they thought.

Eight years later, they lost their wariness while FWC was rising from 40 to 67 per share during a year when it was losing money. All common sense and reasoning was displaced by blind, emotional buying.

This rare combination of actions and earnings is just unbelievable to the average person. Seldom would anyone notice this except by the use of charts. Can the directors of Foster Wheeler give a valid reason for all the juggling of dividend rates? This must have been discouraging to the shareholders when the dividend rate was cut twice, then passed, in 1953 when the company earned $5.05. A mere four years later they paid $1.60 during a year that showed a deficit of $1.39. You be the judge; who do you think sold out during this fast $27 move in this same year?

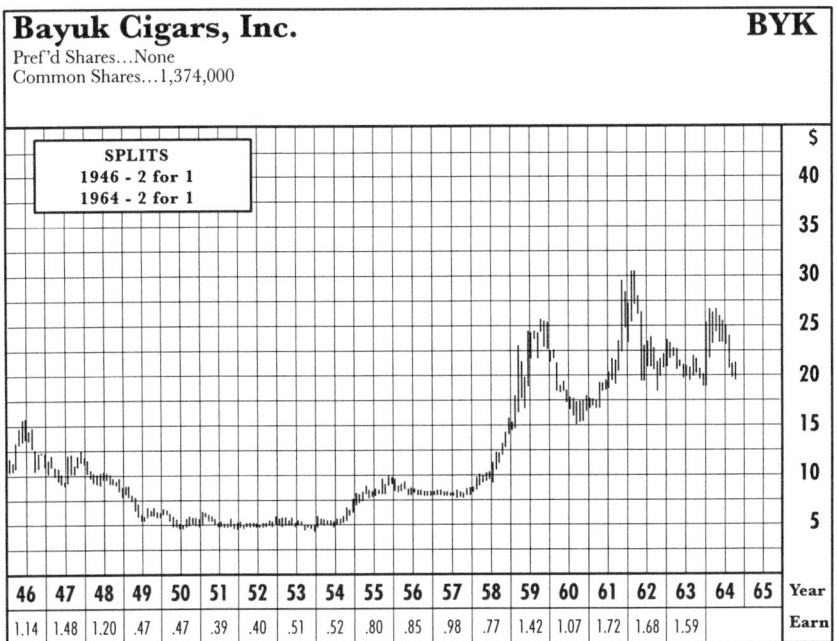

Bayuk Cigars, Inc. (BYK)

Now, let's look at Bayuk Cigars (BYK). In September of 1954 could the hindsight of a fundamentalist, after investigating this company's past, have the foresight to predict that it would have a big rise in a few years? The drop in earnings and the cut in dividends since 1947 would have left him cold. To an "investolator," BYK would have been an easy one to figure out. This was one of those perfect bases. As a chartist, the hindsight of those five quiet years' action was a positive indication of accumulation by the insiders. This accumulation would give the foresight of a big move. Even a chartist cannot help but notice the drop in earnings such as occurred since 1947. At $5, this stock was paying a good dividend, but the public sold during this quiet period. Many more sold out during the following three years' consolidation. How many have been heard to say, "After I sold out it went up"?

From an investolator's point of view BYK was as perfect a "picture" as you can hope to see from base to top. Just by the use of mechanical stops, you would have bought at 6, or later on at 9, and sold on a stop at 22 when the perfect uptrend was broken.

You may say, "but this is all hindsight." True, but it is only through the study of hindsight that you can become the master of foresight.

Watch for similar actions in the future. But don't expect such smooth actions as BYK. The similarities may be only roughly the same, but will be just as positive.

By the use of hindsight through the study of long range charts I hope to teach even the novice how he can make sound purchases and feel reasonably positive that with patience he will make a large profit. Even if the reader refuses to believe that these market actions are not purely accidental, he can't argue with the charts. They show a positive record of past actions forming a bottom that are followed by various patterns—but all eventually have the big move. These sound formations are there to be seen, in the past and present, if you will only look. By the study of these charts you can become the master of hindsight in many cases. A diagnosis of the past can be worth a fortune in the future.

A REMINDER ABOUT TREND LINES. You can learn a great deal about long range price actions as I have done since I first bought a book of charts. But in spite of this accumulated knowledge I outsmarted myself in 1963 while in the outback of Australia, when I sold 11,000 shares of Dr. Pepper at an average price of 31 (before the 2-for-1 split), for a profit of over $200,000, because I thought it was due for a reaction. I still had something to learn. My selling price should have been at 60, the following year when it broke its upward trend line.

Years previously I paid $15 for six lessons purporting to teach me the reasons why markets act the way they do. But here a single lesson cost me $300,000. Actually more, because I could have bought 15,000 more shares of Belding Hemingway and Bond Stores with this extra profit.

In the past I have been satisfied with buying a stock with a sound base and waiting. But since I began writing this book I have studied the long range actions in the charts with more intensity. After all, in order to teach, one should know his subject. (Also this $300,000 lesson was a stimulant for further studies!)

Taking a profit too soon, as I did with DOC, can leave one in an unhappy mood. But it should be considered in a different light. You should feel fortunate at having had the opportunity to make this error. A large profit was realized. You should feel pleased that you were not among those who bought in these high price areas and have taken billions in losses.

EARNINGS AND FUTURE PROSPECTS VS. STOCK ACTION 171

A review of these lessons gained from hindsight, some of which I learned while endeavoring to teach you the do's and don't's in the stock market, should give you the foresight to avoid the pitfalls of which the most common is BUYING TOO HIGH.

The power of foresight comes naturally when you have mastered the viewing of hindsight.

Advisory Services:
A Spider's Web of Conflicting Claims and Confusion

It has been a mystery to me why there are those who struggle for years to build up a business of trying to sell advice on how to beat the market on a speculative basis. If they can beat the market why don't they go ahead and beat it and relax or travel as a tourist or for adventure, or develop an interesting hobby? I remember years ago when I was a "bull" in Pepsi Cola, I saw a small ad in the financial pages of the *Los Angeles Times* by a fellow wanting to sell advice on the market. He implied Pepsi Cola might go into a tailspin. At the time it had made only a moderate rise from where I had bought it, below 10. I showed the ad to my broker who remarked, "Oh, it's probably some broken-down speculator." That's the general idea, if you can't beat the market, start an advisory service. Pepsi did not go into a tailspin.

At this time there are over 1500 stock market advisors registered with the Securities and Exchange Commission and in my opinion the competence of all but a few of them are suspect. New ones are still appearing on the scene. If they can foresee future trends of stock prices, why do they enter this competitive business of forecasting? Is it because self-advice in trading proved unsuccessful? Are profits more positive in selling advice? Most of them cater to the in and out traders who have failed to beat the market on their own. Certainly few would subscribe to a service on a quarterly, or yearly basis if the advice was to the effect that the client would have to wait for three to eight years for a move to mature, even though this could be very sound advice. There are some advisory services that make use of charts in their study of securities, but do they ever mention that the actions that are to be seen are probably guided by market manipulations? Are they not aware of it or don't they believe it exists? Perhaps it is taboo for them to mention this. It could be a very sensitive subject in some circles.

I have been on the mailing list of several advisory services trying to sell me advice. In December, 1963, I received one that said in part, "In a recent special report, our editor-in-chief documents the case for a move to 1182 for DJI by 1972. This case is based upon 65 years of market history. A timetable is included, showing the price level for each year between now and then." This would be a bonus report at no extra cost.

This claim makes my predictions appear like I am a Mr. Milquetoast. Here they are claiming, for a price of course, the price level for each of the next eight years. Who do they think they are kidding? That, you must realize, is an absolute impossibility. It would be interesting to know how many gullible people fell for this line. It must pay off. I am at a loss for words to describe my feelings toward this type of appeal to the ignorant. Besides, to benefit from this you would have to trade only in those stocks that are closely following the DJI. And is there any guarantee they will continue to follow the DJI pattern? If the past is any criterion, they will not. In over 1600 charted stocks at hand I was unable to locate any stock action that was really similar to the DJI in the last four years, let alone the last eight years. The vast majority in fact have far from a similar pattern. Perhaps you might infer that it is then useless to pay attention to the DJ averages. Far from it. This present 1962-66 steep rise of the DJI is really leading the way for the rest of the market. The deadbeats and dogs will wake up and outrun the blue chips in percentage during a period of time in the not too distant future. There are also many fine stocks presently in the "doghouse" because they are not doing very well. They are "sick" at this time. You will be surprised at how much recuperating they will do, given time.

I received another "come on" to sell me advice from an organization now getting market forecasts from computers. They are honest enough to stress that their method is not the "key to Monte Carlo." I had already suspected as much.

At the top of this brochure was this: "O-F-F-I-C-I-A-L A-N-N-O-U-N-C-E-M-E-N-T. Less than 50 charter openings now remain for you to join a small, limited group of sophisticated investors who are seeking large annual capital gains without the usual fears for the ups and downs of the market."

It would be interesting to know how these charter members fared. Did the "large annual capital gains" materialize?

In April, 1964 I received an offer from a well established advisory service to subscribe to their service at half the regular price. Some of their literature had this to say. "When the market moved above 700 for the first time in 1961, it had been rising for so long that the majority was convinced that prices would keep right on advancing. People literally chased stocks." True, this hindsight is perfect. It continues— "Then in the middle of 1962 came the tumble . . . for stock prices and those who had bought so eagerly a few months previously. Now in 1964, the once-burned and twice-shy majority views the market's second move above 700 differently. This time they see it as a prelude to a severe decline."

Now for an example of their foresight. "From a psychological and technical point there is evidence that the market is completing an accumulation phase and now is entering the 'markup' stage." It seems to me they are a little late. The DJI was up over 200 points from the 1962 low at the time they wrote this. And they say it is now "entering" the markup stage. A glance at the DJI chart will show that it had been in the markup stage for seventeen months. Their next statement should get the buyers in the market far above the bottom. "This time the market should keep right on rising—contrary to general expectations."

This is an odd prediction. Do they mean there is no limit to this rise? Perhaps after another big shakeout they will say that it occurred because people chased stocks too high. This kind of advice will encourage people to do some chasing. No wonder they are offering advice at half price.

On March 24, 1964, I received a letter from a well known advisory service stating that they will give me the names of four stocks they recommend, for a price of course. Following is their write-up on one of them: "One of America's best-managed blue-chip companies with an outstanding performance record. Solidly entrenched in one of our most promising industries. Brilliantly managed with an eye to rapid translation of world-wide product and market expansion into tangible dollar and cents profits. Scored a remarkable 30% earnings gain in 1963 and appears headed for new sales and earnings records in 1964. This company never stands still. In 1962 it broke into a highly competitive field, with astonishing results—opening a tremendous new growth dimension that in only two years has brought new rich profit potentials into sight. We see an entire new growth phase ahead. In our opinion you are buying a solid value and a promising future when you buy this stock."

Did you ever see such a glowing word picture? And I believe every word of it may be true. And being quite bullish on the market at that time I agree that it has a good chance of going up. But how much? The price of this security no doubt is reflecting the "astonishing results." Probably this rosy future has been fully discounted. I visualize that it has gone up faster than the DJI. I could agree that it is going higher but I could not agree to buying it. Too much cream has almost certainly been skimmed already. Perhaps it is about due to have a severe setback. It could very well be too risky.

Also this rosy future may be highly exaggerated. After all they have something to sell. The "astonishing results" may be mostly a come-on to sell the advisory service.

Now if they were to write something like this about another company: "This company is a well-known nationwide clothing chain store. We don't know how brilliant the management is, and the earnings failed to cover the dividend for the past four years and the directors recently voted to cut from 31-1/4 to 25 cents quarterly. They have expanded and improved their stores in the past years but for some reason this has not paid off. At this time we do not see any fundamental reason for this stock to go up. The price range of this stock has been quiet in this low area for over fifteen years and it is our firm belief that the smart money has been buying up this stock and will give it a good run in due time. We can assure you it will have a very good chance of rising 300% in three to six years. There will no doubt be a stock split when it nears the upper range. The price is below $17.00 per share and at present it is very unattractive to the public, even though cash on hand is listed at $23.21 per share."

These are the facts on this company and the forecasts are mine. This is the picture of Bond Stores. How many clients would an advisory service get if they sent out that kind of inducement? Most fundamentalists would not touch it and those who did might feel that they were taking a big risk. But I am positive there is little risk and that it will have a very large rise. (At this time of writing I had 17,500 shares of Bond Stores and I had a loss on every share, but I was probably the least worried shareholder outside of those in the inner circle.)

Here is a shining example of an appeal to induce people to subscribe for their weekly bulletins, together with some special reports. "Only $10 for a sixty day 'Get Acquainted' offer." Beneath the name of the service I read in fine print—"A World Economic Service That Anticipates Price Trends and Business Movements." A letterhead like that should instill confidence in the most timid Mr. Milquetoast who finds himself in need of a positive opinion. In the brochure they proclaimed in large red letters, "In 1963, we expect one of the worst business depressions in our history—much money will be lost on stocks."

These excerpts followed: "Boy, oh Boy, are we bearish. And we are not placing any hedges on our forecast. Don't believe it if everyone tells you, you are all right . . . and that some miracle is to be performed which will bail everybody out . . . We hate to be bearish . . . but the events justify that viewpoint . . . If you are caught in this mess . . . we advise you not to fight it to the end . . . In spite of the recent so-called rally, in our opinion, the market decline has already started."

This misguided advisory service's timing is off by at least five years. Obviously they were basing their opinion partly on the fundamental outlook. From a fundamental viewpoint, it would take a sharper "economist" than they, or I, to properly predict when our boom is about to implode. I recognize how easy it is to be mistaken by this type of thinking and refuse to think in terms of whether or not our economy has reached its saturation point, or overproduction.

Those who are in the market and who have been perpetually optimistic all during our rising economy, have been lucky, and should give credit to this characteristic in their nature. They are getting substantial benefits from it. But it will be virtually impossible for them to foresee when our boom is about to collapse. When this time arrives, their optimism will put them at the top of the heap—of optimists, that is.

Many times in the past I have heard it said, "We will never have another depression. The government will not allow it." My answer to this is, "I wish you were right." They are overestimating the power of the government.

I believe this service thought the 1962 break was similar to the 1929 break, and thought the following rally was similar to the 1930 rally. Anyone without a thorough understanding of charts and the manipulation of our markets was justified in believing this. But there was a vast difference. In 1929, nearly all stocks were following the same general pattern. They were extremely active going into an historically fast rise with heavy trading. The 1929 top was a distribution top.

The top action previous to the 1962 break was distribution in only part of the stocks. Many were still in their bottom range, under accumulation, and many others had been in a downtrend for several years. As long as there are many stocks in a low quiet range, the final top in the general market is still several years in the future.

I have often wondered how much proof of knowledge or ability a person should have to qualify for a license as an investment advisor. I decided that the easiest way to find out was to write to the Securities and Exchange Commission for an application form. Upon reading it, I found that a license is not required from them; one is required only to register as an advisor. They ask many questions as to whether the applicant intends to manage securities accounts for clients, furnish investment advice through consultations, issue periodic publications, prepare or issue reports or analyses, prepare or issue charts, graphs, formulas, etc. Also the SEC wants to know if there are time periods involved and what fees are to be charged. They are quite interested in whether or not the applicant has been enjoined by any court from acting as an investment advisor, or if he has been found to have violated any of the provisions of the securities act, and there are many other questions.

But nowhere in the application do they ask anything about *why* a person thinks he is qualified to furnish advice on selecting stocks for others to buy and sell.

The nearest the questionnaire comes to asking the applicant what his ability might be is in a line, "The Education and Experience of—*name of person*—are as follows." I would like to ask, experienced in what? Until *after* he has become registered he has been unable to get experience as an advisor. What kind of experience could qualify him as an investment advisor if he was not an experienced trader?

In other professions one has to make an intensive study and pass a strict examination in order to prove his capability to conduct the work satisfactorily. For trades such as barbering and plumbing, applicants have to go to school or serve an apprenticeship. It is my opinion that it would be virtually impossible to find someone desiring to enter into the advisory business if they had to furnish proof by their trading over a period of years that they could profit out of the markets. Anyone who can do that would have it made, and would have little reason to enter a business where perhaps more effort is spent in trying to think up new gimmicks to induce people to buy a service, than is spent in trying to figure out a future move in a stock. Certainly there is no business in which the ability to give good service is so uncertain.

As it is, almost anyone can be registered as an investment advisor. And I do mean almost anyone. I personally know one lad who was registered at the age of sixteen years. Somehow the SEC found out about his age, and "in the interest of the public" they revoked his registration. On his calling card was printed "The Sophisticated Market Letter." In spite of his youth, his advice may have been as good as most of the services.

"In the interest of the public," I believe the SEC should set up a system that would require the advisory services to report every buy and sell recommendation that they make. Then periodic checks could be made to see if these recommendations are producing profits. A computer could probably handle this task very easily. If over a specified period of years, a service failed to show at least some profit for their clients, their registration should be revoked and the executives forever barred from participating in connection with an advisory service. This could be referred to as a law of "put up or shut up" and I think would eliminate many of the 1500 advisors that are registered, especially those that encourage short term speculation, with their placing of "stops" on nearly every commitment that they suggest, together with their numerous price "objectives." It is instinctive, and it is important, to set price objectives when making a purchase. But there must be a reason within reason, not just wishful thinking. A sound base, seen in a long range chart, provides a valid reason to set an objective.

If there was a rule that required reporting specific price suggestions to the SEC from which results would be computed, no doubt some services would change these practices and avoid being specific. Even today some of them send out rosy reports on stocks without actually advising a client to buy them, thereby avoiding responsibility of a decision.

A rule similar to what I suggest would probably be welcome to the conservative reliable type of advisory services, of which I am certain there is at least one.

According to the Investment Advisers Act Release No. 187, one Paul K. Peers, Inc., 75 Ocean Ave., Brooklyn, New York, had his registration revoked on March 22, 1965. Grounds for revocation were "False and misleading statements in offer and sale of Investment Letter, fraud in recommendation of security and failure to maintain books and records." He had over three years in which to "take" his subscribers at $100 per year, $55 for six months or $30 for three months. This operation was conducted by him and his wife from their apartment. His overhead was low, but his claim to fame and experience was high. He made flamboyant claims as far back as 1926, before he was born. He touted a small water and service company in Florida as being a "Baby Blue Chip."

He did his touting so flagrantly that it was easy for the SEC to pin him down, although too much time was involved. To my knowledge, no penalty was imposed on Paul Peers. Would this verdict of fraud by the SEC expose him to civil suits by his clients? Would they be entitled to a refund on their unexpired subscriptions? Probably not. Who said fraud doesn't pay?

In my opinion there are other advisory services that do their touting so surreptitiously that the SEC wouldn't even begin to suspect them. There are plenty of times touting may be suspected, but the alleged touter is well cloaked by the axiom that "it is human to err." Reverse touting, suggesting selling securities after they are down 50 to 90%, may be suspected at times.

I doubt very much that those who sell speculative advice, such as "buy here and place a stop loss there," do as well for their clients as the clients would have done for themselves if they had bought as investors in the first place during the past years.

Why not be your own advisor by learning how to pick bargains in the stock market by the use of long range charts? They are there to be seen from time to time. If none appear satisfactory to you, stay clear, no matter how disappointing it may be to remain on the sidelines. It is far better to be just holding money, than to be holding a stock that was bought far too high.

The regular fees charged by advisory services, to my knowledge, range from $60 to at least $900 per year. The majority of these cater to speculators and usually publish a weekly market letter which keeps the impatient speculator interested and active.

Most of these bait the public with cut-rate bonus offers or the common $1 offer for a few weeks of advice, before they apply the pressure to subscribe to their service for from three months to a year at regular rates, or even at reduced rates. They also will make an appeal with various types of bonuses (something for nothing appeal). Often they will send along with their literature a beautifully engraved certificate worth $5 or $10 to be applied on the subscription price.

I answered an ad by a well known advisory service with a branch office in Los Angeles for the sole purpose of learning how they operated. They requested my portfolio of stocks which I sent them, but I reduced the amount considerably. I felt they might wonder why anyone with such a large portfolio would be in need of an investment counselor.

My portfolio at this time consisted of American Snuff, Belding Hemingway, Bond Stores, Chadbourne Gotham, Laboratory for Electronics, Seeman Bros., and Servel, all in their bottom or bargain ranges.

I received a three-page letter and two phone calls from them. They were careful not to insult my intelligence, but it was obvious that their opinion of my choice of stocks would not have been very complimentary.

One paragraph in their letter had this to say: "If you decide to make use of our Investment Counsel facilities, we would not have in mind making sweeping changes in your portfolio, nor attempting to revamp it overnight. However, we would anticipate that over a period of time it would be possible to make advantageous switches and to manage your investment funds in such a way as to increase your income and the value of your portfolio to the greatest possible extent consistent with good quality with a minimum risk."

They sent me two copies of an agreement which said in part: "The fee for the first year, and each subsequent year thereafter, unless modified by mutual agreement, shall be $900.00, payable in advance." If this firm's advice was worth this price, they would not need to be in this business. They could merely sit back and use their own advice.

Following are a few excerpts from other advisory services who are forever hopeful of getting clients, or perhaps starve.

"Somebody is likely to make a lot of money in stocks this year or next. There's a distinct possibility that it might be YOU. YOU—that is—if YOU are interested.

"Thousands of people like yourself have made money in this way . . . Your own key to fortune is in following their footsteps, and the rewards can be great in a relatively short time under the proper conditions. Many of our subscribers have found their answers to this in successful stock speculations. This is not as wild-eyed a gamble as many people are led to believe . . . We estimate that it takes at least 90 days for an active market speculator to prove beyond any doubt that it is possible to make money by speculating in stocks."

This paragraph in my opinion contains about the lowest form of advertising and about the most dishonest. It appeals to the gullible and it must pay off, at least enough to keep these outfits prosperous in an apparently thriving business.

Here are a few more samplings from various advisory services' advertisements, all trying to convince you that you are in need of their advice.

- "Then why are we willing to give away this $19.00 bonus kit?"
- "They contain no 'high falutin' theory, no economic 'double-talk.' They are not 'tip sheets.' Every word is factual, down to earth, easy to understand and ready to put to work."
- "The work of our whole organization is brought to bear on your problem and your securities are subject to daily scrutiny."
- "A mature and experienced member of our staff watches your list constantly."
- "Your counselor is kept advised by our security specialists about the issues you hold . . . who have a total of over 800 years of experience to offer you."
- "If you act at once, we will give you seven months of Forecasts instead of six—actually a $5 bonus."
- ". . . Also I'll rush you a detailed report on two exciting recommendations."
- "You can get all this at the regular six month rate of $37.50 or, with the $10 Certificate, for 14 months for only $65. And there's no need to send money with your certificate. We'll bill you."
- "It shouldn't take much imagination to see that just one good investment, chosen from the information sent out each week, could pay for your subscription in short order." (It is consoling to

know that the subscription price is tax deductible even though the choice may be unprofitable!)

- "... members of our staff are always ready to give their particular attention to an individual client's questions or problems. However, the ultimate responsibility is, of course, the client's."

While it is human to err we must concede that even "trained analysts" cannot possibly bat 1000% on short term predictions, but failing to make a "hit" in 10 times at bat should automatically bench the batter.

This is the score achieved by one firm in a double page of recommendations in their report of May 1, 1964. I hope for their clients' sake that their other recommendations turned out better.

These first four were recommended as "Best Buys":

Greyhound Corp., buy 28, stop sell 25-1/2. (Stopped out.)

International Business Machines, buy 456, stop sell 420. (Stopped out 16 points above the following low.)

Outboard Marine, buy 17-1/8, stop sell 16. (Stopped out.)

Republic Steel, buy 43-5/8, stop sell 40-1/4. (Stopped out.)

Republic Steel was given a 300 word ballyhoo and an upside "objective" of 52 was set. Amazingly, the rise failed their selling objective by one-quarter of a point.

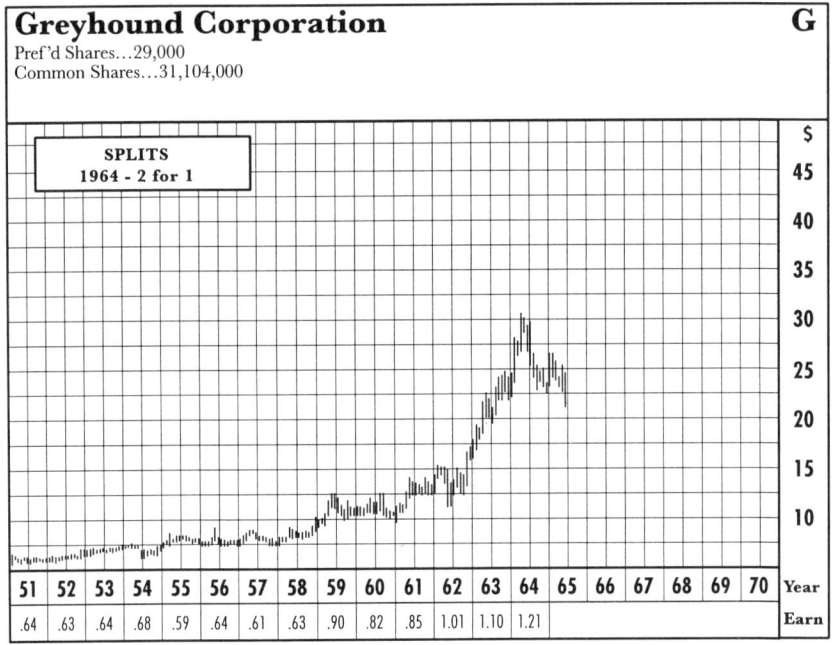

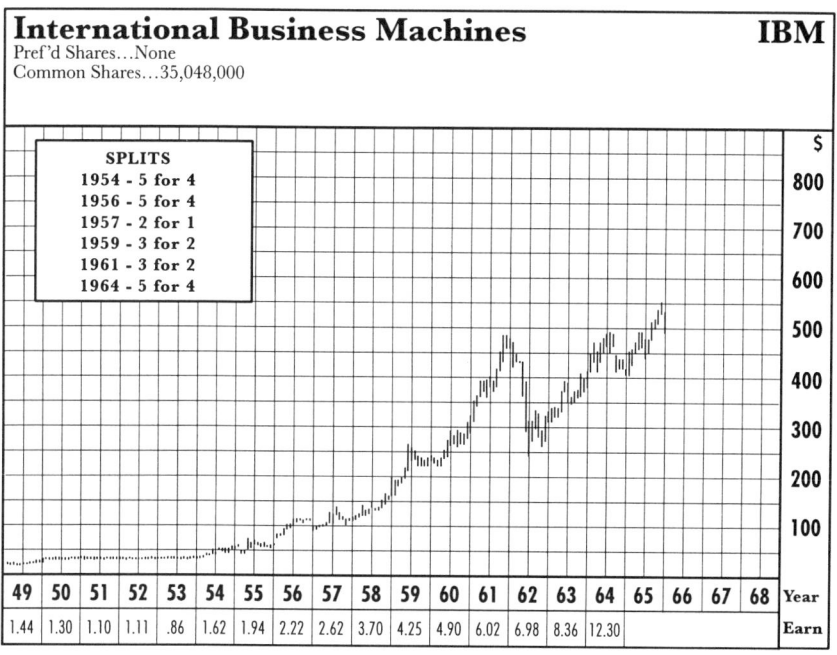

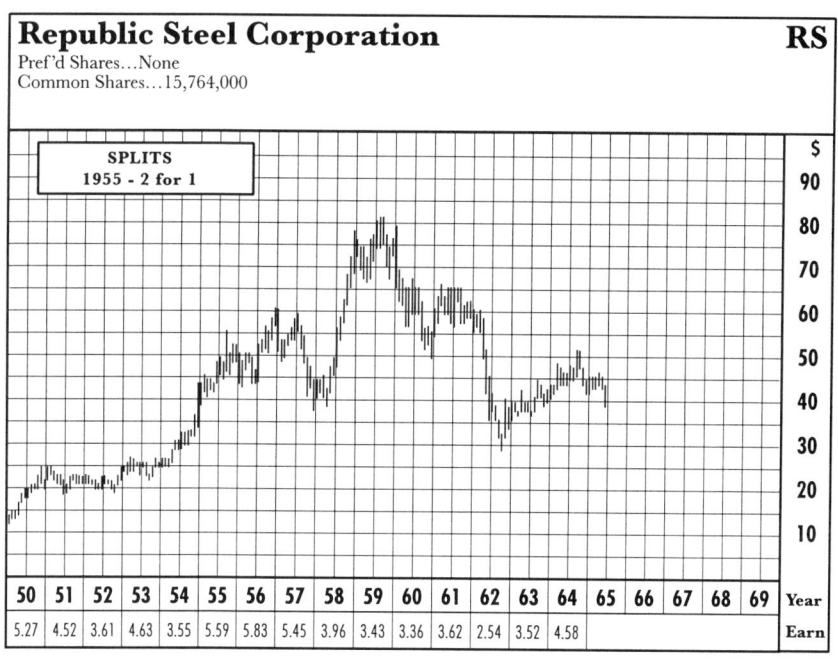

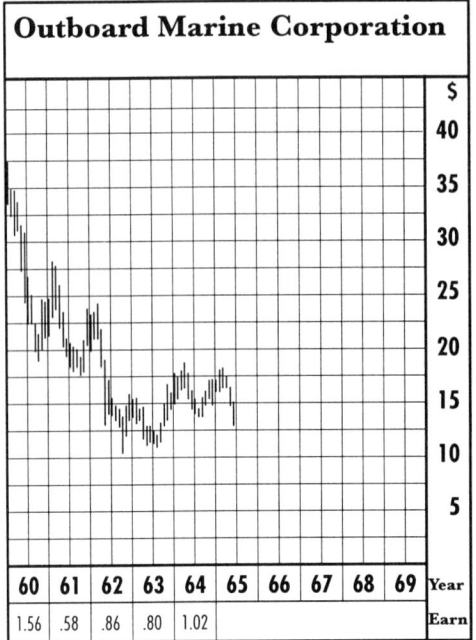

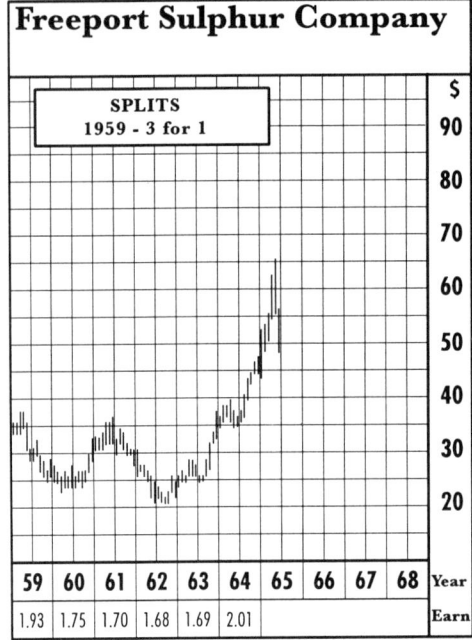

Spiegel, Inc., buy 30-5/8, stop sell 28-3/4. (Stopped out $1 above the following low.)

Freeport Sulphur, buy 35, stop sell 33-3/4. (Stopped out.)

This often happens to speculators. They buy after a 75% rise, then get stopped out on a small shakeout. It then rose above 85.

Reichhold Chemical, hold 11-3/4. Stop sell 11-5/8. (Stopped out.)

Because we do not know where this was bought, we cannot take for granted that this was a loss. But this is the most irresponsible suggestion of the century. A stop sell only 1/8 below the last price is practically the same as a "market" order. Better to sell at once.

Apparently the advice of this firm was no better when advising to sell short.

Abbott Laboratories, sell short 37-1/8, stop buy 40-5/8. (Stopped out.)

Heinz (H. J.), sell short 36-1/2, stop buy 41-3/4. (Stopped out.) Short sale was 3/8 above the low for the year.

Revlon, Inc., sell short

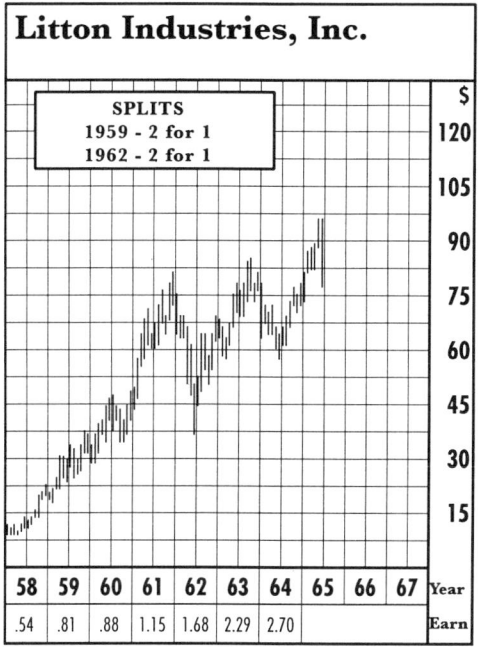

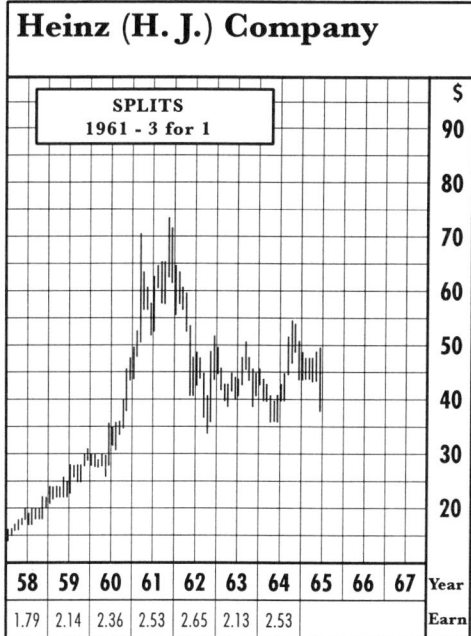

34-1/2, stop buy 39-3/4. (Stopped out.)

Litton Industries, sell short 65-7/8, stop buy 74-7/8. (Stopped out.)

Why pay for this kind of advice? I believe any trader could do better than this.

What a sorry record of achievement. Out of ten trades suggested not one produced a profit, if this advice had been followed to the letter. Any other type of business would lose customers and go bankrupt giving such service. But not an advisory service. Their investment and overhead is so light compared to other businesses. Advertising is probably their main expense. There are so many people in need of advice in the market, that consistent advertising baits new batches of clients. As proven by this example, some advice is worth less than the paper it is printed on.

This company by their indiscriminate use of stop-loss orders could use this as a motto: "Our constant aim is to keep the losses of our subscribers down to a minimum."

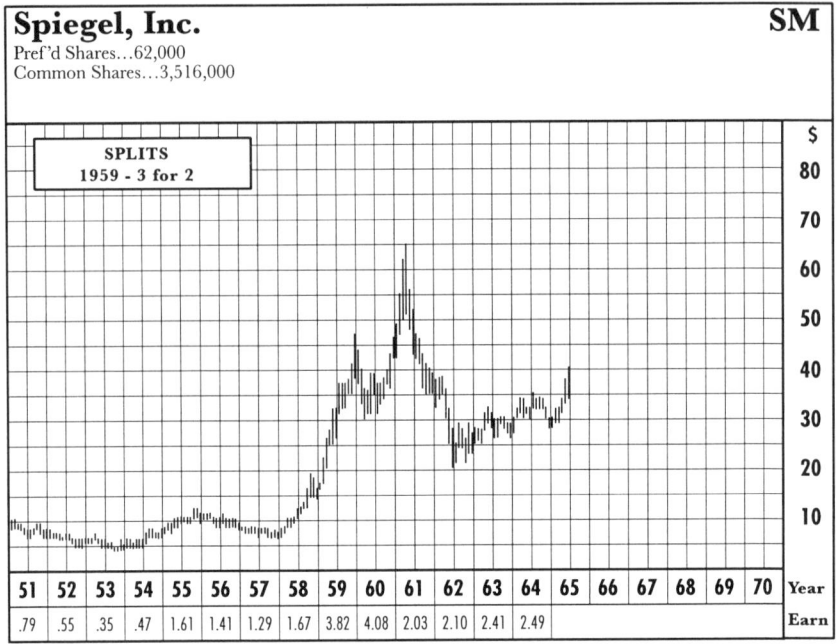

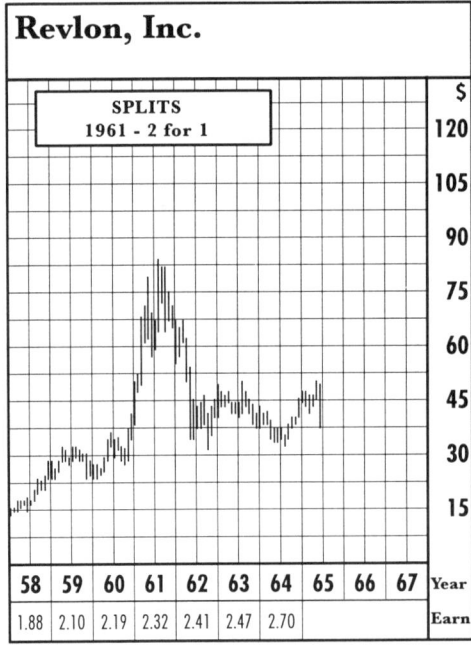

The majority of advisors, because they cater to traders, maintain that losses must be taken. If a client was to be left holding a stock sometimes for years waiting to recover a loss, he would have no need for advice, except to remain patient. The advisor must keep the client stimulated and active. They normally try to keep the losses small in order to keep the account alive. The client is apt to add more cash from time to time, but in case of a large loss he may close his account.

This excerpt from a typical advisory service explains their position more thoroughly: "In such cases, the quicker you get out of a bad

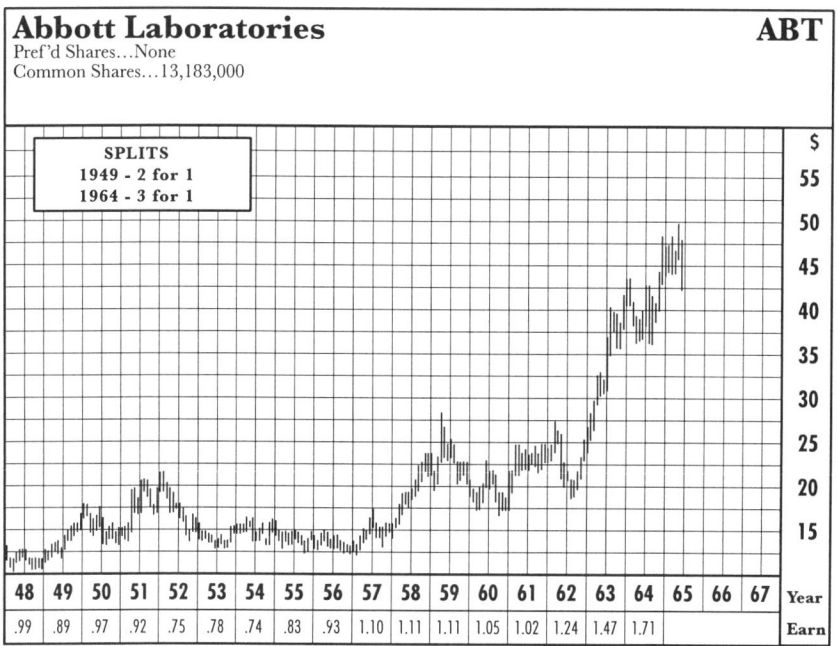

situation the better off you will be. Don't put off taking a loss just because the stock *might* go higher. Every stock will go higher eventually. But a TRADER can't wait indefinitely for a stock to make good. If he does, he will lose all his ready cash. More important, he will cease to be a TRADER."

Yes, that would be important. If a client should be advised to get out of a situation quickly, why was he led into it in the first place? Also, the fact is that many times the bad situation only appeared bad just before a substantial rise.

Your secret to success lies in picking stocks with a sound foundation and cashing in for the long term capital gain. Striving for quick, short term capital gains may only give you an unwelcome tax break. You can deduct up to $1000 in losses against your regular income. But who wants to?

Two Big Advisory Services:
My Predictions and Theirs

I received advertising literature from Standard & Poor's Investment Service, on the front page of which "sell" was displayed in two inch high letters, three times in three combinations of red and white. These headlines would certainly frighten the reader, as if someone had yelled "fire!"

I was not wanting any of their advice, far from it. Here was an opportunity I had been hoping for. An opportunity to match my opinion against that of a stock market advisory service. The list of sixty-three stocks that they recommended selling, and eighty-two that they advised buying, gave me something I could set my teeth into.

When I read this inside the folder, "we believe some stocks have reached the point where they should be sold," I visualized myself being very much in agreement with them, selling stock in a high range. But it would seem that I misinterpreted the word "point" as implying a "high point." It would seem that their idea of reaching a selling point is often far below the previous high and many times, as I interpreted the price actions, in a bargain range.

Here are some excerpts which give an insight in to their way of thinking: "Don't cling to disappointing stocks. Wouldn't you be wiser to weed out your poor performers and reinvest in stocks with better prospects; sell your losers and get into lively situations?"

TWO BIG ADVISORY SERVICES: MY PREDICTIONS AND THEIRS

I can't think of a more positive method of guaranteeing losses. How long would it be before your "lively situation" became a "disappointing stock," and reached a "weak or weakening situation" as mentioned in the following excerpt? "Switching from weak or weakening situations into what you consider strong ones is part and parcel of buying securities to sell later. It is one of the keys to a practical program. It is a reasonable plan. It is a hard-headed plan. The list of sixty-three stocks that should be switched is part of it." Note that there is not even an implication that "sell later" might be at a profit. They made no promise of profits.

This pamphlet was almost totally lacking in promises. The following excerpt is more of a guarantee than a promise: "Selling such stocks now, can give you a free tax ride in the market." You should be interested in paying MORE income taxes, not less. Besides, a free tax ride is NOT free. Most of the sixty-three stocks that they suggest selling would represent a loss to most shareholders, and very often a huge one. Losses are too difficult to regain by purchasing high priced issues AFTER they have recently had some very extended rises as most of the eighty-two issues that they advocate buying have had. Don't buy because a stock has shown a very large advance. It may very easily go higher, but the timing is wrong. As an investolator, learn to buy *before* a stock has its rise, which will almost guarantee not getting a free tax ride.

Immediately on receiving these lists on May 13, 1965 from Standard & Poor's, based on about April 9th prices, for switching purposes, I began checking these stocks with their actual charts and listing them in groups as to what my opinion on them was. Normally when I am looking for bargains I choose only those on which I can form a positive opinion. To the majority of charts I seldom give a second glance. I am looking for those with actions that I can interpret. That should be your primary purpose. DO NOT choose a stock and then attempt to interpret its chart action. This is wishful thinking at its worst. Let the chart action attract your attention to the stock.

The following stocks are of those recommended for sale. I sealed these lists with my opinions, and mailed them to myself so as to prove the date of my own recommendations.

Twelve of the sixty-three were not charted, so I was unable to form an opinion on them.

I was unable to form an opinion on another thirteen. Time will tell whether these twenty-five should have been sold here or held for the long pull.

My opinion on the following group of twenty was, "near term uncertain, long term much higher, three to six years from now."

Recommended Selling By Standard & Poor's

Stock	Price
Colorado Fuel & Iron	13
Continental Copper & Steel	10
Crown Central Petroleum	15
Cudahy Packing	8
Endicott Johnson Corp.	31
Fänsteel Metallurgical	13
Gar Wood Industries	5
General Baking	9
General Contract Finance	6
[1] Gorham Corp.	27
[2] Hall (CM) Lamp Co.	3
Jaeger Machine Co.	12
Penn Fruit Co.	9
[1] Reading Co.	21
Republic Aviation	17
Tractor Supply	12
[3] Transue & Williams Steel	24
[1] Vanadium Corp.	23
Ward Foods	9
Wheeling Steel	26

[1] A sale on these would have resulted in a fair profit for those who had bought in a low range.
[2] The recommended sale price of $3 was one-quarter above the low for the year and one-half above the low for many years. Four months later it sold as high as 7.
[3] Standard & Poor's sights were set a little high on this one, 50 cents above the high at this writing, which would have resulted in a profit for nearly 100% of all shareholders. Can someone explain why so many of the sixty-three stocks were recommended for sale in their extremely low price range, as you will see if you check their charts, whereas for the only sale they recommended that would have resulted in a handsome profit for many, the price was set too high?

TWO BIG ADVISORY SERVICES: MY PREDICTIONS AND THEIRS

How many man hours were required by their analysts (described as "trained field staff") to decide that the following sixteen stocks should be sold at their stated prices? My own opinion on these sixteen stocks was formed in an average of less than sixty seconds, based on the use of long range charts. My opinion is that they are in an accumulation range and are bargains at the price that Standard & Poor's recommend selling them. It is my belief they are forming a base; how much longer it will take can only be a guess. It can very easily take at least a year before they will show an uptrend or a breakaway on the upside. These should give you an opportunity for a large capital gain in three to six years; some may take longer.

Stock	Previous High	Sell Price
American Photocopy	46	8
Anken Chemical & Film	87	11
Brunswick Corp.	74	10
Hydrometals Inc.	43	6
Laboratory for Electronics	70	7
Lamb Industries	9	2
Lionel Corp.	35	5
Marquart Corp.	45	10
National Bellas Hess	16	6
Seeman Bros.	46	4
Servel Inc.	20	5
Standard Thomson	10	4
Stepan Co.	25	7
Trans-Lux Corp.	25	11
United Whelan	23	5
Wyandotte Worsted	13	11

Wyandotte appears to be in a high level consolidation.

A little research on these disclosed that Lionel never sold as high as 5 until six months later and Seeman Bros., which dropped from a high of 46, never sold below 4-1/4 since this advice was given to sell at 4. In fact the low on Seeman during this sound appearing base was 4.

Many of these stocks are so low that if the shareholders sold at these prices, many would be taking losses of 50 to 90%. Seeman Bros.

spent the largest portion of its top action four years previously between 40 and 46. These high-level purchasers have since paid dearly for their emotional instability. This book should forewarn its readers against reaching for these sparkling gems. They can quickly lose their luster. Learn to buy them when they appear dull and are selling cheap. This will take courage. Any touting, then, will be touting in reverse.

Two months before I received this selling advice, I bought 1000 shares each of Laboratory for Electronics, Seeman Bros., and Servel Inc., just to prove that I was willing to back up my opinion with my money. The bases of these three are very similar. Receiving this selling advice only bolstered my opinion. If they were to make their upward move soon, a 100% rise could be expected, but I expect them to spend another year or more in this bottom range. Then a 200% or more rise can be expected. Watch for a possible consolidation period on the way up.

About a week after I had compared my opinions with Standard & Poor's I received a slight shock when I read that the officials of Yale Express had asked to go into receivership. I recalled that this was one that selling had been advised by Standard & Poor's. But I could not recall what my opinion on it had been. Was it one of those I had advised buying? I checked my copy and to my relief I found that I had said about it and Central Aguirre Sugar (CEG), "Still in downtrend, no sign of leveling out for a bottom, but should have been sold long ago." Standard & Poor's had advised selling Yale Express at 7. It was delisted from the exchange after having sold at 2. Then it sold as low as one at a later date.

The suggested selling price on CEG was 23. After having sold at 22 it rallied sharply. As may be seen numerous times, a stock may have a sharp rally during its downtrend. Beware of buying on these. Too often they are just that, only a rally. I could go on and say that often it would be advantageous to sell a stock on one of these rallies. But this is where I refuse to expose myself to errors. One of these rallies can very well extend itself into all-time new highs. It is the safety factor that I am concerned with when I say "do not buy when a stock is dropping." A novice could be lucky and buy during a change to an uptrend, when I would not dare to recommend it. This is too risky. Try to pick the proper time for safety and assurance.

Time proved Standard & Poor's wrong in recommending selling CEG. As I write this paragraph on May 29, 1966, having checked on its weekly price range I found it had closed at 28-3/4 with sales of only 400 shares. This extremely light volume indicates that it has not yet topped out.

Group No. 1 was Standard & Poor's master list of recommended issues for safety and income.

Group 1

Stock	Price	Yield
Amer. Tel. & Tel.	68	2.9
Borden Co.	87	2.4
Boston Edison	47	3.4
Campbell Soup	37	2.4
Chase Manhattan Bank	68	2.9
Chemical Bank N.Y. Tr.	60	3.5
Cleveland Electric Illum.	42	2.9
Corn Products	54	2.8
1st Nat'l. City Bank	58	2.8
Idaho Power	42	2.9
Manf. Hanover	50	4.0
Morgan Guar. Tr.	108	3.7
National Biscuit	63	2.9
National Dairy Prod.	91	2.9
Pacific Lighting	31	4.2
Philadelphia Electric	39	3.8
Quaker Oats	75	2.9
Standard Brands	80	3.0

I consider these far too high to buy at this time, even for an investor. Why buy stocks for an income of 2.4 to 4.2% when you can get almost 5% in a savings and loan company without paying a commission on a purchase? These blue chips are subject to severe reactions. Quaker Oats, for only a short period, had been able to recover 60% of its 41 point setback from its 1961 top in four years. Many years of dividends and then some, would have gone down the drain for a high-level investor if he had sold out during this period. There can be many unforeseen reasons for a sale by the average investor. These "safe" stocks are not immune to panic selling or a long bear market as we go into the next depression. Investors then may be forced to sell in order to eat. It has happened before. Learn to recognize violent tops and broken uptrend lines and avoid one of these forced sales at lower prices.

The following fifteen stocks are from Standard & Poor's buy recommendations in Group 2. I consider them too high to buy at this time; too much cream has been lost.

Stock	Price	Yield
Abbott Laboratory	45	2.0
American Cyanamid Co.	75	2.7
Cities Service Co.	75	3.7
Coca Cola	76	2.2
Columbus & So. Ohio Electric	48	2.7
Consolidated Edison	46	3.9
Consumers Power	57	3.0
General Motors	104	4.6
May Department Stores	59	2.0
Northern Natural Gas	61	3.3
Pepsi Cola	76	2.1
Sears Roebuck	64	1.7
Socony Mobil	83	3.4
Southwest Public Service	42	2.9
Union Oil of Calif.	37	2.7

Among the higher priced stocks, price adjustments will be made on those that will be split.

There were five stocks from Group 2 about which I was unable to form an opinion from their chart action.

This list of fifteen, also from Group 2, I could not recommend buying at this time. They may very well be a good purchase, but are subject to more of a setback or consolidation.

Stock	Price	Yield
Allied Chemical Corp.	56	3.4
American Can Co.	44	4.5

Dow Chemical Co.	77	2.3
Dupont (E. I.) Co.	237	2.1
General Electric	102	2.2
General Public Utilities	40	3.4
Gulf Oil Corp.	53	3.4
Illinois Power Co.	44	3.2
Montana Dakota Utilities	40	3.5
Niagara Mohawk Power	58	3.8
Public Service Electric & Gas	40	3.4
Standard Oil Calif.	69	3.2
Standard Oil Ind.	42	3.8
Standard Oil Ohio	51	3.5
Union Electric	29	3.9

I agree that this following list of six should be bought, but there are far better bargains elsewhere for percentage gain.

Stock	Price	Yield
Columbia Gas System	32	4.0
Eastman Kodak	151	2.1
Ford Motor Co.	56	3.6
Johns-Manville	61	3.3
Kroger Co.	41	2.9
Shell Oil	58	2.9

I can very well agree that this next group of four should be bought, but there may be a long wait for the big rise to begin.

Stock	Price	Yield
Continental Insurance	66	3.6
General American Transportation	78	3.5
Oklahoma Natural Gas	37	3.8
Union Carbide	127	3.1

This final list of six from Group 2 I highly recommend buying for the long pull and a very good rise.

Stock	Price	Yield
Borg-Warner	50	4.4
Lone Star Gas	27	2.1
National Fuel Gas	35	4.0
Otis Elevator Co.	52	3.7
Phillips Petroleum	54	3.7
Reliance Insurance	35	3.8

Note that this list yields a higher average return than the others. When these rise to a price where I may say they are too high to buy, naturally the yields will diminish considerably unless the dividends have been increased. They are, of course, always subject to a minor reaction.

Standard & Poor's had a separate group of fifteen listed as "low-priced stocks" and had this to say about them. "Low prices do not necessarily imply low quality. These are all well-situated companies with promising prospects; some are 'name' issues. Low-priced stocks are ideally suited for the small investor, enabling him to obtain a degree of diversification not possible in the higher price brackets."

I agree with this. Notice, though, that their idea of low-priced stocks are in the $11 to $25 bracket. In the past, and at present, there have been many bargains available under $11, but seldom will a broker, or an advisory service, suggest buying them.

Belding Hemingway at 19 is the only one of these fifteen that I can highly recommend buying at this time. It has an eighteen-year base and is in strong hands. It is always, of course, subject to another setback.

This list of six in my opinion have an incomplete base. A purchase here could be perfect in timing, but is more apt to be two years too soon.

Stock	Price	Yield
Allegheny Corp.	11	1.1
National Tea Co.	18	4.4
Potomac Electric	24	3.3
Tennessee Gas Transmission	24	4.2
United Gas Improvement	24	4.2
Wisconsin Public Service	21	3.8

On the remaining eight from this group I could only make a guess.

My opinions, derived by a simple and short study of long range charts, I have pitted against an organization that is staffed with trained analysts, that includes coast-to-coast investigations, gathering data "in arriving at sound investment judgments and timely decisions," and which has over 100 years of experience behind them.

Here is an opportunity for the reader to check the results and keep score over the next few years and see for himself whether in the future he wishes to subscribe to an advisory service, or make his own decisions by the use of long range charts.

Standard & Poor's chose these stocks, so actually I am submitting opinions on some that are not clear enough to justify an opinion that has a proper assurance of being correct. Among these, I expect a bigger margin of error, whereas among stocks that I would choose upon which to make a prediction, I would expect to be nearly 100% correct.

Dow Theory Forecasts Inc. On October 2, 1965, along with several pages of other literature, I received a list of 181 stocks that Dow Theory Forecasts recommended selling. I had no chart on thirty-five of these but closely checked the other one hundred forty-six.

Apparently they do not apply any system in making decisions as to when stocks should be sold. At least I could detect none. These selling suggestions came in a range from a high price level representing very large profits, to prices that were barely above the lows for many years standing, which would mean losses of far more than 50% for many shareholders. Laboratory for Electronics, Servel and Seeman Bros. which I had considered to be in an accumulation phase, or in other words, incomplete bases, were among those suggested to be sold. Standard & Poor's a few months earlier had also suggested selling these. No wonder these three stocks became depressed in price. These advisory services were advising thousands to sell. Why? Were they advising to sell these when they were 300 to 500% higher in recent years?

Conceding that they were also advising large profits to be taken in some stocks, by what method, formula or reasoning do they arrive at these decisions? Is it possible that they are using the hit or miss pin method? In my opinion they may as well be.

I also received some buy suggestions, one of which was American Photocopy Equipment (APY) at 10-1/8. At a glance there would seem to be much similarity between the chart of APY and that of Seeman

Bros. (SEE) during 1963-64. Both may be in the process of making a base, but I am not confident that APY is doing so. I like the 2-1/2-year, very discouraging action of SEE much better, especially the last six months when it sold as low as 4. Many large losses were taken by badly frightened shareholders below 10.

But Dow Theory Forecasts advised buying APY around 10. I have some doubt that 6-3/4 is the final low. There was a nearly two-year false bottom above 8, from which it had two fair-sized rallies. It then dropped to 6-3/4 from which it rallied to 12-3/8. Volume increased heavily on this rally which indicated the public had become excited. It is my opinion that the price should have soared on this heavy trading, but it didn't. Did the smart money sell heavily on this rally? Someone did. If so then we are likely to see a new low range where these buyers are taking their losses.

If APY does not drop below 6-3/4, I am wrong. Remember, this kind of error in judgment does not create losses, but buying at 10 could mean a long holding period with a paper loss. At this time there were plenty of other stocks showing positive bases, both on a low-level and at high-level consolidations as recommended elsewhere in this book. Study them for a better understanding when similar actions are seen.

The following sixteen stocks were taken from the list of one hundred eighty-one that Dow Theory Forecasts recommended selling. The price quoted was the last price previous to receiving this list. These sales would represent huge losses to many people. My opinion on these is that they are in a bottom range that perhaps is incomplete. Some may yet make new lows.

A. J. Industries	2-5/8	Hardeman (Paul)	2-7/8
Aerojet-General	33-3/4	Hazeltine Corp.	8-1/4
Alpha Portland Cement	13-3/8	Kawecki Chemical	16-1/4
American Distilling	33	Laboratory for Electronics	12
Atlas Corp.	2	Seeman Bros.	7-1/4
Certain-teed Products	17-1/2	Servel, Inc.	4-3/8
Commercial Credit	35-1/4	Sheraton Corp.	8-5/8
General Development	5-1/8	Standard Packaging	10-5/8

The following sixteen stocks were also advised to be sold by Dow Theory Forecasts. These stocks topped out years ago and should have been sold long ago. I cannot detect action in these low ranges that I consider to be accumulation, although some may have begun to form a base, Studebaker for instance. However, even here I now look for weak appearing rallies in this new low range and generally discouraging action. This will influence many shareholders to abandon any hope of recovering their investment and they will sell with relief—and a loss.

American Motors	10	Helene Curtis	12
Chock Full O' Nuts	10-3/4	High Voltage Engineering	18-1/2
Duffy-Mott	25-3/4	Marquette Cement	23-1/2
Elgin Watch	9	Newberry (JJ)	18-3/4
Financial Federation	24-1/4	Seilon, Inc.	9-3/4
First Charter Financial	24-5/8	Studebaker	18-1/2
First Western Financial	6-5/8	Technical Material	11
Guston Beacon Manuf.	18	United Financial, Calif.	9-1/8

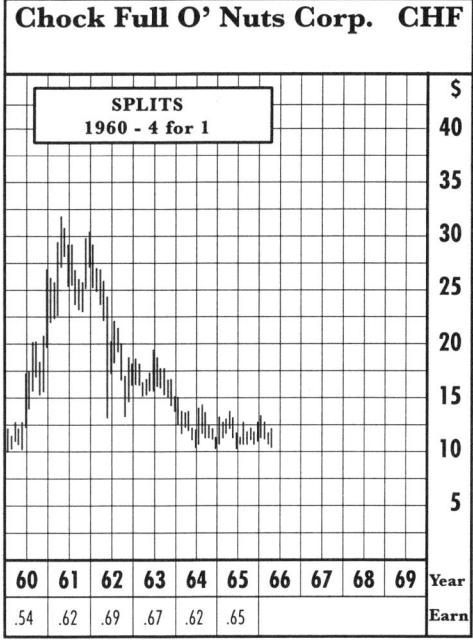

These items on Dow Theory were sealed and mailed to myself for the purpose of accurate dating.

In May, 1966, Chock Full O' Nuts broke a false bottom at 10-1/2. Whether this will be a mild shakeout, or will develop a base in a new low range can only be a guess at this time, but should prove itself within a year. Compare this false bottom with that of Marquette Cement and with that of Vanadium Corp. and you will recognize what I mean.

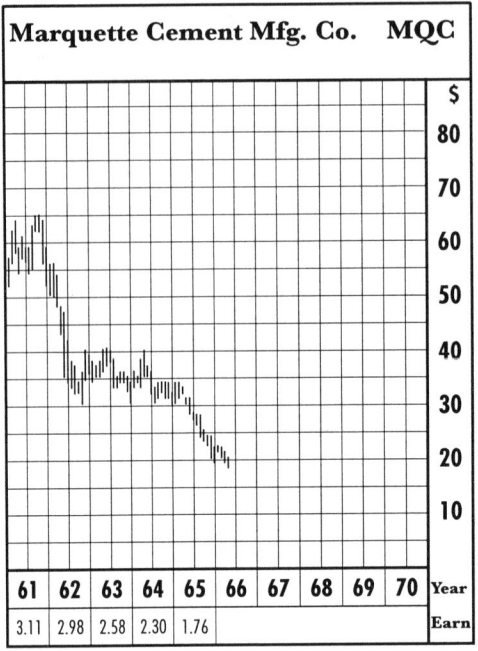

Watch closely in the near future for sound bases in the above four "Financial" stocks listed above. The Installment Financing group will be developing some real bargains.

The Pro's and "Con's" of Investment Courses

The reader may examine the financial pages of any metropolitan newspaper and find advertisements by large brokerage firms giving dates and places for free investment lecture courses. I recently examined an ad that listed thirteen locations in the Los Angeles area where they would be given. To me these ads are appropriate. The public should know more about the market. There are many people who should be investors but have a long-standing fear of the market. The "crashes" of the past give them the impression that the odds are too much against them. Many of these timid souls do not worry about crashes when taking to the streets and highways in spite of the heavy toll in deaths and injuries. And even though some of these are the very ones who cause many of the casualties by their lackadaisical driving, they wouldn't risk a dime in the market. The chance of total loss of an investment is slight if a person buys only on an open market. A market crash need not be serious—only frightening. If you bought a stock outright, you did not have to take a loss. Most stocks, if you did buy in a top range, usually will come back and go higher given time. And you would be getting dividends in most cases.

These free lessons by brokers are not motivated by altruism but by a desire to build up their own business, through commissions, a normal enough motive in our capitalistic system. After all, the profit motive is the incentive that indirectly creates our high standard of living. However, it is most unfortunate that a large majority of these people get the idea they know all about the market after taking these lessons. They have only scratched the surface of learning what makes the market tick. The new student thinks he is now at about the same stage as the medical doctor when he has passed his course as an intern. But the market student on a comparable basis is about where the doctor-to-be is when he takes the admissions exam to medical school. In the stock market you get the TEST first, and the LESSON afterward. And should a market student pick a winner the first time, he really thinks that he is a master of the markets. This is the beginning of his downfall.

It is noticeable that these free lecture ads seem to bloom best after the market has had a big rise, when obviously they bring a better response. Were there many of them during the summer of 1962 after the bad market scare? That is when the free lectures should have been given. Most of our corporations were on the bargain counter. There are still plenty of bargains at the time of the writing of this manuscript, but how many of these bargains will be recognized and bought by those attending these classes? Very few, I can assure you. They will be attracted by those which have already moved up by at least a fair amount. The lecturer will almost certainly be the last to recommend a stock when it is on the bottom. He is not a successful trader; he is usually an account executive for a brokerage firm.

Another brokerage firm on this date advertised lessons in COMMODITY TRADING. It said: "Trading in Commodity Markets offers the potential of high profits with a minimum of capital. The risks are great, but many traders who can afford to carry high commitments are switching to commodities. Learn what sophisticated investors need to know about commodities at our COMMODITY SEMINAR."

There is no law against an ad like this. But in my opinion it is misleading. The ad was honest enough to admit the "risks are great," but not honest enough to say how great to the uninformed. And this is the first time I have ever heard of a trader in a futures market being called an investor, sophisticated or otherwise. I am sure that they cannot teach the novice futures trader how to beat the market—for they do not know the method themselves. But, of course, the ad did not say that.

It said "you would learn—*what you need to know about commodities."* Could they mean that they would teach you the difference between a kernel of oats and a coffee bean? This firm was so greedy for commissions that they were quite willing to lead the gullible into taking heavy losses. Not that they want it that way. Far from it. They would like to have the traders make good profits. That would result in more commissions. But, would an audit of the broker's books over the past twenty years show over 3% of their futures traders closing their account with a profit? I certainly doubt it.

We have many laws intended to protect the public from dishonest schemes, but there are none that I know of that would protect them from being led into something like this. Nevertheless, it is ethically dishonest even though they are not taking any money away from the trader except legitimate commissions. It is not their fault that the trader is not sufficiently sophisticated to keep from taking losses.

It is my suggestion that any course given on stocks should include one evening on the subject of how swindlers and gypo artists operate. Perhaps, though, this would have little lasting value. Each person thinks that being gypped is something that only happens to the other fellow. A thorough coverage of this subject would require many evenings.

In April, 1962, I gave a stock market lecture at the Los Angeles Adventurers Club of which I am a member. I made some very positive statements as to the future trends of several stocks and the DJ averages. Unknown to me, one of the members tape recorded this program, including the questions and answers.

At our next week's meeting, a member who has been a stock broker for thirty-five years told me in an apologetic manner that "no one could be positive as to what a stock would do." I believe that he was afraid that I would be forced to eat crow. I explained to him that these positive statements as to the future would prove to be correct and that I would continue to make more in the future.

It is only in the timing of a move about which I cannot be positive. My "guesstimating" then can easily be from six months too late to three years too soon.

Why You Can Distrust Trust Funds

High-pressure salesmen have induced the public to put their trust in Mutual Trust Funds by the billions of dollars. An attractive appeal to many, no doubt, is that the responsibility of making decisions is shifted to others who supposedly are experts in this field that so few understand. The salesmen are trained to gain the confidence of the timid souls, people who, when they think of the stock market, shudder in memory of crashes. They are putting blind faith in strangers who are in the business for the sole purpose of feathering their own nests. Beginning with the usual 8% or more commission, they have a well laid out plan to do just that.

The "financial experts" who head these funds seldom make buy and sell decisions in their stock market trades. This would limit them to a mere salary, and if their salary is over $60,000 a year, the SEC may want to discuss this with them.

The usual deal is to set up their own advisory company. Up to 60% of the funds' directors are allowed to have connections with the advisory company according to SEC regulations. In all probability, buying and selling decisions are actually made by the funds' executives in the first place, but the "dummy" advisory company is paid one-half percent a year which can amount to many millions charged to the investors. It is difficult to imagine a business such as these "dummies" having such a large income with so small an overhead. Only a small office force and floor space are required, no transportation, inventory or packaging problems, no products to lose favor with the public and no striving to invent new ones, no unions, no competition, and no advertising.

The mutual funds of today are considered to be far more sound than the investment trusts of the 1920's. In theory these trusts were good and still are, but they were soon subjected to abuses. Many of the managements of these trusts became speculative pool managers. It would seem that every device and scheme available was used to fleece the public during the bull market era of the '20's and the bear market of the early '30's. Trust funds were among these.

As long as we are in a rising economy and the management of trust funds is average, they can hardly help but give fair returns to their investors. One wonders are these managements merely optimists who have the rising economy and subsequent rise in common stocks going in their favor? Or have they been able to determine that there has not been any serious threat to our continuing prosperity? It is very doubtful to me that they will recognize the final top of our stock market when they see it. Perhaps they will get "carried away" by the overwhelming wave of optimism that will sweep the country when this top comes. That was the lame excuse for much of the mismanagement that took place in 1929. Won't some of the present trust funds be tempted to use this excuse also when the crisis has passed? It is my opinion that the public have been so imbued with false confidence in these trust funds that few would consider cashing in their holdings at a critical time. If they were holding the shares of individual corporations they might be tempted to take huge profits when available. Even if they sold too soon, they would be lucky, or they could be among those that frightened quickly when the break began. I am going on my prediction that our economy will wind up with a boom and bust which may come before 1970. I wonder how many investors are under the illusion that we will not have another depression.

Many believe that we cannot have another depression for the simple reason that our government will not allow it. These people have false faith in the ability of government, ours or anyone else's. When a depression begins, it is like an avalanche; no government can stop it, except perhaps by starting a war, which would only postpone the inevitable depression.

Now let us theorize on what would happen in the event that all mutual funds and investment companies were to see the handwriting on the wall before a predepression stock market boom ended, and then decided to sell all their holdings. The news would soon leak out and a large percentage of the public would be influenced into selling their holdings of individual stocks also. This could develop into a premature break. The manipulators could lose control of the stock market and they would find themselves holding a lot of unsold securities. It would be an impossible situation with the holding companies, the insiders and the majority of the public all trying to sell at the same time. In comparison, the 1929 crash would be a Sunday school picnic.

That, I can assure you, will not happen. It is my belief that the trust funds will be holding a tremendous amount of public money, which in turn will be invested heavily in stocks that should have been sold, and the public as usual will be holding the bag. The managements would not be guilty of anything worse than poor judgment. But with human nature being what it is, I will be surprised if there aren't some red hot scandals that will come out of this after our boom has turned into a depression.

Statistics show that the gain in mutual funds in 1965 was about 19%. This was better than 5% over the gain in the DJIA. 1965 was one of the better years for the mutuals. I averaged the gain of several stocks picked at random and found that the average stock gained over 25% in 1965. There were many losers among these.

In twenty years beginning January 1, 1946, the DJIA has averaged a 24% gain per year or a total of 480%. Would the average mutual fund have gained as much?

As an investolator, using this book strictly as your guide, you should have done far better than this. You should have been able to cash in on a large move at least three times during the twenty years.

Theoretically, if you could have bought $1000 worth of the DJIA average at 200 in January, 1946, you could have sold with a 480% profit in January, 1966, or $4800 before taxes. If you had picked a bargain about that time with $1000 as an investolator, and sold at a 200% gain, you would have cleared $1500 after the long term capital gain taxes were paid. With the $1000 principal you now invest $2500 again in the bargain basement, for another profit of 200% or $5000, minus a tax of $1250. With this $3750 and your $2500 principal, you now have

$6250 for reinvestment. Another 200% profit would amount to $12,500 for a total of $18,750 before taxes compared to $4800 with a possible purchase of the DJIA. There also would have been a larger total of dividends. Your profit may very well have been higher. This example is figured on a minimum of 200% profit on each commitment which is the minimum percentage that should be taken on any purchase made by an investolator from a well established base. A profit of 200% over an average of over six and one-half years should be within reason.

When buying a mutual fund you still must make a choice, requiring a great deal of "skill and research." Do you believe that you have this skill? If you don't, there is an easy way out of this dilemma; just let your salesman tell you which one is "best for you." He will glibly explain to you which one will "fit your need." I dare say that for his share of the usual 8-1/2% chunk taken from your principal, he will gladly tell you anything, except that rarely will these mutuals pay off what are claimed for them.

If you really believe that mutual funds are what you want, why not buy the "no-load" funds that have no sales charge. There are nearly 40 of them. Ask your broker about these.

For diversification of stocks, which is a sound claim of the mutuals, it is better to buy a closed-end investment company on the open market as you would any other stock. You can never expect the wide swings though as in other stocks, because their value can be gauged more or less by the value of the stocks they hold. It is more like buying an "average." By the use of charts on these you will have a better chance to avoid being a high-level investor. More satisfactory than the mutuals.

Don't ever sign a contract to invest so much a month for a ten-year period. The fund is allowed to charge 50% of your first year's payment as a sales charge. If you were to quit at the end of the first year you automatically lose 50%, moreover, the price of the fund may be lower when you sell.

Why do people buy insurance funds which they are compelled to sell at the end of ten years? If you wish to continue your investment, you will have to repurchase them with the usual 8-1/2% sales charge. No discount is offered for being a ten-year customer. These funds are so rigged that you feel that you cannot afford them during the first few years.

I baited a mutual fund salesman into paying me an evening's visit in order to get more information for this section. Posing as a neophyte investor, while writing a book on how to invest put me in a very hypocritical position. It was not an enjoyable acting experience.

I can now readily understand why so many people have been high-pressured into buying mutual funds. It would take rugged sales resistance to ward off the glowing word-picture that was presented to me. He would have had the average person feeling sorry for himself for not having gotten onto this gravy train years ago.

The SEC, no doubt, would be interested if I had a tape recording of not only what he implied, but in statements and warnings that he omitted. Those who sell investment company shares are warned not to "represent or imply" that an investor will receive any definite percentage of return, or any regular, continuous return, or indeed any particular rate of return, or, that shares can be redeemed at a profit, without adding that they can also be redeemed at a loss, or that SEC registration and regulations are not to be referred to without pointing out that management is not supervised by the SEC. Numerous other omissions are to be avoided. In my opinion these rules are a futile attempt at forcing honesty in salesmanship.

I have only scratched the surface in covering what needs to be said about mutual funds. My attitude toward mutual funds is very well expressed by the names of two books: *"Mutual Funds: Legal Pickpockets?"* by Dean Palance and *"The Grim Truth About Mutual Funds,"* by Ralph L. Smith.

Advice from Books?

Through curiosity and with the thought that I would learn more about what motivates the moves in the stock market, I spent some time in libraries during forced periods of idleness such as while waiting to sell our seaplane at Anchorage, Alaska in 1964, or when I was an outpatient at the Mayo Clinic in 1965. I read little that was satisfactory to my way of thinking. There was never any hint of any probability of manipulation today. Nearly all authors were fundamentalists and none that I read made any claims to having made their stake, if any, by trading in stocks, except Nicolas Darvas who claimed to have made $2,000,000 in the stock market. Apparently the Securities and Exchange Commission did not consider his writing as being instructive because they did not require him to be registered as a market advisor.

These volumes impress me about as much as would a book entitled "How To Raise Children" if written by a lifetime bachelor.

If a novice were to read several books on "how you should do it in the stock market," he could believe that he would be well qualified to pick a winner or he would be thoroughly confused by: – book value, – par value, – intrinsic value, – value analysis, – value line, – profit line, – advance-decline line, – equity, – normal prices, – actual prices, – wholesale prices, – balance sheet, – earnings ratio, – liquidity, – profit margin,

– marginal companies, – credit, – funded debt, – private debt, – bank debits, – gold supply, – money supply, – floating supply, – demand and supply, – how to sell short, – puts and calls, – trailing stop-loss orders, – techniques of buying and selling, – market measurements, – panic levels, – moving averages, – key stocks, – principal stocks, – general qualifications, – magnitudes, – safety, – judgment, – timing, – business cycles, – market cycles, – cyclical swings, – cyclical clues, – cyclical stocks, – business activities, – business indicators, – competition, – carloadings, – commodity price influence, – related industries, – assets, – liabilities, – capitalization, – amortization,   projected working capital, – management inventory, – retail sales, – mode of distribution, – appreciation potential, – growth and stability indices, – odd lot index, – index of prosperity, – checking hypothesis, – hypothesizing an economic environment, – autonomous action, – trends, – trend characteristics, – clusters of symptoms, – correlation, – external correlation, – dependent variable sensitivity to volume, – test for group conformation, – dollar inventory amounts, – average monthly liability per business failure, – monthly construction awards, – cumulative data, – internal data, – current data, – short cut in computation, – frequency of probability, – theory of probability, – divergencies, – special situations, – discountable news, – meaningful concept, – corroborative evidence, – permanent components, – genesis of the climax, – technical systems, – internal behavior against external developments, – internal stock market phenomena, – internal evidence approach, – difficulties in value concept, – methodological difficulties and emotional difficulties.

When you have gone through that and more, you are liable to be afflicted with some of the latter. I was dumbfounded when I made up this list gleaned from various books on how to make money in the stock market. The "internal evidence approach" applies to the study of chart reading. Those who did comment on the use of charts, implied that there was little if any value in their use. Their ignorance of chart reading and their prejudice was showing.

If a Philadelphia lawyer was to study all of these above subjects advising how to buy and sell stocks, he still would be in the dark as to whether the market was going up or down. The speculator can beat his brains out hashing over all this information and can come up with some positive decisions, but if he makes a good one he is just plain lucky (although he would disagree with you if you told him this). But the fact is that those who are so often wrong were just as positive when they made their decisions.

Advice by one author is to the effect that the reader should go into every possible source for information. I can't see where the average person could possibly digest anything to his benefit from the many of these that were suggested: Federal Reserve Board Bulletin, The Survey of Current Business, The Bureau of Labor Statistics Monthly, The Economic Year, Congressional Inquiries, National Bureau of Economic Research and many, many more. Then came newsletters, bank letters and bank figures. It went on and on. I wouldn't be able to understand most of them, let alone get any idea from them as to which way the price of a stock would move. It would be too much of an intellectual wrestling match for me. I wonder if anyone really took this advice seriously and tried to read up on all of it.

I found myself in disagreement so much with these authors, that I feel compelled to mention some of the highlights of their secondhand advice. Most of them give much credit to brokers and others for their advice in compiling these instructions on how to trade in the stock market.

The author of one book confesses that he received most of his knowledge from such sources as Alan C. Poole of N.Y. Securities Co., Edmond and Anthony Tabell of Walston & Co., Morris Goldstein of F.I. duPont & Co. and others.

This book was revised by the author's daughter, and she admits doing much research and was also given much aid. She comments she had dipped her nose into more than one hundred books and would hesitate to recommend more than five.

This book makes the dangerous recommendation that you should buy on the rumor and sell on the confirmation—but make sure you're not the only one buying. This means that if the mob is buying, join them. Even the author admits that you take some risk when you're doing this.

This volume of "advice" also tells you to buy stocks when they are making new highs, not when they are down at the bottom where nobody loves them.

This is the very opposite to the advice I give. The risk is too great. There is one thing in its favor I will admit—it is safer than Russian Roulette.

I have yet to read an author who does not advocate taking losses. This kind of advice is common: "Never hold onto a loser. Sell it." How far must a stock drop before it proves itself to be a loser? That apparently is your problem.

You are also advised by many authors to get out of the market if you feel frightened and make your profits at a later date when you are, for some reason, more confident. That is what the speculator is always hoping to do, but seldom does—make it back on the next trade. To me this means that one should buy dangerously and sell when scared. I might add, speculators scare easily.

One author does favor the use of charts as an aid. But his teaching of chart reading was confined to short term, speculative trading. He acknowledged receiving aid from several people. He could only promise that the chartist would be right more often than wrong. He explains all about boxes, flags, pennants, wedges, diamonds, islands, reversal days, breakaway gap, common gap, measuring gap and top reversal gaps.

If a person insists on speculating, I am very much in favor of him using charts. But it is doubtful that he will understand them well enough to benefit from them. This is when he is faced with the real trickiness of manipulation. The short range moves are loaded with false moves that deprive you of profits.

This author asks you how much you are prepared to lose. You can't say he didn't warn you.

In yet another volume a professor of economics who is credited with having written eighty articles and books on economics and finance suggests that a study of steel output, automobile production and the construction industry will enable you to make statements about general employment, national income, gross national product and general economic conditions—if you also study the Federal Reserve Index on Industrial Production.

I ask you, whether you are a novice, or one who has studied fundamentals for years, do you think that after following this advice that you can come up with a decision in which you can have full confidence? While you could be right, the manipulators of the stock you bought or sold, could very well have their own idea as to how they are going to move their stock. You must assume they are going to do it their way. Why not learn to go along with them? I did.

If you had followed the advice of this professor, you would have assumed that the Federal Reserve Index of Industrial Production has reached a peak at 138 in March, 1953. He reasons that when most of the total labor force is employed, as he claimed it was at that time, there is not likely to be expansion since further expansion depends upon more workers. If you had also come to this conclusion in March, 1953 you would very likely have sold your stocks and lost your position in a generally rising market during the following years. The fact is that at this writing, production has been increasing almost steadily, and the DJI has risen (not so steadily) over 250%.

Probably the most astonishing recommendation published in a book is the following: "If you bought it at 40 and it goes to 39, a good smart trade would be to sell at 39. The first loss is often the best loss."

If you thumb through a chart book and check the charts of stocks that you may have bought at 40, whether rising or falling, you will see how seldom you could have come out ahead if you sold at 39. And those times when you were stopped out at 39, would there be a guarantee that you would have taken the profit when available? It is very easy to carry a stock over a 5 to 40 point rise and still sell out at 39.

Now, if you were to apply this rule of selling 2-1/2% below any purchase price, you would sell a stock at 19-1/2 if you bought it at 20. One bought at 10 would be sold at 9-3/4 and one bought at 5 you would sell at 4-7/8. Don't you agree that this idea of protecting yourself against carrying a stock below the purchase price would be ridiculous? Too much safety applied by this method would result in few profits, but the attrition would be positive and persistent. Using this selling formula, you would seldom have the opportunity of holding your stock long enough to carry it out of its bargain range.

Another writer who has been a broker for forty years and has built up for himself quite an enviable reputation claims that making money in the market demands a lot of 'genius' or 'flair.' He says that no amount of study or practice can make you successful if you really are not cut out for it. Yet an important theme of his writing is the more you trade, the quicker you learn to be successful. He says that mastery of short term investing has very much more the elements of dependable business than the windfalls or calamities of the long pull.

Amazingly he finds that there is much more peace of mind in frequent turns where you take a fresh view often. The truth is that "frequent turns" will keep you in constant turmoil.

Moreover, he advises that cutting losses is the one and only rule that is always correct in the stock market. This advice helps create brokers' commissions.

Does he really mean that taking a loss is the most positive advice he can give? If he is teaching cutting losses short, it must be that his students and clients are doing some high-level investing. Ask any speculator how many losses he has taken which later proved the wrong thing to do. He recommends that if your investment shrinks by 10% you should sell out and try again. These 10% losses, plus commissions too often will overwhelm your profits.

Taking losses quickly will invariably prevent you from taking large profits, and shows a lack of confidence in your commitment. If you are a high-level investor, then I also recommend cutting your losses quickly. But you should never buy a stock without full confidence that a large portion of it is held by strong interests. At times this can be seen clearly in charts. Any other reason is only guesswork. No major rise can be generated unless or until powerful interests are ready to move it.

He does add this, with which I am in agreement wholeheartedly: "One should bend every effort to determine what the tendencies of the public are, right or wrong, and profit from them." But he gives little information on how to detect the public's tendencies, other than watching the tape, which he recommends highly. He follows with a criticism of charts that is mild compared to the opinions of most authors. Why doesn't he tell you that most tape-watchers go broke, or give up before they completely understand it? Tape reading is really similar to chart reading, but on an hourly basis. Chartists who operate on a daily basis cannot see the forest for the trees. Tape readers cannot see the trees for the brush. They are often whipsawed, paying a commission each time to "you know who."

In addition, this broker tells you to buy a stock as it starts to get dearer. But I could not locate a part of the text where he explains how you are to decide this. Furthermore, he admits that in all his years of giving investment advice he has not found the real key to success and does not expect to.

The theme of my book is to show you how to make money in the market, and how to prevent you from losing it. These authors have the right to their opinions, and to write what they wish; so I think I have the right to criticize their opinions. The best way I can do this is to counteract the attempts they make in encouraging you to speculate.

ADVICE FROM BOOKS?

I heard a nation-wide brokerage firm broadcast on the radio: "If your stock drops 10% below your purchase price, you should sell." They must have been hungry for commissions to make a statement like that. Most of the profits, large or small, that I have made could seldom have been possible following that kind of advice. Check the charts. You will see how often you would have sold out unless you bought just right on a rising market. Of course if you bought in the top range or on a falling market, that would be good advice.

Let's take Dr. Pepper as an example. In 1946 it sold as high as 48 and in 1957 it sold as low as 8 after spending nine years in its twelve-year bottom range. Following this formula, every Tom, Dick and Mary holding DOC at this time would have sold out, except those who bought below 8-7/8. What a ridiculous situation if this rule had been followed to the letter. And what a deluge of selling this would create. The 1929 break would appear to be a Sunday school picnic in comparison.

I was holding DOC when it sold at its low of 8 (pre-split price). Since then I have profited from it by over $200,000. I assure you, I could not have done that if I had followed this broker's advice.

In one book, Bernard Baruch's statistician was quoted as having said, "If you are ready and able to give up everything else — to study the whole history and background of the market and all the principal companies whose stocks are on the board as carefully as a medical student studies anatomy — to glue your nose to the tape at the opening of every day of the year and never take it off until night — if you can do that, and in addition, you have the cool nerves of a gambler, the sixth sense of a clairvoyant, and the courage of a lion, you have a China-man's chance."[1]

If the reader accepted this statement at its face value and swore off speculating, he should consider the cost of the book as being money well spent.

---

[1] *The Stock Market,* Joseph Mindell, American Book-Stratford Press Inc., New York.

The Abuses of Floor Trading

I quote an author who writes, "Brokerage commissions are the primary reasons for the existence of the organized stock exchanges; without brokerage commissions, there would be no Wall Street Casino."

This could imply an evil motive. If this statement applied correctly to the stock exchanges, then it can be said that there would be no butcher shops without a profit motive, or a barber shop without fees for a haircut, or theaters without a charge for tickets. A stock exchange exists because there is a demand for it. One can only guess how many times, when our capitalistic system was in its early development, shares were sold to friends or anyone who had faith in the person who needed venture capital. Then came a time when some of the owners of these shares wished to resell. (No doubt many wished they had never bought them.) Eventually someone recognized the need of a market in stocks and became a dealer on a commission basis. I dare say there were many small dealers of this type before our stock exchanges came into existence.

Of course, we know our exchanges have developed into something far beyond the need of investors, namely, the largest gambling game ever devised. If the game was a mere contest among people as are most games, this gambling would not be so serious, but the rank abuses in the past by those in control of our markets have fleeced the public of billions of dollars. Years ago, those in control learned that the public thinking could be guided by manipulations of stock prices or by financial reports, either true or false.

To curtail some of these abuses the Securities and Exchange Commission was formed. There were many rules put in force, but in my opinion they do not have enough teeth in them. In spite of the SEC riding herd over our stock exchanges, we have had scandals only recently on the American Stock Exchange. Is anyone naive enough to believe that the guidance of prices can be prevented? There are times when it is obvious to an experienced market observer that prices are held down by someone other than the public when the tendency was for the price to rise. Many times the market is noticeably supported in a way that was meant for it to be noticed by the public. But neither the SEC nor anyone else can prove that this buying or selling was committed for any motive other than an honest opinion. As long as I can continue to make positive forecasts and be right most of the time I will continue to think in terms of how our markets are being guided. If my thinking is misguided, is there a better way of being right than by thinking wrong?

An old Wall Street adage that "the public is always wrong" will continue to be correct as long as there is a public. It is my opinion that the floor traders and specialists have a hand in making them wrong. When such a huge percentage of total daily trades are done on the exchange floor, free of commissions, what else can you expect? The specialists on the exchange floor are not only permitted to trade against the public, but are required to buy when the public is selling and to sell when the public is buying. By doing this they are supposed to keep the market acting in an orderly manner. Doesn't this provide them the power to control prices?

Let's do a little hypothesizing. If the sponsors of a stock wanted the price to rise and the natural demand was greater than the supply, there would be no need for helping it. But if there was a tendency for the price to sag because of a greater supply, mostly because there was a lack of buying incentive, the specialists could very well buy against public selling and to the tape watchers, this would be noticed as good support and would create a buying incentive. This increased demand would cause a price rise which would in turn encourage more buying by the public. The specialists then can take a profit on a rising market which is now strong enough to absorb it. The price, in fact, could have a firm close. Mission was accomplished at a profit and no illegal motive could be proven.

Now suppose a bullish overnight report caused a buying wave in a stock. The price could very easily open higher with a dollar gap, more if it would normally continue higher during the day and close on or near the high. Normally, more buying would appear next morning and higher prices would result. If perchance, this stock was in an accumulation phase and the sponsors were not ready for the price rise, a friendly group of floor traders and/or specialists could sell against the public demand either the first or second day, creating enough supply so as to stop the price rise. The tape watchers seeing that the rise was wavering in the face of bullish news can only take for granted that there is too much stock for sale and buying will then slow down. Disappointment will set in by the public and their selling will start a reaction and the stock will reenter the accumulation phase of selling by worried longs. Obviously, if their stock cannot go up, it must be going down. If the sponsors who had been buying over a period of many months or even years had openly sold temporarily in such a manner and later continued to buy, the SEC detecting this could conceivably accuse them of manipulation, but the odds are very slight that they would notice it. They could not trace the many incidents of market control, nor prove there was control if they did.

There is considerable effort from various sources trying to show a good image of the specialists on the exchange floor. Louis Engel in his book *How To Buy Stocks*, practically glorified them when he said, "The genuine service which the specialists render in maintaining a balance in the market and ironing out temporary disparities between supply and demand, at considerable risk to their own personal solvency, was perhaps never better demonstrated than on Monday, September 26, 1955. That was the day after Eisenhower's heart attack, the kind of unforeseen crisis on a national scale to which the stock market is always vulnerable. That Monday when the market opened, sell orders far outnumbered buy orders. It was virtually impossible to open trading in any stock. The sell orders would have depressed prices beyond all reasonable levels before buying sentiment could be generated. The specialists met the challenge. They bought steadily for their own accounts at prices only moderately below the levels that had prevailed at Friday's close. All told one quarter of the stock purchases that day were made by the specialists—1,759,360 shares with an estimated market value of $80,000,000. Eisenhower's recovery enabled the specialists as a group to work off the stock they bought without loss—indeed, with profit—but when they took the risk, they did not know but what they might be wiped out."

Who does Mr. Engel think he is kidding? The specialists would not risk a dime for the sake of the public. They are on the exchange floor for the simple purpose of making money for themselves which includes earning their salaries for performing their duties as specialists. Their risk is nil. At almost any given time when the market is dropping they have the power and know how to support it and to sell out on the following rally. They did this no less than seven times during the severe downtrend in 1957 and several times on the 1962 break, thereby keeping the public in for the final fleecing at the bottom. If they are the public's benefactors, why did they not support the market at the same level two weeks after Eisenhower's heart attack, instead of allowing it to drop another 15 points on the DJIA? They allowed it to drop further so that someone could pick up more bargains that were sold by the nervous public. It's that simple.

One of their obligations is to provide a fair and orderly market. Just what constitutes a fair and orderly market? Doesn't that imply control? In my opinion they are in control just as much as a good traffic policeman at an intersection.

It was known that there would be a deluge of selling on the news of Eisenhower's heart attack; sell orders were flooding the pits before the opening. The market should have been closed. In a few days the panic would have subsided. Even if Ike had died, a few words from Richard Nixon as the new president would have calmed the shareholders. There would have been no need for the specialists to support the market "at considerable risk to their own personal solvency."

Mr. Engel said they bought at levels only moderately below Friday's close. Many stocks sold down more than 10% that day, some opened down with a gap of 8%. Would you call this only a moderate drop in one day? If they did this for the benefit of the public, why didn't they support it at a higher level? Selling would have subsided sooner.

President Kennedy's assassination took place during market hours. The public panicked far worse than if he had died a natural death.

Perhaps some imagined a political upheaval far beyond a mere assassination. Imaginative rumors can spread far faster than facts.

This serious news hit the exchanges so suddenly that the specialists were caught far off guard and unorganized. The exchanges were closed with the DJIA down 21 points. Over the weekend the shareholders not only recovered from the shock, but reacted with a flood of buying orders before the opening on Monday, November 25, that carried right to the closing gong, giving the DJIA the largest one day rise in its history, up 32 points. Within two weeks it was making new all time highs and extended the rise to 228 points before the big shakeout of 1965. The assassination proved to be only another incident in the course of the market's rise.

The Securities and Exchange Commission, and also Congress, seem to be quite aware of abuses as practiced by floor traders on our national exchanges. The Commission believes it has a mandate to attempt regulation of floor trading, and adds that, "if such regulation does not accomplish the statutory purposes, the alternative, expressly provided by Congress, is prohibition."

For years the Commission has tried to adopt rules governing floor traders that would give the public a break, but the exchanges seem to have an underlying power to prevent this. They always get by with promises to eliminate abuses by making their own rules.

The following excerpts are from SEC Release No. 7290 April 9, 1964, concerning a proposed rule restricting floor trading.

In a letter to Congress, dated July 23, 1963, the Commission commented,

> "In light of the very serious and basic problems presented by the continuation of floor trading, the Commission agrees that a rule proposal abolishing floor trading on the New York and American Stock exchanges should be developed, unless those exchanges demonstrate that its continuance would be consistent with the public interest."

All these years the Commission has relied upon the regulation of floor trading by rules adopted by the exchanges.

> ". . . the Commission's staff, as a result of numerous studies, consistently concluded that regulation by the Exchange was inadequate . . ."

> ". . . a review of the exchanges' enforcement of these rules over

the past 10 years demonstrates that neither these nor any similar rules administered by the exchanges serve to restrain floor trading in the slightest measurable degree."

In the light of this, one wonders if there is pressure from some source that restrains the Commission from adopting their own rules with teeth in them, and enforcing them. They know what they want to do and the reason for it. Here are some of the reasons they give.

> "The floor trader . . . by his short-swing speculations frequently interferes with the orderly execution of public brokerage orders in a normal fashion through the facilities provided for that purpose by delaying consummation of a public transaction or causing it to be executed at a different price than it otherwise would, to the detriment of one or the other of the public customers involved. The public has no way of knowing the impact of floor traders' activities on the functioning of the market generally or in particular securities. In certain stocks floor trading has amounted to over 35 percent of total reported volume on selected days; during shorter periods, floor traders have, on occasion, participated in virtually every transaction in particular stocks."

Doesn't this back up my opinion that floor traders are parasites, chiseling $1/8$'s and $1/4$'s off of the public's trades, besides making their normal profits? No matter what trades they make, no one can prove that they weren't based on an honest opinion. But when they "participate in virtually every transaction," you can rest assured that stock is being manipulated to satisfy the wishes of the sponsors of that stock.

Participating so actively in a stock by floor trading can be substantially the same as creating "wash sales," (which is done by matching many buy and sell orders against one another), and at times is no doubt intended to serve the same purpose, but it cannot be proven that this activity was so intended. The use of wash sales in the stock market is as dishonest as using loaded dice in Las Vegas. Until forbidden by the SEC years ago, it was a gimmick used by pool managers to give an impression of great activity and demand in a stock, thus actually inducing a demand by the unsophisticated public.

> ". . . trading activity may be observed minutes before it appears on the tape, and bids or offers may be made or withdrawn in a matter of seconds. In addition, presence on the floor carries with it the

benefit of what has been termed the 'feel of the market' ... a heightened sense of market tenor and trend. This is attributable, among other things, to the exchange among floor members, and familiarity with trading techniques of specialists or floor brokers, with a resulting ability to foresee short-term market movements by informed observation of the activities of other persons on the floor.

"Being first on the scene as a market movement commences, the floor trader can buy a stock quicker, and at a lower price, or sell it quicker at a higher price. This, of course, is done at the expense of some members of the public.

"A floor trader, familiar with the fact that certain commission brokers handle a large number of orders and do not execute them all at once, can anticipate from their appearance in the market that further substantial buying is forthcoming; and, it is extremely doubtful whether trading on this information, which is unavailable to the investing public, is consistent with 'fair dealing' or with the anti-fraud provisions of Rule 10B-5 under the Exchange Act.

"Where floor traders rush to a security in which buying exists or is anticipated, and, by a succession of purchases at rising prices, interspersed with those of the public arouse and capitalize upon public reaction to the activity shown on the tape, the consequences are hardly distinguishable from those of manipulation ... Similar questions arise where he trades in anticipation of the rally which is apt to follow the 'clean up' of a large sell order overhanging the market. In the nature of things, it is impossible to determine how often these things happen ... while the exchange endeavors to prevent such abuses, its efforts to do so have not been successful."

The Commission's study and comments seem to be only concerned with how floor traders take advantage of or cause rising prices to the disadvantage of the public. I will relate an experience that I had in which I feel certain someone on the floor was more concerned about keeping the price down. After all, manipulation of a stock includes preventing a rise when a rise is undesirable.

During January, 1964 I bought 2500 shares of Bond Stores. I seldom set a price, so all of this was bought "at the market." Because the trading was very light I spread my orders over a four-day period in multiples of mostly 200 shares every hour or so. On the 15th of January after ordering the last 400 shares by phone I drove into Los Angeles and visited with my account executive late in the session. On arrival he told me that my orders had not yet been filled. The last trade had been made at 17-1/4, which was also the high for the day, and that New York had wired that they were "holding" my order, meaning that they would not bid higher for my stock unless they had to. Not many minutes before the close of the market my broker remarked, "Well, it looks like you are going to make a new high for the day." I agreed with him. There had only been a few hundred shares traded at 17-1/8 and 1/4 earlier in the day. I watched the tape closely. Just before the close 400 BND went over at 17-1/4. I could be wrong, but I doubt very much that this 400 shares came from public selling. Someone did not want BND to show any strength by selling at 17-3/8 or 17-1/2. Someone on the exchange floor, perhaps the same one who executed my order, accommodated them by selling the 400 shares so as to hold the price at the ceiling 17-1/4. It seemed obvious to me. I saved money by it so am not complaining, but did mention this to my broker. Now in all due respect to the firm that I deal with, and there are none that have a better reputation, I don't believe that their man on the exchange floor was so concerned over my interests that he delayed my two market orders of 200 shares each. My opinion is that this delay was occasioned by the expectation that public selling would fill my order, at 17-1/4, and if not, a floor trader would then sell against it. Bidding for my stock may have put a close of 17-1/2 on it. The market was thin. Only one day in the last eighteen had BND sold as high as 17-3/8, but did close at 17-1/4. Six days after I bought this stock, a block of 3000 shares traded at 17, and it promptly closed at 17-3/8. The low during this time was 17. This was positively good accumulation action. I can't help but wonder, was this block of 3000 a forced sale by an estate that the insiders had previously learned about? Was someone waiting to pick it up at 17? BND later rallied to 17-7/8, then dropped and held for two weeks at 17, which by now obviously was a twelve-week false bottom. The directors then cut the dividend and it sold as low as 15-7/8. Selling, even on this discouraging dividend action was light. The stock was in strong hands.

About two hours after the market opened on July 12, 1965 I phoned my broker in Los Angeles and I first inquired as to the price of Bond Stores. It was at 21-3/4 down 3/8 and had only one sale of 100 shares up to this time. The price in the previous five days had only a range of 3/8. Trading was light. This lone sale was no doubt prompted by an order to sell "at the market." I placed an order to buy 500 "at the market" and to buy another 500 about an hour later. I figured there would be a chance of more shares being offered before the second 500 were bought so that my order would not be forced to bid a higher price than it may have on the 1000 share order. My first order was filled 100 at 21-7/8, and 400 at 22. The second 500 was filled 200 at 22-1/8 and 300 at 22-1/4. Here is an example of how alert the tape watchers are to a display of strength in a stock accompanied by an increase in volume. This purchase of 1000 shares triggered the tape watchers into bidding the price up to 23-1/4 before the close, on a volume of 4700 shares for the day. If my 1000 shares had been bought at once, instead of in two lots one hour apart, the price may have been bid up to 22-1/2 in order to fill it. This may have attracted even more buyers. This proves how the tape watchers are inclined to buy only when they observe someone else is buying. The market on BND could have been thin enough that a bid of 300 shares could have moved the price up to 22-1/4, but it would not have attracted as much attention as the 1000 shares did.

This is an example, on a minor scale, of how the public are attracted by a fast rise on heavy volume. This is why they are so inclined to buy in the extremely high price range of a top, and why "wash sales" are forbidden. This may still be accomplished at times when floor traders and specialists trade heavily in a stock.

It is noteworthy to mention that it was apparent that no one on the exchange floor was determined to hold the price of BND around the 22 level on the day of my 1000 share purchase as when I made the purchase of 400 shares at 17-1/4 that I previously mentioned.

Also it may be noted that if I had been the floor trader who had made this 1000 share purchase, I could easily have sold it commission free at 23 with a nearly $900 profit. In fact, in view of the following setback I believe there was organized selling at 23-1/4.

The Commission's comments continue. "These problems are compounded where commission brokers handling public orders simultaneously engage in floor trading. A conflict of interest at once arises between the commission broker's duty of fidelity to his customer and his opportunity to personally profit from his customer's investment decisions—perhaps at the customer's expense."

Referring to past attempts to prevent abuses by floor trading, the Commission says, ". . . under present concepts of floor trading, these efforts could hardly be expected to be successful except perhaps by an inordinate expenditure of time and money."

Let's hope that in the near future the SEC will exercise the mandate that was given it by Congress and prohibit floor trading. No one should be denied the privilege of owning stocks, but why should these 400 plus have the privilege of flagrantly weighing their thumb? I believe the same restrictions should apply to them that the SEC has applied to their own personnel: they may not sell any stock that has been purchased within one year.

It could be said that a controlled market is a necessity. That I will agree with if the control is held within justification. If a market was merely supported to the extent of buying the stock that the public are foolishly selling and then allowing the stock to stabilize around its true value, there would be no complaint. But the evil of controlled markets is that they go to extremes as does everything else that man does if his power is not curtailed. Instead of our markets being merely supported in the bargain basement, they are maneuvered in a way so as to keep them there, thereby holding the public in fear that the price is unable to recover. That, in a nutshell, is why we have these long dragged out bottoms.

If there was no guidance in our markets, perhaps a large percentage of our stocks would idle along with only slow and moderate changes, except an occasional stock with a "hot" item such as Brunswick Corp., or the Texas Gulf Sulphur ore strike in 1964 which came as a surprise—to the public, that is. How high could one of these stocks carry if the smart money did not sell large quantities in the top range? On the other hand without artificial stimulation and touting there would be far fewer speculators. Commission-hungry brokers would then be the only ones to bait the public into the market.

On every stock that has an important top the public has bought heavily even though the price may have failed to make any headway over a period of many months of activity. On these tops you can be sure there was concerted selling by someone who was quite certain of what they were doing at the time. This, then, is distribution. Without this heavy selling by other than the public, the price rise naturally would continue. And as long as it continued the overwhelming incentive would be to buy. Who could say where it would top?

If we had uncontrolled markets, then public buying and selling would be on balance or nearly so; no one would know where the rise would end. A normal amount of stock held by insiders could easily be sold too soon or held too long, the same as it could be by anyone else.

Losses by the general public in this type of market would not be as serious to the economy, because outside of commissions they would be nearly offset by their profits. There would not be the heavily-weighted odds against them—odds that were well known and admitted by authorities when pools and insiders operated freely.

New York Stock Exchange President Keith Funston has defended the often-attacked floor trader as important in helping maintain the liquidity "so essential to a healthy public auction market."

I agree that they keep the market liquid all right, but certainly this kind of "liquidity" is not healthy from the public viewpoint. In my opinion they are the pool managers of today.

The New York Stock Exchange reported that the specialists' purchases and sales in 1965 totaled 453,000,000 shares in their role of maintaining a fair and orderly market. These transactions amounted to about 14.5% of total volume. 91.2% of these transactions were of a stabilizing nature, which means that the purchases were made at a price below the last different price and the sales at a price above the last different price. You may safely guess that the other 8.8% were "stimulating" transactions which helped to stimulate price moves so that profits could be made on these "stabilizing" transactions. You may wonder how many of these purchases prevented someone else from buying stock on a lower bid, or forced a "market" order to bid for and pay a higher price. You may also wonder how often these "stabilizing" purchases were made in order to give an illusion of strong support of a stock for the purpose of stimulating public buying at a higher price when a stock was actually in a downtrend or during distribution. Or how often enough "stabilizing" sales were made in order to create a false resistance level to induce public selling during an uptrend or an accumulation period. After all price stabilizing is not a one way street.

Your guess may be better than mine as to what the average profit per share was taken on these 453 million purchases and sales.

My Experiences While Helping Others to Market Success

Ever since I have had enough confidence in my own opinions to help others make an easy dollar, I have been willing to do so. Most of them were in the lower brackets and were in a position to appreciate a few dollars. But it had its problems.

My standard procedure when I find them to be interested is to show them a stock chart book and point out how stocks have formed quiet bottoms of many years before a big rise. I explain how the public are selling these stocks at a heavy loss during this discouraging action.

To the novice, it is only common sense that this is when stocks should be bought and he is surprised when I tell him that few people have the courage to buy during this time and that few brokers will recommend them. They are also affected by the doom and gloom action. I advise that stocks during this period should be bought with confidence and held with confidence. The novice is also surprised when I explain that in my opinion the markets are guided this way, and that it is only a matter of time before the sold-out public will buy back at far higher prices.

I always tell them that the first part of the move will be normally slow, and explain the reason for this is to give the impression that the stock is acting "tired." This encourages profit-taking. This sluggishness is a false front to hide the real technical strength that will show up at a later and at a much higher level. I explain that normally it is impossible for the average person to judge when this strength has been spent, but that a large majority of stocks can be sold at a huge profit without forming an opinion. This statement, of course, is accepted by the listener as being highly exaggerated until I show him how the stocks either have a very fast rise to an important top, or form a long uptrend line of over 45 degrees, which when crossed indicates a change of trend. This, I explain, is the time to sell.

I have never advised anyone who bought a stock at my suggestion to take a loss. Several have taken small losses because they lacked the patience to hold on, or became too nervous. Several had to sit with a loss for a long time because it dipped to a lower level during its bottom action. Desoto Chemical is one that took a lot of patience. At the time of purchase it was called United Wallpaper and had a reverse split later on of 1-for-5. It is now being moved up very nicely and I should be able to pick a high selling point for them.

I refuse to give any advice to people who want to speculate. They are apt to hound me on every move the market makes whether they are in trouble or not. I try to get speculators to simmer down, buy something I suggest, and sit tight. They have losses that they are anxious to recover and go right on taking more. Next time they will be right, they think. They prefer great risk to the long ordeal of a period of patience.

I usually caution my friends against telling others how I, as a common laborer, and with only a 6th grade education, have become a successful speculator in the stock and futures markets. I explain that if word gets around that a person with my background can beat the markets, many people will get the idea that with their better intellectual status, they should be able to do it also. If they followed this thought with active speculating, they would only get into trouble. Successful people in other endeavors, are perhaps the last to realize the depths of knowledge to be gained by an intensive study to what makes our markets tick.

When a friend, or sometimes a mere acquaintance is willing to take my advice, I give them a little lecture along with it that goes about like this: You are buying in the bottom range, if it goes lower, don't worry about it, it is just a part of the bottom. I can't tell you when it will go up or how high it will go. But it will have a big rise and I will let you know when I think it is time to sell. Don't watch it too closely as it may influence you to start thinking, and when you start thinking you will form opinions which invariably will be wrong unless you have had proper experience in counteracting the influence of market actions.

This happened to a friend who failed to heed my warning. Some time after my wife and I had returned from our second trip to Alaska he told me that he had sold his Curtiss Wright which I had advised him to buy. "Why did you do that?" I asked him. "You were not here and it looked like it could not go up," he replied. This type of action "baits" the unsophisticated into taking a profit at the wrong time. After moving up from 10, it had turned quiet between 12 and 14 for a perfect three and one-half month consolidation. This gave him the impression it could not move higher. It was now time for CW to move. For eighteen years it had topped out five times in a range of 12 to 13-1/4. Two years later it sold at 49.

Unless these people already have a broker, I try to get them to buy through the one I deal with. He has a list of these persons and what shares they hold. This is especially important when I am away from home. He relays my sell suggestions to them by phone and they then give him the order.

In the spring of 1961, I gave sell orders on Coty International, on the way to Alaska from a phone booth on the Hart Highway in British Columbia, including sell suggestions for other persons.

In 1956 I suggested to an elderly lady that she should sell her 100 Eastern Stainless Steel that she had bought on my advice and on which she now had a profit of 200%, and buy 300 Dr. Pepper with the proceeds. From the expression on her face one would think I had asked her to kick an old friend in the teeth. She sort of stuttered, "But I won't get my $1.00 a year dividend." I informed her that 300 Dr. Pepper would pay her $1.80 a year instead. That seemed to relieve part of the shock. She made the switch. But the next fall after our return from Alaska, I was slightly stunned when she apologetically informed me that the broker had told her to sell her 100 Eastern Stainless Steel and buy 300 Dr. Pepper. I thought it would be very embarrassing to her if she found out how short her memory was. Not getting credit for this was not important—so I did not tell her that I had suggested this.

At a later date she told me that she called her broker, but he was on vacation and the phone operator connected her to another one.

She asked him to suggest a good stock to buy as she had more cash available. He suggested National Castings, and she bought it at 45 during an active top, only $3 from the high. It has sold below 19 since. She should have bought more Dr. Pepper. Perhaps she wanted to diversify. She, perhaps like many people, has the impression that it is a simple matter for the average broker to give good advice. I am hopeful that her bad memory will not credit me with this gem of advice.

Perhaps she thought if I could give good advice, a broker could do even better. If it is merely a question of buying a good stock, that's fine, if you don't care what price you pay for it. If your broker is smart enough to give advice that would enable you to beat the market, very likely the next time you called him the switchboard operator would say, "Sorry, he doesn't work here anymore; he has retired."

It was nearly nine years later before National Castings recovered to 45. If she had bought more Dr. Pepper at that time and held it, she would have had nearly 400% profit at the time National Castings had merely recovered to its purchase price.

Back in 1951 I bought Pepsi Cola below 10. A tape watcher acquaintance ridiculed me for buying it at the time. "It's just lying there doing nothing," he told me. I explained to him that was what I liked about it. The public was selling it in disgust, I explained, and the insiders were picking it up. This didn't impress him a bit. The dividend had been passed for two years and to him it was a sad reflection on any future prospects. He didn't know it, but this is the type of comment I like to hear when I am enthusiastic about a stock that I consider to be on the bargain counter. It backs up my opinion that the public does not like it. It proves that I can tell what the majority are thinking by analyzing the past price actions of the stock.

I voiced my opinion to friends about Pepsi and one fellow bought 100 shares above 10 in 1953 even though he refused to concede that there was any sense to my reasons for buying it. I guess he only bought it because some of my enthusiasm rubbed off on him. But only a few weeks later he told me he sold it at a bare profit. He explained that he and his father had figured that it could not go above 15 and that he decided to sell now. The coincidence is that Pepsi's first move stopped at 15 and it reacted to 11. Of course this proved him to be the expert and proved me to be all wrong. But not for long. At this writing it has sold at 83-3/4 and has not yet topped out. The final distribution top will easily cross 100.

With the Pepsi money he bought Schenley Industries at 27 when it was in a downtrend. Several years later, the bottom action of Schenley wore him out and he sold at a good-sized loss. Then later, on a fast move, it rose to 48. How many of my readers have had a similar experience?

Once again in 1957 my enthusiasm rubbed off on him enough to buy Bond Stores when it was selling at 14-1/2. He ignored my advice, always buy "at the market," and bid 14-1/4 for it and luckily got it. Only once after ordering it was there an opportunity for his order to fill. Once again he was smarter than I. At this price it paid nearly a 9% return on the investment. But he almost missed a bargain by not buying "at the market."

A few years later while spending an evening with him and his wife, I told him I had bought more Bond Stores. He said he had recently sold his. He said he had anticipated the dividend cut. Of course the real reason was that he had become worn out waiting for the big move that I had promised. It was now selling below 17. He was now thoroughly convinced that I was wrong about Bond. But to my amazement he now thought Dr. Pepper at 55 was a good buy, but he would not buy it previously when it was in the bottom range below 20. This was just before it split. We argued like a couple of opposing political fanatics. This always happens when we get together. I frankly told him that he was a good subject for me to write about in my book and that his way of thinking perfectly represented the majority of traders as I know them. After all, the real basis of my chart reading is what I believe the majority are thinking during various actions of a stock. I just can't convince him that his mind at times is being brainwashed by the price actions of the market. He has taken a course on the stock market and is thoroughly sold on the study of fundamentals. He refuses to concede that Bond Stores can go up very much from here. I reminded him that that was similar to when he didn't think very well of Dr. Pepper or Pepsi Cola when they were low. But now he maintained that DOC would go up more from the present level of 55 than Bond would from 16-1/8. I could not agree with that. For argument's sake I asked him which one he would make the most money in, DOC if it went up 50 points or Bond if it went up only 40 from here. He quickly answered that DOC would of course. I cautioned him to do a little simple arithmetic and told him he was not seeing beyond his nose. After several minutes he could not see it. I then explained that you would make $12,000 on Bond but only $5,000 on DOC because you could buy 300 shares of Bond for the price of 100 DOC. I am not writing this for the sake of ridicule . . . but to give you an insight of how most traders think. Actually he is only thinking in the way that comes naturally as a speculator.

A number of times when I have suggested to acquaintances that a stock should be bought, I urged them to do it *now*, but often they did not. I think they were merely timid and waited. But later on when it went up 4 or 5 points, they bought near the top of a rally, and had to wait out an extension of the bottom with a loss. It would seem in a case like this that when the price rises it confirms to them that my opinion was right. Then they are inclined to be embarrassed when they tell me they had bought at the higher price. In these cases, though they did not realize it, they were influenced emotionally. First by a timid attitude, then the upward move gave the necessary urge to buy. The same urge in a greater degree, that overwhelms the speculator into buying in top areas.

One woman bought Dr. Pepper, belatedly because of the emotional influence just described, then did not sell for a good profit and switch to Bond Stores when I suggested it. I was sure DOC was not toppy, as it did not have heavy enough volume. I thought though, at 44 that it was time for a setback or consolidation. But DOC kept right on moving up. Some time later I phoned her on a different matter just after DOC had sold as high as 56-1/4. At this time I had supposed that she had sold when I first suggested it and was prepared to console her about selling too soon, in that the switch to Bond would be far more profitable in the long run rather than holding DOC for the final top. She would have as good a chance to sell her 200 Bond at 80 which would give her a gain of over $12,000 or over 300%. DOC would have to be sold at 88 in order to get $4,400 or 100% more than the price at which she would have sold it. Before I could get on my intended subject she told me that she had not sold DOC and before I could tell her that that was a lucky break, she was lamenting the fact that she could not make up her mind to sell or not. I did manage to break in long enough to say that if it was a good sale at 44, it was certainly a better one now at 54, and that if it was mine I would certainly make the switch now. She was in such a quandary that she sounded as if she had not understood what I said. She continued, "My broker won't tell me what to do, he says he has no other client in it and has not paid much attention to it and does not have an opinion. I don't know what to do. All the information I can get on it doesn't seem to help." As far as I know at this writing she still holds it. She was not dealing with my broker. He would probably, in a case like this, merely have referred her back to me for my opinion, as he would have known that I had recommended it to her in the first place. On the phone I did not have time to think this out. But this switch now at this price appeared better than it did at first glance. Bond was now selling over a dollar lower in the 17 to 17-1/2 range. She would be able to buy 300 shares of Bond on a switch. On this she could, in my opinion, gain a profit of over $15,000 but perhaps would be lucky to get $3000 more in DOC, and would also get far more dividends during the holding period. To me it would have been one of the easiest decisions I could ever hope to make in the market. But to her it was a tough one. She was trying to get the last dollar out of DOC.

A small businessman who had accumulated a good amount of cash became interested in the stock market after I had showed him my charts. I picked out five that appeared to have sound bases. He timidly bought 100 shares of each. He could have bought far more. When later on, one of them rose to a price that I thought would be a good switch to one of the others, I called him up to suggest this. He then told me that he had sold all of them some time back at a small profit. He gave no reason for selling. I thought I had him thoroughly convinced as to the safety in holding these stocks. I told him I did not know when they would move up, but I was sure they would, and they have.

I find it very difficult to help elderly people. They become overcautious and often lack the will to do. They prefer the status quo to making any change. While they seem to have confidence in my opinion, they are afraid that this time I may be wrong. A common attitude is that why bother, they probably won't be around long enough to benefit from it anyway.

For many years now one old lady predicted, each time my wife and I would leave on an extended trip, that she would probably not be around when we returned. But she still is. Before we went to Australia I tried to get her to sell her Pepsi Cola that she had held for many years, and buy Dr. Pepper. She could buy three times as many shares with an increase in dividends, and the chance for capital gains was far greater. But she refused. She is now about to enter a home for the elderly. The higher profit she could have had on Dr. Pepper would buy her a few more comforts in life or even a higher grade of rest home. And if she had taken my advice she would have switched to Bond Stores since then.

What I want to point out is that a person is never too old to buy a stock providing they buy after it has established a long base—as can be seen in long range charts. If they did pass away in a year or two after the purchase and before the stock moved up very much or none at all, what difference did it make? If they are still around five to fifteen years or more, they have gained from it. And couldn't it help their morale at a time when they need it most? And it could be an added interest in what may be a dull life.

On the other hand I have the impatience of youth to contend with when trying to help a young person. I show them a "picture" of a company whose shares have been on a quiet bottom for many years. I explain that I can't say just when it will move, but that when it does it will be a big one, and that it may be five to six years or even more before it has a rise of 200% or more. The answer I get? I think you have already guessed it. "I can't wait that long." It leaves me cold. When I look back and think of the years that I have spent trying to save a few hard-earned dollars, it is difficult to understand those who can't wait a few years for some very easy profits, plus dividends. They are the type that fast promoters are looking for. If it's fast profits that they want promised, these boys are the ones that will give them. Moral: A sucker and his money are soon parted.

An acquaintance who has for several years been reluctant to concede that my buying suggestions have been anything more than luck, finally accepted one of them. He bought Bond Stores at 16-1/8, only a quarter above its low of 15-7/8 after the dividend had been cut. The timing on this purchase was lucky. I told him it would have a move above 70. After its run-up to 23-1/4 on a false rumor of a merger, he told me he had sold it at 22. In a plaintive voice I said, "What did you do that for? You will probably lose your position." His answer was noticeably hostile when he said that you can't go wrong taking a profit. He was going to buy it back at 18 and sell it if it went to 26. He used the word "if" as if he was not too confident that it would rise that high. The previous close on BND when this conversation took place was

21-1/4. I told him he should hold for possibly 80 in five or six years. He said it did not have a chance to go that high in that period of time.

This man has had only a limited experience in buying and selling stocks. Yet he forms positive opinions. He grabs the figures of buy at 18 and sell at 26 right out of thin air. Of course he would probably never admit it, but I doubt that he has any basis for these figures; they are mere guesses. And no doubt he is just as positive that BND should be sold at 26 as I am that when it hits 26, it is at the breakaway point of leaving its 16-year base, and should be bought, not sold. If enough traders are aware of this, it could generate a fast move at this level. But there will be premature profit-taking by persons who have grown weary of holding this stock.

This man instead of feeling kindly toward me for good advice and for trying to help him, winds up with hostility and ridicule for my opinion. It is impossible for him and also many others to believe that anyone can make the positive predictions that I make and be right. He told me that if anyone could do that they would get rich. I asked him, "What do you think I have been doing?"

He is no doubt misjudging our financial position by our appearance and the mode of life we lead. He does not know I made $200,000 on only one stock. If we tried to "live it up," we would have to learn to lead a new life. We might find ourselves a little like those on the TV program, "The Beverly Hillbillies." We would be out of our element. Keeping up with the Joneses has been the least of our worries.

Women accept my opinions far quicker than men. When I explain to them through the use of a long range chart why the past action of a stock acted that way, I don't believe they grasp the idea with any greater facility than do men, but they are far more apt to have an open mind. Many men with experience in the market are convinced that there is no other way to study the market except through fundamentals. It takes time to pry their minds open.

I believe that women are inclined to think that the market is a man's world, and advice is more acceptable by them. But men who have been in the habit of forming market opinions, even though they are very often wrong, would have to under-rate their own before accepting mine. Human nature being what it is, that is not easy. Perhaps if I charged a fee, my advice would be more acceptable.

Whenever there has been a hesitancy by only one of a couple to follow my advice, it has nearly always been the husband who was reluctant to do so.

Late in 1961 a friend phoned me and asked if I knew anything about Grayson-Robinson Stores. My answer was no. She told me she had just seen an item in the newspaper about it. I don't recall now just what it said, but it praised the company so highly that she decided to buy some of its shares. Partly through curiosity, she decided to ask my opinion on it first. To me, this item had all the earmarks of touting that is so difficult to stop.

I looked at the long-term Grayson-Robinson chart. It required only a glance to decide it was too dangerous, and I told her so. It had a fast rise early in 1961 from 8 to 19 followed by several months of boiling action. She did not buy. Time proved that my opinion was more correct than I thought possible. Three years later Grayson-Robinson was bankrupt. If I had publicly accused the management at this time of causing this touting item to be published, I probably would have been sued for slander.

The chart shows that this company earned an average of 80 cents per year for the previous six years. How can a retail store be mismanaged into bankruptcy so quickly? Could it have been planned that way? Is it possible that under our bankruptcy laws it can be profitable to go broke?

The chart action of the stock shows that it boiled for eleven months in 1959 after a fast rise, with a high of 16-1/4. Typical distribution action. After a reaction in 1960 it had an even faster rise in 1961. Obviously the insiders knew what they were doing when they sold out, with the help of newspaper touting.

If my readers will only take the advice that I offer, they can at least save themselves millions. But knowing human nature as I do, I know that far too many will fail to bear down on themselves and ignore touting and emotional impulses that overwhelm them. Too many will think, if they think at all, that my advice does not apply to them.

I have been asked, "If everyone should follow your advice the whole market action would be changed." I explain that there is not a chance of this happening. I could never get that kind of a following. There will always be people with popular illusions who will think, when a stock shows extreme strength, there is no reason for it to go down again. There will be enough gullible people around to enable me to sell Bond Stores with a million profit, when it gets to above 70 or even 80, providing I don't switch to another in the meantime.

Many fundamentalists are so prejudiced against a product that they will not buy shares of the company that manufactures it. You know the type. They have bought the same make of car for years and consider all other makes to be inferior. One acquaintance would not consider buying shares of a soft drink company because he did not like the taste of its drink. Why allow prejudice to deprive a person of a profit? I don't like snuff but I bought 2400 shares of American Snuff.

Many people buy shares of companies merely because they are well acquainted with them, perhaps having done business with them for years. A typical example is a friend in a small town in Montana who has known me since the winter of 1935-36 when I was spreading hay out on the snow for a herd of cattle at $30 per month and board, with no days off. In late 1964 I suggested four bargains to him, among them Belding Hemingway and Bond Stores. He is well aware of my success in the market and seems to respect my opinion, but a few months later he bought Montana Power (MTP) at 43, right in a top range. It is obvious to me that he was influenced emotionally because MTP was like an old friend to him—and it was high. Since then it has sold as low as 32-1/4. If he lived in Idaho no doubt he would have bought Idaho Power.

Perhaps he never doubted the soundness of my suggestions. Perhaps he outsmarted himself by thinking (so easily done) that if my four recommendations would have a healthy rise why wouldn't Montana Power also have a healthy rise. Everybody knows it is a good stock. So he became a high-level investor, which is the easiest thing to do in the stock market. Anyone can do it.

Several times in the past, townsmen, and surrounding farmers where my Montana friend lives, have been swindled. A very humorous book has been written based on the great muskrat swindle that was pulled on this town and its vicinity many years ago. These people were talked into buying pairs of muskrats (on paper of course) for breeding purposes. Rather like buying shares in a fur farm. They were also taken on a wildcat oil well.

There is a wide variety of reactions from people when I am having a "chart session" with them, pointing out the important price actions. Elderly men with market experience are the slowest to see through this concept of market forecasting, and some are really reluctant to do so.

The other extreme happened in March 1966, when after about a thirty-minute "chart session" with a young lady whom I had known since birth, suddenly, as we leafed through a stock chart book, she pointed to a stock and exclaimed, "There's one I like!" It was Polarad Electronics. (See Page 78.)

In my opinion there are no better bases to be seen during this period. This girl's mind was uncluttered with what you must "know" about a stock before you buy it. She did not start "thinking" as most sophisticated people do, "What's wrong with it?" "Is it going broke?" She already understood why it was so low. It was undergoing accumulation. She asked for my approval of it, which I gave without hesitation.

She was a doer, not a "should have done it." She bought 150 shares the next morning at 4-3/4.

If she can pick a bargain so can you.

At one of our regular Thursday night meetings of the Los Angeles Adventurers Club, a fellow member who is a well known eye specialist asked me with apparent confidence for a suggestion of a good buy in the stock market. Bond Stores was then trading quietly above 17 and I explained to him why I thought it to be a bargain. He seemed enthusiastic about my suggestion. Two weeks later I asked him if he had bought it. He said he hadn't but that he was watching it. This idea of "watching it" is typical. Invariably this "watch it" type will buy after a stock has risen several points. This rise apparently proves my opinion to be right.

Several weeks later after Bond had cut their dividend and the price was hovering quietly above 16, I again asked him if he had bought. He now appeared quite concerned when he said, "You know, Warren, I have talked to some of my clients about Bond and some brokers and clothing men and . . ." I interrupted him with "and probably not one had a good word for it." He agreed and went on to tell how some of them thought the company was going broke, that they had closed some stores and that you couldn't get any information from the management. This should have had a very depressing effect on me. But when he finished I told him, "What you have said is like music to my ears. This helps back up my opinion that I am right." I told him I now had a loss on all my Bond shares but that I was probably the least worried of all its shareholders. I reminded him that when Dr. Pepper was on the bottom range I had predicted it would have a big rise. He agreed that I was right, but that this time he was afraid that I was wrong. He was not argumentative. He was really concerned that I could be making a terrible mistake. I told him then, that this conversation would be one of the highlights of my book, explaining that this is proof that a successful, intelligent, well educated man is no more capable of thinking properly in terms of the stock market than the average person. He is just as apt to take his advice from the wrong sources. He has not learned how to screen the logic from the illogical.

These "clients, brokers and clothing men" who could not see any encouraging future in the shares of Bond Stores at 17-1/4 did not realize their opinions were largely influenced by Bond's discouraging action. When it sells above 70 in a very few years, these seers will discover some very sound reasons for buying it, that were invisible at 17. Few recognize that the soundness of a sound reason is severely dissipated after a stock has risen to an unreasonably high price. This is one reason why so many of them become high-level investors.

If this noted ophthalmologist should advise a serious operation on a patient, would the patient ask his numerous friends as to whether he should accept this advice? Of course not. But this man seems to think his acquaintances are qualified to have an opinion on the stock market. They have a right to their opinions, but they should never be taken too seriously. Some very insidious logic can be heard both in and outside of brokerage houses. Though few are qualified in forming an opinion on the future course of the market, few will ever admit to not having one.

Sample Charts and Comments

A.J. Industries, Inc. (AJ)

I'd like to tell you an experience in forecasting a move in Alaska Juneau gold mining (now A. J. Industries) back in September, 1954. I became

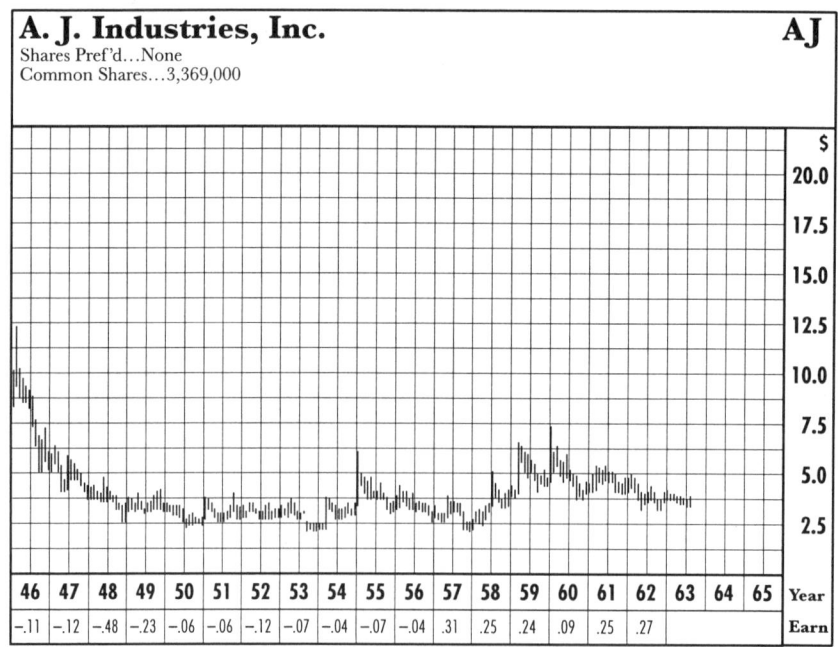

well acquainted in Anchorage with a long time resident of Alaska when my wife and I were on our second trip up there. He happened to mention that he had worked for A.J. years before and had speculated in their stock. It so happened I had been charting it daily for several years. I was curious to see how a stock would act while the company was not in business. I told him that I had reasons to believe it was going up. He disagreed with me. He explained that their mine had filled up with water after the shut-down early in the war and that it would not be profitable to reopen it at the present high cost of labor. I showed him my chart on it and pointed out the extremely quiet action below 3-1/2, which was a good shakeout. Then a small rise followed, which I considered to be good consolidation. I told him it appeared that the insiders were buying, and if this was so, then the price would move up and somewhere the insiders would unload to the public. He claimed it could not go up. Notice on the A.J. chart the fast 100% rise to 6 in January, 1955. It was announced that the company was going into the pulp business. This took the public by surprise and they bought heavily and "you know who" generously sold their stock to "meet the demand." The company never went into the pulp business. Naturally, A.J. dropped down and went through a reaccumulation period, completing its base in early 1966. While we are on the subject of A.J. Industries, I want to point out that I have stated that the price of a stock nearly always moves slowly out of its lower range in order to prevent the traders from getting excited too soon. Notice that A.J. moved up 100% in about one month. Anytime the price moves as quickly out of its low, quiet price range as this one did, you had better not wait for the 200 to 400% profit that I advocate. You had better consider it to be the sucker bait move and sell out quickly.

From a high of 33, A.J. dropped to 1-1/2 in December, 1941. In 1942 the Government forced the company to close their mine because of the war. It has been said that the machinery was lend-leased to Russia. For eleven months in 1942 someone willingly picked up the stock at an average price of 2, and again willingly sold back to the public as high as 12-1/4 in 1946 when the public were anticipating the reopening of the mine. Doesn't this prove that so many times when the public form an opinion by thinking what comes naturally, they are wrong? They sold at a huge loss when their company closed their mine, and then became high-level investors when they anticipated the reopening after the war.

During the 1950's A.J. bought out several small businesses and are not doing badly.

When the price of gold is eventually raised, one wonders if A.J. will find it profitable to reopen their gold mine near Juneau, Alaska. Perhaps they will do this during the next depression when labor and other costs are low. Do not be a high-level investor in the future, by buying during a fast rise in anticipation of this.

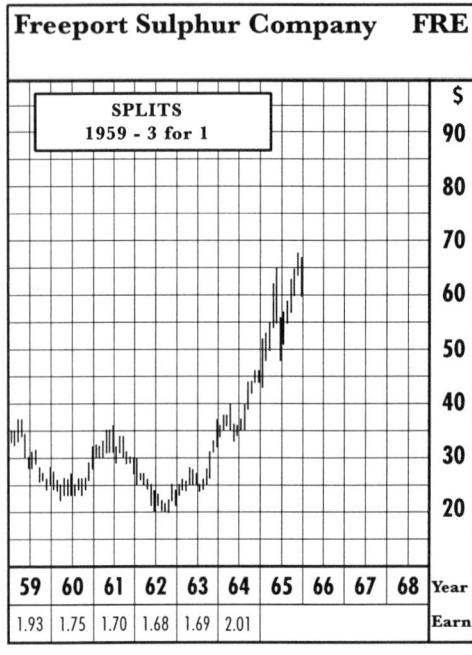

Freeport Sulphur Company (FRE)

I happened across an appraisal in 1960 of Freeport Sulphur by a partner in a brokerage firm, in which he wrote that the more he watched busy speculators bidding for popular merchandise, the more he found himself rummaging on the bargain counter while their backs were turned. That is exactly the type of thinking that an investolator should follow.

He analyzed the chart action of Freeport Sulphur (FRE) in 1960 below 27 as a probable indication that the floating supply had moved into "strong hands." He noted the resistance that appeared at 26, but he most certainly evaded making a positive statement, such as "buy when crossing 27." Instead he said that it "should be accorded more than passing attention."

This was a sound suggestion for a short term trader. And being a broker, I am sure that he specializes in holding the attention of the short term traders. After all, commissions are what keep a broker in business. His hinted suggestion to buy proved to be correct, temporarily that is.

Backed by the behavior of many stocks in the past, buying when a resistance level has been overcome can be the perfect timing of a purchase. But I advocate doing so only when there has been a minimum of over two years after what would appear to be accumulation. The action of FRE on which this broker based his technical analysis was too short to warrant confidence in expecting a large rise of 200% or more. There may be one, but too often it fails.

Now place yourself in the position of a speculator who bought FRE at 27. You would have been very fortunate to have taken a $6 profit out of the 8-1/2 point rise that followed. If you had sold when it broke a minor uptrend line, you would have sold at 30 or less. Or you might have held over the next rally to 33. As a speculator you should have sold at 28 when it broke a triple support level above 28. If you did not sell then, as a speculator you would almost certainly have panicked into selling below 25 during the 1962 market break, missing the large rise that followed.

I maintain that the odds were not enough in one's favor when buying at 27, after breaking a resistance level of such short duration such as this.

Fruehauf Corporation (FTR)

Study the action of Fruehauf Corp. in 1947-48. It is almost identical to that of FRE in 1959-60. If you had bought this as a speculator

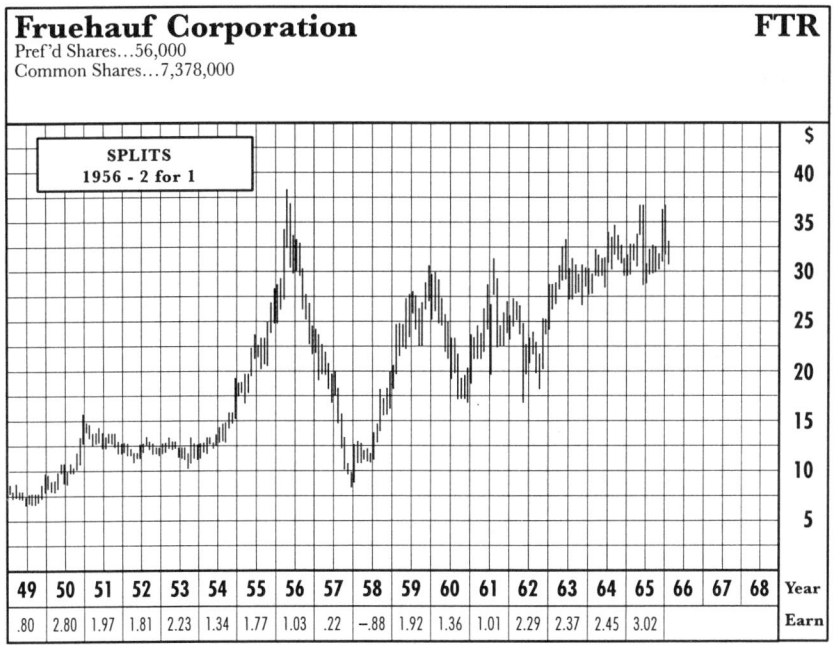

at 10, after it broke its recent high of 9-1/2, you would have found yourself in trouble. This proved to be a false start. It is seldom a speculator's intention of carrying a stock very far at a loss, so you would have sold out very quickly as it dropped.

There followed nearly a year of extreme quietness on the downside. Few speculators would be able to see any good in this type of action, but this is one of the actions for which an investolator should be on the alert. It is the same action as Boston & Maine and several others mentioned in the chapter on Stock Trends. That final five-month quietness was the signal to buy "at the market" or with the use of a stop buy at about 8-1/2 in November, 1949 as it broke the two-year trend line drawn through the thrust move above 10, which took place in October, 1948.

As an investolator you must understand that this kind of action weakens the faith of the staunchest shareholder. You must realize that this action should give you the confidence to buy and the confidence to hold for the inevitable large rise.

As an investolator in FTR you should have had the faith to hold out during the long consolidation during the early '50's. Based on your purchase price, your better than 10% dividend on your investment should have bolstered your faith. Following the selling recommendations that I have made elsewhere, you should have sold on the fast two-month rise from 27 to 38, at around 35, or at no less than 31 when the steep trend line was broken.

Kresge (S.S.) Company (KG)

The chart on Kresge (S.S.) Co. (KG) would have tried the patience of an investolator who could have bought it with sound judgment, but too soon. It has about the most perfect, slow six-year downtrend ever seen, the basis of a sound bottom. An alert investolator could have been tempted into buying during the quiet period at about 29 in early 1956 and again at 26 in 1957, each time expecting that the next move would break upward through the trend line. The positive cue to buy came at 27, after a small but sharp shakeout during the 1957 panic selloff, followed by breaking through the downtrend.

It then appeared to have a perfect three-year consolidation at an average price of 32, with a double top and false resistance level above 34. But the manipulators of KG came up with a different gimmick. A

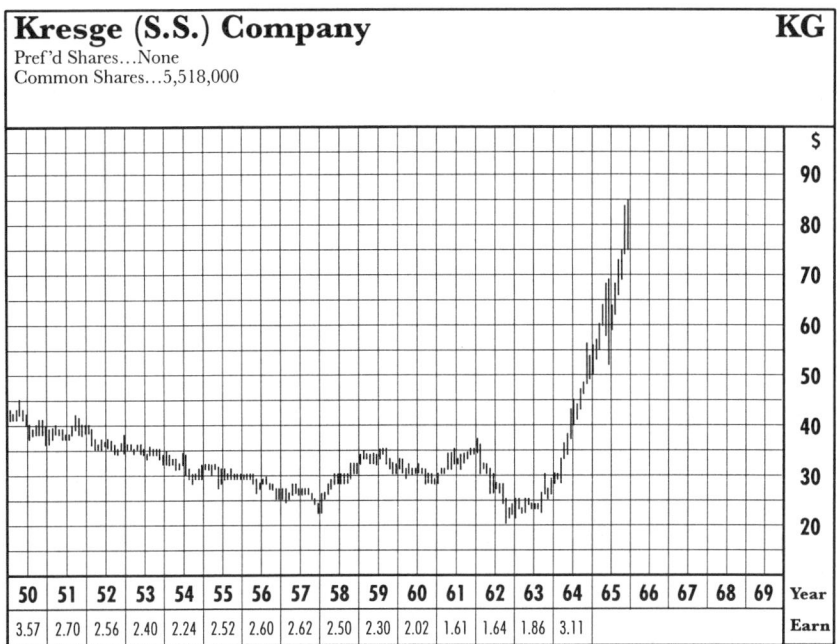

false upward start in January, 1962 turned down. Only an experienced investolator would have gone through this 17 point drop with full confidence. It ended with the 1962 general market panic. You could be confident that there was a sound base of accumulation by someone who knew what they were doing, and this someone certainly had not sold out on the higher level because its action had been too quiet for distribution on a large scale. This appeared to be normal consolidation action. The shakeout was aided considerably by the 1962 panic selling in May and the Cuban crisis in October.

Douglas Aircraft Company (D)

Douglas Aircraft (D) is a perfect example of how stock prices will sell at lower levels on increased earnings, during 1962-64, compared to 1959-61, proof that people overwhelmingly will sell a stock for no better reason than that they had a loss on it and feared that it would go lower.

Notice the rare two-year flat top. Normally a breakdown would occur long before it did. My guess is that for distribution to have taken place during those final five months around 90, there must have been some powerful touting by advisory services or from brokers. Without it, there would have been much profit-taking by the public as Douglas

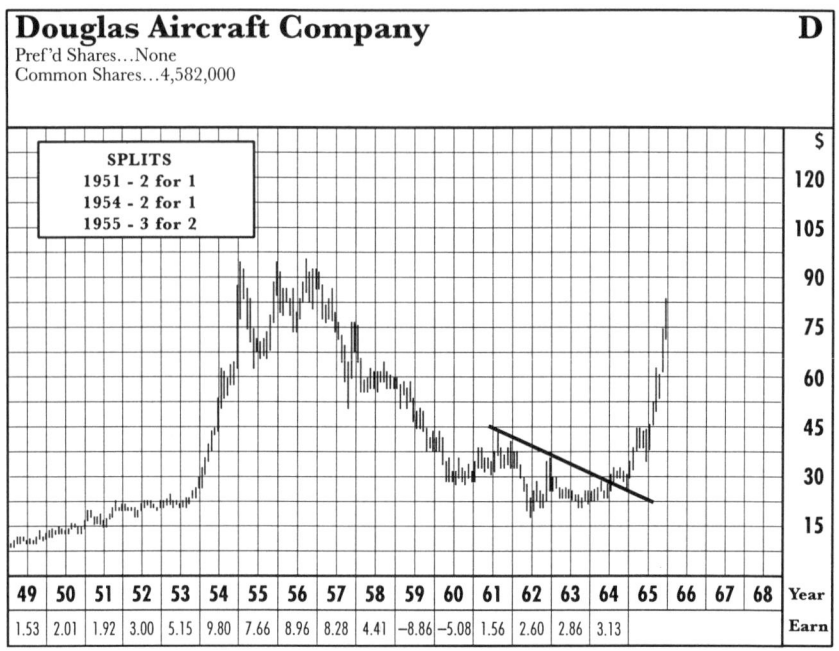

hovered at the two previous highs. Buying would have been very cautious. Plenty was lost by high-level investors who couldn't resist buying a "good stock."

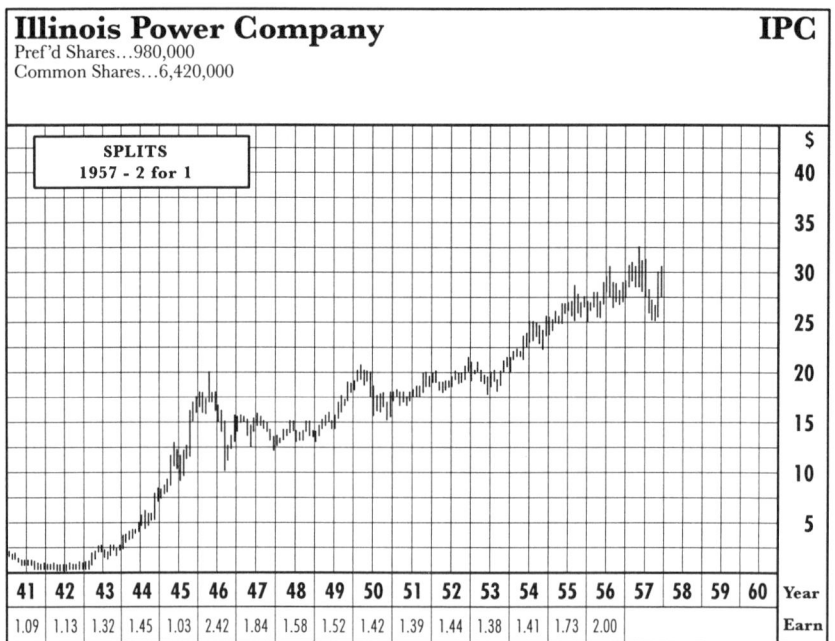

Illinois Power Company (IPC)

For at least six months during 1942, the public sold Illinois Power Co. (IPC) shares at an average of 50 cents a share. This after a sound record of earnings totaling $7.87 during the previous five years. It earned $2.26 in 1942.

If 1942 had been a depression year as was 1932, it could be conceivable that people would sell a sound stock at such a low price when many were forced to sell for various reasons, if only to eat. But 1942 was a period of fairly high employment because of the war plant activities. The public sold blindly from war fears and because the stock was so low. If, for instance, IPC had sold at around 5 during 1942, up from the previous level, no doubt fewer people would have sold. The low price depresses the public so thoroughly that they are induced into selling. Has this happened to you?

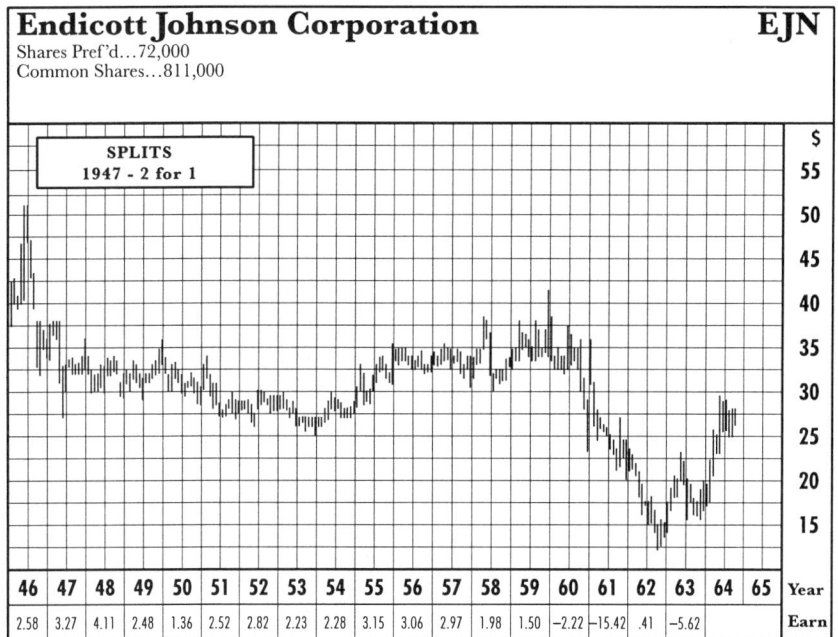

Endicott Johnson Corporation (EJN)

Endicott Johnson (EJN) had action in the past that could have worried an investolator. There was a six-year period of patient waiting with a small profit.

From a high of 51 in 1946, EJN dropped to a low of 25-1/2 in 1953, during an extremely quiet period. Although there were dozens of stocks at that time with better "pictures," an investolator may have bought this stock. The following double top above 35 appeared to be a false resistance level. Perhaps the insiders were moving EJN according to a long range plan for a large rise. But obviously someone saw storm clouds ahead in the way of heavy losses. For those with a 20-20 hindsight, a four-year deficit of $22.85 can now be clearly seen. But someone with a 20-20 foresight decided they wanted out. So a new plan was developed. First, I am certain that the fast breakaway above 35 attracted a large following. Failing to see the price carry through, in spite of heavy volume, speculators sold heavily and forced the price down to 30 where it was supported.

In 1959 too much activity developed at a time when EJN should have normally been moving up quietly, without exciting the public. Only a person with an understanding of market manipulation could have reasoned this out. One may wonder if the sponsors of EJN were entirely successful during 1959-60 in distributing their holdings before nervous selling developed into a break. The 12-point, fast rally from 23-1/2 was no doubt stimulated by reports right from the horse's mouth to the effect that this storm cloud that had now become visible to some of the public had a lot more silver lining on it than was visible to the naked eye. Someone, you can be certain, sold more stock on that $12 rally than they bought on the previous break.

After the $15.42 deficit report, the public continued to desert the sinking ship by tossing their stock overboard. After the stock was salvaged by those who knew what they were doing, that severe leak was miraculously stopped and another market cycle was well on its way.

Do not allow this example of EJN failing to carry on to its logical rise to frighten you into worrying that other stocks which you have bought may turn sour and do the same. If you bought during a sound base or consolidation you must hold with confidence. But, if a stock, at a time when it should be moving up quietly and unnoticed, should develop spasms of activity on the upside with very heavy volume, but is unable to make headway, you should realize that there is trouble ahead that is not yet visible over the horizon — to the public that is. To an experienced, long term chartist, storm clouds may be seen when the gyrations of a stock become too active at a time when it should be moving up quietly.

If you had sold at a time like this, because you were suspicious of too much volume and activity on the rise, at a time when it should have been moving up in a quiet, sluggish manner, and time proved your judgment was in error, your error was not so serious. You did avoid an unhappy market experience. In the meantime you probably saw another sound base and joined up with its insiders, uninvited, and unwelcome.

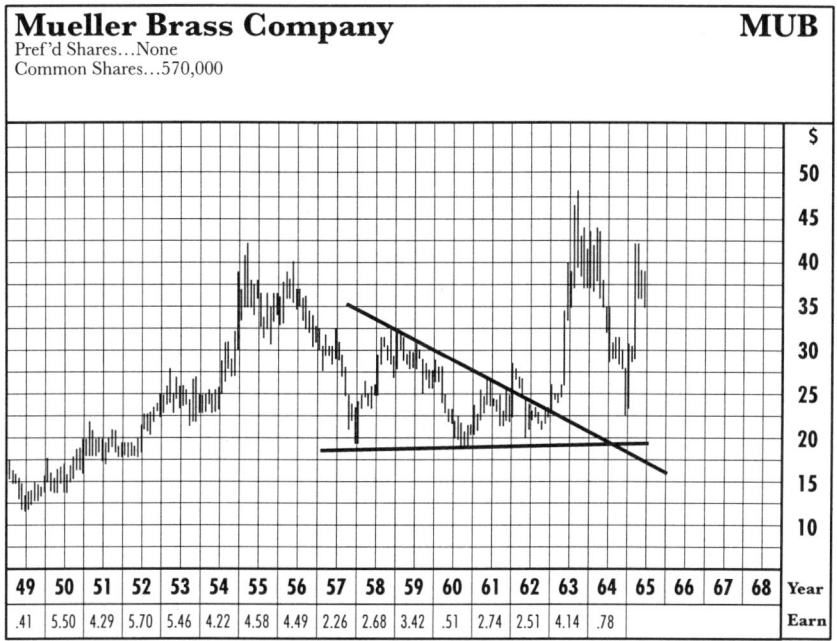

Mueller Brass Company (MUB)

A friend who has taken a deep interest in helping me write this book and also in the study of determining future trends of securities by the use of a chart book, drew my attention to the parallel of Mueller Brass (MUB) past action with that of Woodward Iron. He is doing just what I want the reader to do: Studying these charts closely and comparing. Certain past actions of stocks prove that others in the future will follow a similar action, with some variations of course.

A line drawn from the top in 1955 to the top in 1961 and one drawn from the low of 1957 to the low of 1962, form a perfect triangle. A sharp breakout on the upside in January, 1962, was quite possibly started by a rumor and subsequently denied. The price then sagged and broke sharply during the 1962 shakeout. You will seldom see an eight-year triangle filled out as completely as this one.

A chartist who quite logically bought Mueller Brass at 26 or 27 on the breakaway was given a bad time during the 1962 break. Taking an early loss here and buying back at a lower price would have been profitable. But if you had been frightened into selling at a loss, you would have been too frightened to buy back at a lower price and then would have lost your position.

This long triangle indicates a very sound formation and the buyer, as this broke out on the upside, should be prepared for a shakeout and should hold on with determination, knowing that this is a last attempt at frightening the public to sell out.

Normally, from a sound base such as this, I advocate holding for a 200 to 400% profit, depending on what price a steep uptrend line is broken, or selling after a very fast rise, no matter where this fast rise takes place.

MUB, you will notice, had an untypical action. It had a very fast start from a low range and a fast finish less than five months later. Because of a fast move like this, you must forget your objective of 200 to 400% profit. The public was given the "bait," they struck, and were hooked. You should recognize this after studying the many other fast starters and sell. This is no time to do wishful thinking that it may go higher. Logical thinking is what gives you the profits. No doubt it will go higher. But after this kind of a rise it may take years before it does. Now forget it, except on your next income tax return, and pick out another stock with a sound base or consolidation.

One wonders if there was a juggling of figures or inventory in 1963 which created high earnings of $4.14 that year, and perhaps depleted the normal earnings in 1964 which dropped to 78 cents. At least someone foresaw the drop in earnings and engineered that fast rise. There was apparent haste in unloading stock that had been bought during the triangle.

Mueller Brass has been absorbed by U.S. Smelting.

I like the picture of Woodward Iron better than MUB for a larger rise, but of course there will be a longer wait. In other words, its action during the eight-year triangle, appears more conducive toward worrying its shareholders, which appears to be the object at this time.

Julius Kayser & Company (JKS)

The fifteen-month quiet base of Julius Kayser (JKS) in the early '40's was the beginning of an investolator's dream come true: a 350% profit, plus an average of over 10% dividend per year, all by merely using mechanical stops. By instituting a stop buy at 5 on the breakaway, and by following a rising rounded trend line with a stop-sell order at 23, an extremely large portion was taken out of the middle of this move.

The various short consolidation periods on the way up, especially the false resistance level at 13 were meant to encourage you to sell. Nearly every person who sells out on the way up is a potential buyer at a higher level.

Note the increased earnings and higher dividends during 1947-48. The fact that the dividend was raised over 100% during this period was almost proof that this action above 15 was not accumulation. Seldom will a dividend be increased during a base. Name has been changed to Kayser-Roth Corp.

Checker Motors Corporation (CHC)

Checker Motors Corp. (CHC) completed a sound base in 1954 with two consolidations and a vicious shakeout in 1957. An investolator

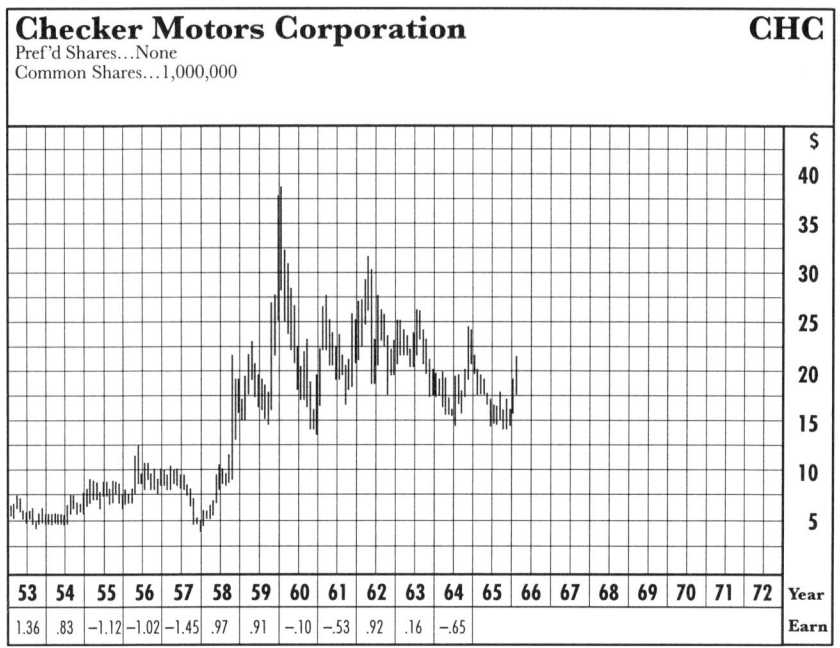

should have enough confidence in its previous action to prevent being panicked as many others were in 1957. The smart money picked up much stock on this shakeout. An investolator would have been tempted to sell on the 12-point fast rise. If he had held on, he should easily have decided to sell above 30 following its fast three-month rise.

On April 18, 1966 when this was written, only 100 shares of CHC were traded at 16-3/4. This light volume is a cue that it is under accumulation, but still subject to lower prices. A year or more of quietness, subject to a small shakeout or false downward move could indicate the final action of a base.

Chadbourne Gotham, Inc. (CGI)

In 1960 and early 1961 I bought Chadbourne Gotham, Inc. (CGI) because during 1960 its action positively indicated accumulation. The main base was formed in the 1956-58 period when it had a perfect, quiet downtrend ending with a twelve-month head and shoulders bottom at an average base price of about 2-1/4.

CGI developed a perfect uptrend line in 1961, and after selling at a high of 9-1/4, it broke the trend the following month as the 1962 panic selling began to set in.

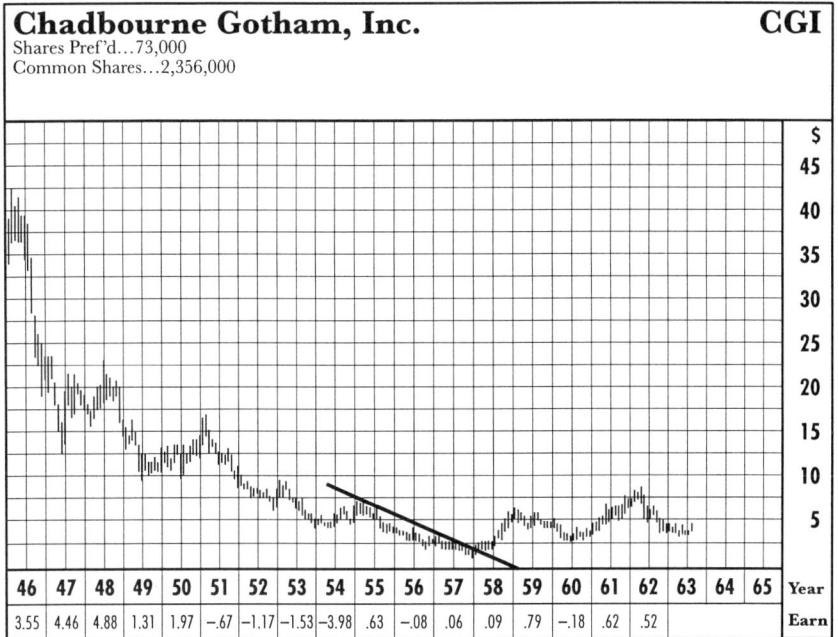

I failed to sell. Why? Partly because I had my sights set for a higher price, but mostly because during the time when it broke its uptrend in May at 7-1/4, I was in Sydney, Australia busily helping a caravan manufacturer build a camper for me. My wife and I toured 31,000 miles with this rig on a four-wheel drive pickup. No one in Australia had ever built such a camper before. I had taken the measurements of every piece in our American camper and indexed them. I knew from memory where almost each piece belonged.

Learning to drive the new pickup on the "wrong" side of the road with the steering column on the right side (but the "wrong" side, for me), outfitting our home on wheels of fifteen months, and then adventuring up the east coast was sufficiently distracting that I did not knuckle down to paying enough attention to the market.

In spite of my advocating selling a stock when it breaks an uptrend line of over 45 degrees, providing it had had enough of a rise from its previous base, I goofed by not selling CGI at above 7 in 1962 when it broke its uptrend. If the chart of CGI was on a 50 cent scale which would be proper in that price range, the uptrend would have been barely over 45 degrees. While I was well aware of the value of trend lines at this time, I had not yet formulated this rule of selling when a steeper than 45% uptrend is broken.

I was also aware, during the 7 to 9-1/4 range that a number of buying waves occurred with fairly heavy volume. This in itself does not prove that CGI could not have been run up much higher on heavier volume in the near future. But it should have alerted me that the breaking of this trend line could be important. But instead of a "doer," I became a "should have done it."

This is to prove to you, that a rule has no value unless you follow it. Avoid allowing other activities to interfere and dull your alertness when your stock has risen to a possible selling point. The trend line was there. I saw it. A stop-sell order at 7-1/4 would have been so simple. This order would have been triggered into an "at the market" sell order while we were camping and skindiving on a coral island off the east coast of Australia.

The only reason that you may be justified in not following this selling rule is when the volume obviously has not increased to an extent where distribution can possibly be taking place. If the volume is noticeably light, you will know that higher prices can be expected. Breaking a trend line then means only a normal reaction and consolidation of doubtful duration. It could be a toss-up then, whether it would pay to wait for a further rise or sell and wait for a new commitment to get underway.

As this book goes to press, CGI has established an additional sound base in 1964. It may be that the 1954-66 period is a long base. A cue as to whether this may be so will be if CGI holds quietly, perhaps around the 9 level for a year or more. This action would encourage profit taking at a time when it should be bought. Only time will tell. The final top from this base, should be well above 10.

As this manuscript goes to the printer, I do not advocate buying it as there are many better bargains at this time.

Fifty Predictions from Me to You

These predictions were made by me after the close of the stock markets on March 13, 1964 and upon receipt of the latest issue of my chart book. These will be sealed and mailed to myself, to remain unopened, until my book on long range chart reading is about to be published.

The Dow Jones Industrials are in a sharp uptrend, and have a very good chance of going above 900 before breaking this trend, then there will be a good shakeout or a good consolidation period or both. Then we will have perhaps the last fast final move. The final top cannot be made within three years. How much later, can only be a guess at this time, the DJI will go far higher than the average person can imagine. I am very doubtful that it can top out under 1200.

Most stocks will go much higher than they are today. And the average one will have a better rise percentage-wise than the averages. I cannot give any near term predictions on but a few of them, as most do not have that kind of clear cut pattern of action. Many of the stocks charted are still in a downtrend, many may stall, or react again before the big final move.

The figure following the name of each stock is the closing price on March 13, 1964.

A.J. INDUSTRIES. 2-7/8. Insiders sold on 1959 and 1960 fast rises. Now again under accumulation.

ALLEG. POWER. 53. Nice uptrend. Fast move ahead. When? Probably several years more.

ALLIED STORES. 60-3/4. Nine-year ragged consolidation period. May start up anytime. Hold for big rise.

AM. CEMENT. 10-1/8. Watch this. A year of extreme quietness below 10 would look like a good base.

AM. CHAIN & CABLE. 53. Very good cons. Big rise coming. Gen. Cable is now showing you how it is done.

AM. SNUFF. 24-1/4. With this terrific base and two-year consolidation at 20, should certainly have much higher to go.

ATCHISON & S.F. 28-5/8. Very good consolidation triangle. Strong move coming. Should remain in triangle another year. Could even drop below 25 as a false move before the start.

ATLANTIC THRIFT CEN. 5-1/2. Speculator could catch a good rally when breaking downtrend. Remember I said speculator. For the long pull, it may also be a bargain.

BELDING HEMINGWAY. 17. A seventeen-year bottom. What are the insiders waiting for? Trading is so thin that there were many days in the last six months there were no trades. Distribution cannot take place on this kind of volume, so it has to be accumulation. It appears that a big move is coming up.

BOND STORES. 16-3/4. This one is begging to be bought. A fifteen-year bottom and not yet complete. A recent twelve-week false base at 17 was broken last week when the quarterly dividend was cut from 31-1/4 cents to 25. This brought out fresh selling and it sold down to 16-1/2 last week. It no doubt will drop further this week, and someone will really pick up some bargains. After this news has lost its effect and is the cause of a final shakeout, it will then probably be sluggish on the upside and slowly break the upper trend this year. This is typical bottom action.

BORG-WARNER. 47. This flat topped triangle makes a "beautiful picture." This nine-year top is really wearing out the public. It is one of the best consolidation periods of all time. How few will see that it is a strong base? It may not go through 52 until 1965.

BRUNSWICK. 10-1/8. A speculator that insists on speculating could soon pick this up as it rounds out further.

CHADBOURNE GOTHAM. 2-7/8. Having good bottom action.

CHRYSLER. 48. This looks like a top from the appearance of both the daily and monthly chart. The rally now taking place, appears to be more of the top action and may carry through 50. Only the gullible would buy here.

COLLINS & AIKMAN. 32-1/4. Showing the results of a perfect eleven-year bottom plus a perfect two-year consolidation period. Profit should be taken any time that the uptrend is broken and proceeds put in a sleeper.

CONS. COAL. 55-5/8. It is being marked up nicely after nearly eight years of consolidation. Selling here would be far too soon.

CONT. BAKING. 56-1/2. The only question here—will it move up now, or continue to consolidate?

COOPER-BESSEMER. 32. May remain in triangle another year. The verdict is up, of course.

CROWN CORK & SEAL. 29. If you like living dangerously, this is a good one.

DANA CORP. 43. Perfect false resistance level. Not too high to buy.

DECCA RECORDS. 46. What's cooking here? Never saw anything like it.

DR. PEPPER. 53. Charting this daily. A rare piece of manipulation. It was marked up 200% in fifteen months, 19 to 57, without exciting the public. Very little increase in volume. I bought too soon on this base, but it was worth the wait. It is not yet high enough to attract the gullible. Doubt if it will top out under 80. When? I can only guess. Has been split 2-for-1.

EASTMAN KODAK. 130. Three-year head and shoulders bottom. A head and shoulders bottom does not have to be on the bottom. Need I say more?

EX-CELL-O. 38. Another good consolidation not too high to buy when it goes through 50.

FEDERAL PAC. ELEC. 7. Shaping up nicely. But is it too soon to buy?

GEN. CABLE. 71-1/2. This is a predicted move from a new base. Could stop here for its second wind, but I doubt that it needs to.

HAZEL BISHOP. 7. Hazel has a honey of a bottom curve, but is it complete yet? Hazel has one of the most depressing two-year bear markets ever recorded. Not a fair sized rally on the way down. Hazel's handlers certainly have picked up a lot of bargains around 5.

For a human Hazel Bishop to have attracted a crowd down on the beach, like Hazel Bishop, Inc. attracted a crowd in 1961, she would have had on something less than a bikini. What was the attraction? I don't read *The Wall Street Journal* or the dope sheets around the broker's office, so I don't know. Whoop! I almost said the dope sheets are only for dupes. Something must have appealed to the fundamentalists to buy from 20 to 43-1/2. I can't imagine a chartist buying in this range, unless he kept a daily chart and was an active trader as in futures. In that case he had better be pretty active, or else. Did the crowd think that because Hazel lost 72 cents in 1960, that the earnings could only improve in 1961? And if so it would go up in 1961, but the loss increased to $1.64. What went wrong here? Was there a single fundamental reason for setting off this buying wave that ran it up to 43-1/2? Can a fundamental reason be found for selling two years later below 5, when it earned 23¢?

For me it is easy to understand. It was done by well planned manipulation and no doubt some nicely scented reports were handed out that the outlook was rosy, etc., etc. And so, the old story of love turning to hate when Hazel dropped from 40 to 5.

HOTEL CORP. 2-7/8. Making a very attractive bottom. Perhaps too soon to buy.

KVP SUTH. PAPER. 29. This action can be considered the same as consolidation. Breaking the trend line on the upside will indicate the beginning of the big move.

NAT. UN. ELEC. 2-1/8. Two-year bottom appears too perfect to hold. Will almost certainly have a shakeout below 2, and could remain there several months. Should then be bought.

PEPSI COLA. 50. I chart this daily. Double top is part of a long consolidation coming up. Will go higher. I believe it is too soon to buy though. If in 1966, or later, it goes through 60, it should then be bought.

REVERE COP. & BRASS. 57. Turning up from a high base.

ST. JOSEPH LEAD. 59. This one is becoming very attractive. To the gullible that is. At 25, they were afraid of it. Now, a year later, it has become a wonderful stock at 59.

SEEMAN BROS. 7-3/8. Can you blame the insiders for running this one up and unloading to the public around 40? The next year there came a $3.62 deficit. They are now buying back at a huge discount. I have an impulse to sell another stock and buy this. I could do far worse.

SHELL OIL. 48. Appears to be breaking out of its shell. Its embryo should grow to 100 plus.

SHARON STEEL. 21-1/4. It is now tight against the downtrend line. The only question is (and only time will tell), will it break through now, or have another setback first?

UNION BAG-CAMP. 38. A very strong picture shaping up. But don't be left holding the bag at 80, after it tops out.

VANADIUM CORP. 13-3/8. The fourteen-month false, quiet support level has been broken. Should be bought here or when breaking trend. Expect change of trend soon. The very lack of rallying ability in this range is action that is very depressing, and worries the public into taking losses for fear it will go lower. This action does not just happen. It is guided this way for the purpose of appearing weak. Notice the waves of strength Vanadium had at higher levels. Those rallies were caused by temporary oversold conditions and baited the majority back in again. And this also, did not just happen. Now the stock is changing to strong hands.

Plenty of stock came out for sale around 14 during this false bottom. Then when selling slowed down, the price was let down merely by withholding purchases at this level, then a new wave of selling came out, caused by the support level being broken. Simple, isn't it?

WELBILT. 3. Bottom shaping up.

WOODWARD IRON. 27-1/4. Last but not least. Almost perfect triangle. Upper line now at 28. Buy in triangle or as it moves up through 29 or 30. Woodward then will go skyward.

You can see every type of action at this time. When you see them all moving up fast at about the same time, with extremely heavy volume, look out. Time to get out, and stay out.

JANUARY 16, 1965. Predictions on Dow Jones Industrials unchanged. Steep uptrend may hold for several months more. Uncertain.

Compare present comments on predictions of March 13, 1964. Figure following name is closing price on that date. Second figure is closing price on January 15, 1965.

A. J. INDUSTRIES 2-7/8 – 2-1/2. Very quiet under a perfect five-year downtrend. May be bought soon or wait for trend to be broken as shown in a stock chart book.

ALLEG. POWER. 53 – 29-1/2. Split 2-for-1. Prediction remains same.

ALLIED STORES. 60-3/4 – 69-1/2. Hold for higher price.

AM. CEMENT. 10-1/8 – 11-7/8. Bottom action appears incomplete.

AM. CHAIN & CABLE. 53 – 61-3/4. Rising slowly, which is proper at this stage. Gen. Cable is still showing how it is done.

AM. SNUFF. 24-1/4 – 28. Predictions more sound than in March. Previous base indicates far higher prices.

ATCHISON & S.F. 28-5/8 – 33-7/8. Strong move from consolidation triangle has begun.

ATLANTIC THRIFT CEN. 5-1/2 – 8-3/4. Recent high 10-1/8. Now subject to more reaction or a consolidation period.

BELDING HEMINGWAY. 17 – 19-3/4. Insiders still taking their time. Base appears better than ever.

BOND STORES. 16-3/4 – 22-1/2. Sold as low as 15-7/8 after dividend cut. Many of my friends bought this in the 16-1/8 – 1/2 range. Should easily cross 25 level this year, beginning its big move above 70.

BORG-WARNER. 47 – 50-1/2. Big rise may begin anytime now.

BRUNSWICK. 10-1/8 – 9. Has rounded out further. Heavy volume has me confused. Leave it for the speculator as previously suggested.

CHADBOURNE GOTHAM. 2-7/8 – 3-7/8. Expect a resistance level to develop at 4 for many months.

CHRYSLER. 48 – 60-5/8. Rose higher than I expected. The bears sold it heavily and gave it added strength. A perfect uptrend has developed. Beware when broken.

COLLINS & AIKMAN. 32-1/4 – 25-1/8. Did you sell as I suggested when uptrend was broken?

CONS. COAL. 55-5/8 – 53. Prediction still holds. Just having a normal setback or shakeout action.

CONT. BAKING. 56-1/2 – 55-1/8. Prediction remains the same.

COOPER-BESSEMER. 32 – 34-1/2. Triangle now complete. Big rise should begin soon. A perfect picture.

CROWN CORK & SEAL. 29 – 35-1/8. Very risky.

DANA CORP. 43 – 45-5/8. Acting sluggish. A healthy sign.

DECCA RECORDS. 46. Changed name or something.

DR. PEPPER. 53 – 28-3/8. Rose to 70, then split 2-for-1. Steep uptrend broken, but positively has not topped. Volume was too light. Based on new price, will rise to above 50, but not soon.

EASTMAN KODAK. 130 – 146-1/2. Action is proving the value of a head and shoulder bottom.

EX-CELL-O. 38 – 41-5/8. Consolidation appears more positive than ever. Exceptionally sound base.

FEDERAL PAC. ELEC. 7 – 10-5/8. It was not too soon to buy.

GEN. CABLE. 71-1/2 – 47-3/8. Equivalent to 118 before split. Not yet under distribution. Could sell soon and buy Borg-Warner, Belding Hemingway, Ex-Cell-O or Cooper-Bessemer.

HAZEL BISHOP. 7 – 9-5/8. Had fast rise. Immediate future in doubt.

HOTEL CORP. 2-7/8 – 3-5/8. Consolidating at 4.

KVP SUTH. PAPER. 29 – 29-1/2. Past fifteen months of quietness are cue that perfect 10-year downtrend may soon be broken.

NAT. UN. ELEC. 2-1/8 – 12-3/4. One-for-5 split. I cannot have confidence in the two-year perfect support level at 10. Appears phony to me.

PEPSI COLA. 50 – 61. Definitely going higher, but in spite of having broken the 60 level, consolidation does not appear complete. Pay strict attention to those "pictures" that show a period of quietness that indicate a consolidation phase has about ended. And act on them.

REVERE COP. & BRASS. 57 – 45-1/2. I was right too soon on this one. Had a false start. Do not sell.

ST. JOSEPH LEAD. 59 – 46-3/8. Split 3-for-2. This is now too risky to hold. May go higher but sell signal was given when long uptrend was broken. Others are begging to be bought.

SEEMAN BROS. 7-3/8 – 5-1/8. Appears to be in final quiet period before breaking upper trend line.

SHELL OIL. 48 – 58-5/8. Has broken out of its shell.

SHARON STEEL. 21-1/4 – 19-7/8. President Johnson's fracas with the steel companies has given an excuse for a last and final shakeout after having broken the upper trend line.

UNION BAG-CAMP. 38 – 35. Triangle nearly complete. Still a bargain when crossing 40.

VANADIUM CORP. 13-3/8 – 18-1/2. Near term uncertain, but long term higher.

WELBILT. 3 – 3-1/2. Now consolidating under 4.

WOODWARD IRON. 27-1/4 – 29-1/2. Rise is slow but positive.

There are many stocks that are in the early part of an accumulation stage, and may fluctuate in this low range for several years. Why buy these, perhaps far too soon, when there are others with sound bases, that appear ready for the big rise?

Don't hesitate to sell stocks that are up several 100% from their base, no matter how sound they are or how bright their future. A few more samples of predictions and comments.

ARMSTRONG CORK. 61. This may go higher, but steep uptrend line was broken in October. That was the cue to sell.

ASSOCIATED DRY GOODS. 67. Hold. In steep uptrend. Sell when trend line broken or after fast rise of $20.

BURLINGTON IND. 58-1/2. Sell when steep uptrend broken or after fast rise of perhaps $20.

CONS. CIGAR. 52. If you did not sell after fast rise to 65, you were expecting too much. That was 1200% above base of 5.

CURTISS WRIGHT 20. In accumulation phase. Too soon to buy?

EVANS PROD. 44. Sell after fast rise or when trend broken.

GEN. CIGAR. 48. High 79. Did greediness prevent you from selling on fast rise? Present picture on Am. Snuff similar to previous action on this one. Hindsight on Gen. Cigar gives you the foresight on Am. Snuff.

INTERLAKE STEEL. 34-1/2. Being moved up nicely from triangle.

MARATHON OIL. 66. This is what you can expect from a near perfect seven-year consolidation picture, during which the public was induced to sell out. Notice the resistance this had against the 1962 break. This proved technical strength. The stock was in strong hands. It is not yet high enough for the emotional speculators to buy.

At this time only a small percentage of stocks appear really dangerous. Many are in the buying range. Most are subject to reactions at any time, but if you tried to anticipate one, and sell, you would probably lose your position. Most will have a fair to large rise before this bull market has ended, which may be four to eight years ahead.

STOCK PREDICTIONS FOR 1966. These predictions are written during the 1966 Memorial Day weekend. The DJI has just had an eight-day 33-point rally to 874 with the volume dropping off to less than 5,000,000 share days, extremely light at this time. In my opinion, there is a strong possibility that the DJI will close below 800 with a selling climax on very heavy volume. Whether it does this or not, the end result will be the same, the market will rise above 1500. When? I can only guess. Perhaps within four years.

This opinion is based on the fact that so many stocks have positively not yet topped out. Many are undergoing accumulation. Many stocks are in strong hands, proven by the fact that only a few hundred shares a day are traded in them, sometimes none. In these stocks most weak holders have sold and there is little incentive for the public to buy. That incentive will come several years from now and 100 to 500% higher.

Following this present market break, watch for stocks that sell off on very light volume and are quick to recover. These are the ones that will show their technical strength by making new highs this year or early next, and will be headed for far higher prices.

These stocks appear to be in a process of making sound bases. Watch for that final quietness before turning up.

Acme Hamilton Mfg. Co.	L'aiglon Apparel, Inc.
American Cement Corp.	Lehigh Portland Cement Co.
American Dist. Co.	Libby-Owen-Ford Glass Co.
American Machine & Foundry Co.	Lionel Corp.
American News Co.	Seeman Bros., Inc.
Creole Petr. Corp.	Servel, Inc.
Desilu Prod., Inc.	Spencer Shoe Corp.

Drug Fair—Comm. A.
Duro-Test Corp.
Echlen Mfg. Co.
Edison Bros. Stores
Granite City Steel Co.
Hazeltine Corp.
Ideal Cement Co.

Stephan Co.
Suburban Gas
Talcott (James), Inc.
Tractor Supply Co., A
Univ. Controls, Inc.
U.M.S. Industries, Inc.

This list consists of a wide variety of high-level to near high-level bases or consolidation.

A year or more of quietness usually indicates that these bases are nearing completion; you may then become confident that the mark-up stage is about to begin.

Borg-Warner Corp.
Continental Motors Corp.
Cooper Industries
Crown Zellerbach Corp.
Dana Corp.
Eagle-Picher Industries, Inc.
Ex-Cell-O Corp.
Firestone Tire & Rubber
Inland Steel Co.

Keystone Steel & Wire Co.
Mack Trucks, Inc.
Mead Corp.
National Tea Co.
Phillips Petr. Co.
Revere Copper & Brass, Inc.
St. Regis Paper Co.
Union Camp Corp.
Woodward Corp.

All the above stocks appear to be forming various types of bases that have proven themselves in the past. These stocks can be safely purchased, providing that you ignore that final shakeout that may occur. Hold with patience and confidence for that major rise. Years later the vast majority of speculators may wish that they had bought these stocks instead of chasing the high-flyers.

These two stocks appear to be in the early stage of a high-level consolidation. Check these for a buy opportunity in the future.

Hercules, Inc.   Hershey Chocolate Corp.

PART THREE

Editor's Note to the 1998 Edition

In these final three chapters, Ted Warren applies his remarkable charting techniques to commodity trading. You may be surprised, and perhaps even a little amused, at the tone he takes when discussing commodities. He warns of the inherent dangers and decries the degree of manipulation. Readers should take all this with a grain of salt. After all, Mr. Warren himself titled the first chapter in this section "Poverty to Wealth: My Experiences in Futures" and, indeed, it was in futures that he began to build his fortune.

Also, keep in mind that in Mr. Warren's time, long-term commodity price charts were not easily available, which restricted the power of his charting methods. Today's technical trader has access to charts showing price activity over many decades. This allows easy identification of long-term trends and comparison of current and past prices. Additionally, new trading alternatives have been introduced, including mini-contracts and options, that considerably enhance a trader's ability to maximize profits and control risk.

I'm the first to agree that trading futures can be risky, especially for the uninformed. The key to successful trading is to use sound technical principles. I myself have made millions in the commodity markets using Mr. Warren's charting methods—applied in a way that keeps the risk within my comfort level. (I tend to be conservative with my money. I like to sleep nights.) I've taught this approach to more than 300,000 people around the world. Every day my office receives letters filled with success stories. My company publishes a 3-month course that explains, step-by-step, how anyone can build a fortune in commodities. For more information, call The Ken Roberts Company at (541) 955-2700.

Ken Roberts,
Grants Pass, Oregon

Poverty to Wealth: My Experiences in Futures

While this book has been written primarily for the benefit of those who are interested in the stock market, I think I would be remiss if I did not include a section on the commodity futures markets. My education and understanding of market manipulation and the psychology of the public came from the many years of speculating in commodities. During this struggle to success, using charts from which I formed my opinions in initiating a trade, my worst enemy was my emotions. When mine and my wife's hard earned money was involved, fear became my master. Too often fear caused me to take losses because I feared having to take larger ones. Fear can come under different disguises and the masters of manipulation are experts at instilling fears. I now realize that fear of missing a move was primarily my worst weakness, causing me to get into the market too often.

Fear of losing hard earned savings was deep rooted in my memory. I had lost over $1800 in my first battles with Wall St. ending before the stock market hit bottom in 1932. As a twenty-eight year old laborer, just emerging from a backwoods environment, with false confidence I headed into something of which I was completely ignorant. The timing of my entry into the art of speculation was untimely. If I had entered the market at a more favorable time I may have taken enough profits to have survived the ordeal of going broke.

During this time I was a worker on the assembly line in the Ford plant in Seattle. Production was eventually cut from 160 cars per day to 18 and to only one or two days a week; then the plant shut down, another victim of the depression. Previous to the shut-down, all production workers had been cut to $5.00 per day, still a high wage for those times. Saturdays and other times when the plant had been closed, I spent in the broker's office becoming acclimated and getting over the feeling of being a misfit in these surroundings.

It is easy to get acquainted in a broker's office. The tape watchers are easily drawn together by their misfortunes. One of my first acquaintances was a fellow who from time to time would explain to me about his pet subject, chart reading. This idea that he propounded about past actions of a stock having a bearing on future actions did not make sense to me at first. Finally, as he explained more about how these manipulated price swings of the market guide the fears and hopes of the public, I began to see through it, having experienced some of it myself.

A couple of fellows who were operating an advisory service called "The Graph-forecaster," and who published a weekly market letter based on their interpretation of charts, found that there were many who wanted to learn something about chart reading and arranged a number of evening classes of six lessons for fifteen dollars. I attended their first classes.

We were each given a textbook with charts of various stocks that showed the 1929 tops, the following break and the 1930 rally. With the use of a blackboard, our instructor showed the various main formations and many of the finer details, such as the importance of volume changes, and explained why this could show bullish or bearish tendencies. It was soon apparent to me the importance of manipulation in the market and the psychology of the public which is the basis for interpreting future actions of the market. This is a line of thinking so different from our normal way of life that perhaps this was the reason most of these fellows failed to grasp it. Most of the "students" were along in years. Perhaps the maxim that you can't teach an old dog new tricks held good in this case. Perhaps they had become set in their ideas of the market, while I had little to unlearn.

If I could have learned to overcome my natural optimistic thinking, and applied properly what I had been taught, I could very well have been far ahead instead of being broke, when the bear market ended in 1932. But I had to start THINKING and went against some of the rules I was taught, partly because I lacked the confidence in my ability to judge what I really interpreted by the chart action. If I had entered the market at a more favorable time my money may have held out long enough for me to acquire enough experience to avoid going broke.

I can't recall the trades I made during this period, but most of my losses were in Case Threshing Machine. Several times after it dropped, and I had taken another loss, it would move sidewise with an upward tendency, for from two to five weeks. I was taught that this type of action should be considered to be a continuous formation, meaning that it will turn downward again. This same formation in reverse often applies the same way in a rising market.

Very seldom in those days did a stock move counter to the general market. An exception was Auburn Auto. They were ballyhooing the Cord car, named after the president of the company. It had a front wheel drive and for awhile sales on it were fairly brisk, which sparked a speculative spree. The price of its stock rose from below 100 to 217, when it made what I thought was a good top. I was charting it daily, and after seven days it had moved sidewise enough to break the upward trend line. I sold short. It dropped 30 points, 17-1/2 of it in one day. It then formed a perfect eleven-day triangle and I interpreted this to indicate it would have another rise from here, and took a profit, one of the few profits that I took in this bear market. But I did not have the nerve to back up my opinion with a purchase. These two opinions showed that I was catching on. While the Dow Jones averages kept dropping, Auburn Auto rose from 185 to 295 in four weeks. On the way up it stopped long enough to form a seven-day triangle and again I predicted it would continue up. But again I lacked the nerve to follow through.

It became natural for me to go back to losing money in my favorite stock, Case Threshing Machine. When it fell below 50 I began convincing myself that people would not sell below these prices. But they did. What I had not learned was that the public will sell at any price when they are scared, or when they are pressed by margin calls, or for many normal reasons when they are in dire need of cash. As the depression came on, these reasons became all too numerous.

During this period of idleness I went to the library and copied wheat futures quotations from the newspapers for years back and charted them for study after realizing that profits in the commodity markets could be made far faster than in the stock market. These charts proved to my satisfaction more than ever the value of studying market manipulation. Some of those years showed the smoothness of control during months of a quiet bottom, the markup with increasing speed, and then the fast spurt which could be called the sucker bait, followed by boiling action of sometimes only a matter of days when the insiders sold out to the excitable speculators. And then of course prices fell off and again the traders would take their losses and wonder what went wrong.

March 4th to 15th – Exchange Closed – Bank Holiday

If there is anyone in doubt about our markets being manipulated I think the eighteen-week head and shoulder bottom of 1932-33 is proof beyond question. The timing could not have been more perfect. I remembered that there had been a frenzy of buying on the August and September double tops, and had heard it said that on one of those days, there had been the heaviest trading in wheat futures that had ever taken place in one day. Such is the power of manipulation, that speculators were influenced into a buying spree, that easily overwhelmed the normal movement of actual wheat to the elevators. In fact, this bullishness of the speculators I am sure rubbed off a good deal on the farmers and no doubt many of them held back on their deliveries of wheat in expectation of higher prices, as always happens at a top. Notice a nearly perfect head and shoulder bottom. After the rebound from the head of this formation, May Wheat settled down to 7 weeks of quietness. Note that there was Saturday trading at that time. Then after the final setback in this period, it broke out on the upside on March 3rd. The next day the market was closed because of President Roosevelt's inauguration. Then Roosevelt declared the bank holiday and all markets were closed. On March 13th the market reopened and wheat opened much higher and trading soon stopped up the limit of 5 cents. Roosevelt announced plans to pay the farmers to curtail wheat production. The next morning May Wheat opened higher, but closed weak and the previous enthusiastic buyers were inclined to sell on the following perfect shakeout. Wheat then rose on the Roosevelt boom to near the $1.25 level. Can anyone deny that the timing of this eighteen-week head and shoulders bottom wasn't planned many months ahead? Even the August and September tops were timed at an unusual season so that there was time for the decline and accumulation period to take place before Roosevelt took office. The Roosevelt plan for the reduction of wheat acreage was obviously well known to the insiders and they had the market well prepared for the bullish news. The insiders of Winnipeg wheat futures were also in on the secret plans. Their May wheat did not have the same bottom action as Chicago but no doubt had the same bearish effect on the traders, and the timing coincided with Chicago. It had its false resistance level at 49, giving the impression it could not go higher. But it did during the Chicago closed period. Then it had a perfect shakeout after the Chicago market reopened, heading for much higher prices.

There was a 4 cent break on December 16th. I was told by a Canadian that this was the culmination of a manipulated deal that not only forced many traders to sell out because of margin calls, but also forced the Canadian farmers indirectly to sell millions of bushels of their wheat right at the lowest prices. As he explained it to me, the Canadian banks had loaned the farmers 18 cents a bushel on millions of bushels, at around 55 cents. This amounted to almost the same as an 18 cent margin on the purchase of futures. The farmers were led to believe that this would take much of the pressure off the market and wheat would then sell at higher prices later on. But, as always, when it seems obvious to the majority that a certain action may take place, they are wrong. No doubt the traders were aware of these wheat loans and because of this, were bullishly inclined and were long. That apparently is what stabilized Winnipeg wheat at 55 in October.

When this 4 cent break took place, the banks called in their loans because the price had now dropped nearly as much as the loan. Few farmers were able to meet the call, so were forced to sell at once, similar to a margin call. Most of this of course was hedged by dealers and millers by selling short in futures and the insiders then were able to buy these on the bargain counter. Because of freight rates, the price of wheat on the farms averaged several cents lower than the price quoted on futures at Winnipeg. The farmers were actually speculating just as much as the bulls were in the futures market.

In May, 1933 I received a wire from Alberta, Canada, that my Mother had a nervous breakdown. That wire no doubt changed the whole course of my life. I had been going steady with a young lady for nearly two years. She was working for $30 a month as a housemaid. In my financial straits I had no thought of marriage, but now I could not bear the thought of going to Canada without her.

I tossed all the vague ideas that I had in the past about being financially independent before getting married, and proposed at a time that I was probably the most dependent in my life. But I guess we both thought we didn't have much to lose. At least this way, we would not lose one another. We were married as soon as we could make arrangements. She had enough money for her ticket and I borrowed some from a friend working at Boeing for part of mine and we were on our way.

My stepfather had passed away in 1931 and left my Mother with a small general store which they had opened about three years earlier when they quit the farm. They had homesteaded near the community of Tomahawk, Alberta, in the spring of 1912 when I was nine years old. They migrated to Canada from South Dakota where Dad had been the proprietor of a hotel in a small town. He had become an alcoholic and lost the business. Dad built our first log shack in early spring, on a flat area over the snow with poor drainage. When the snow melted and the ground thawed out we were in mud. A crude floor of straight jack pine poles was hurriedly put in. These we packed on our shoulders from a muskeg "island" nearby. Our bunks were made of poplar poles and were covered with hay for a mattress. Flour sacks were in place of glass for two of our three windows. We owned a few chickens and held a half interest in a cow with an English bachelor neighbor.

Because my parents were cooking for a crew in a railway tie camp the previous winter, and because of the lack of a school in this district, I missed three years of grammar school. But I certainly acquired a thorough education in the school of hardship while pioneering in this cold climate. I learned how to work and knew the value of a dollar. As a boy I became an expert with the axe, chopping and splitting wood for our stoves. One winter I ran a day-and-a-half trap line twice a week for weasels, wading in snow through the woods and stopping overnight with a bachelor in his cabin. This was a great experience for me. It was an education in self-reliance.

When my wife and I arrived in Alberta, we luckily found my Mother's condition was not as serious as the wire implied. Her neighbors had been very helpful. Waiting on customers, many of them old acquaintances, was a new experience for me. Here I had an insight into what the depression really was like. My Mother, a very generous person, had extended credit beyond her means and was deeply in debt to the wholesalers. Many Ukrainians had recently settled on nearly worthless wooded homesteads nearby, where I had formerly hunted moose and trapped weasels. Most of them were destitute. They came into the store with $10 relief checks per month for a family. It was illegal to sell them anything purchased with this money except absolute necessities, a list of which was furnished by the government. My Mother paid 5 cents a dozen for eggs—and lost the amount of 30 cents a crate, for the truckers' freight charges to Edmonton—a subsidy she could ill afford.

In a couple of months, my Mother had fully recovered and I was wondering where I could earn some money. In August I joined two friends who were sons of Russian neighbors in the early days of homesteading. We headed for the prairie harvest field in a truck one of them owned. They had some business to attend to in Edmonton and I took advantage of this stop to go to the library and copy the last three months of Chicago and Winnipeg wheat futures quotations from the local newspaper bringing my charts up to date. I found the Roosevelt boom in wheat had topped out in July and had made a four-day break. Wheat futures rallied from this break and had now nearly completed a triangle, which to me was obviously distribution. The price would break out on the downside from the apex of the charted triangle. Later, when I rejoined the fellows, I showed them the chart and lamented the fact that I knew what the wheat market was going to do next, but that I had no money to back up my opinion. I explained to them how I could make money by selling short. They were not the only ones that have had difficulty in understanding how you can sell something you don't own. It turned out that a short sale here would have been perfect.

WINNIPEG WHEAT PEGGED TRIANGLE. We three landed a job harvesting with various farmers near Killam. Because of the tremendous unemployment, we considered ourselves fortunate. A railway passed close to where I worked and every day the freight trains carried dozens of men looking for work. Younger generations cannot visualize how bad conditions were in those days. In normal times there was more likely to be a labor shortage in the harvest fields.

The farmer I was working for subscribed to *The Edmonton Journal,* and I was keeping my Chicago and Winnipeg wheat charts up to date and studying them as if I had thousands of dollars involved. Wheat had broken sharply for three days from the apex of the triangle as I

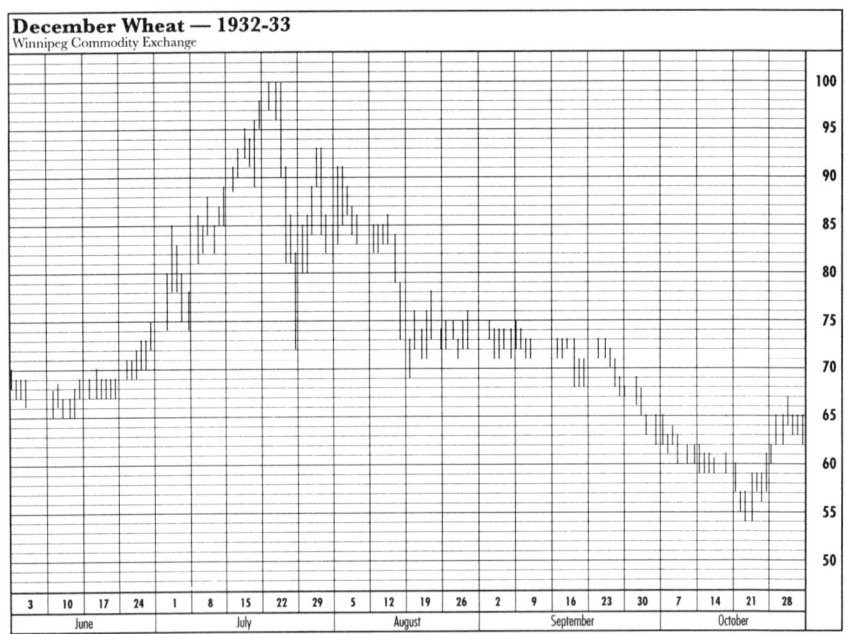

had anticipated. The Canadian government pegged the price of wheat futures at the closing price of the third day. That, on the face of it, seemed to be a fine thing to do. Both the speculators and the farmers were being protected from a further drop. The farmers' price is controlled by the futures gyrations. The farmers had plenty of praise for this decision to protect their income, which had already shrunken to an extremely low level.

On a rainy day toward the end of the season, the thresherman stopped in to chat with this farmer whom I was working for. Of course the price of wheat was an important topic of their conversation. I happened to be a listener. After a while I joined them on the subject. I felt sure that they would be interested in what I had to say. I told them that I thought the government was going to pull the peg about next Monday. This was on a Wednesday. They were polite enough not to say what I am sure they thought. Here I was an American, working ten hours a day for $1.50 per day when it wasn't raining, trying to tell them what their government was going to do. That peg, they argued, was put there for their benefit. My reply was, "That's what you think." To try to prove my point, I invited them into the bunkhouse to see my wheat chart. I showed them the triangle which had formed with a flat bottom following a three-day break. I pointed out the various rallies from the pegged price, with each succeeding rally being less than the previous one. I asked them who they thought was doing the buying during these rises. They said they had no idea, which was the answer I expected. After all they were not expected to have any knowledge of this sort. I explained to them that it was my opinion that the speculators were buying here with confidence because obviously there was only one direction the price could go. It just could not go down. Then I asked them that providing I was right, who then, did they think was doing the selling? Again they had no idea. If they had ever given thought to the subject they probably would have had only a vague idea that the buying and selling in a future market was merely a difference of opinion among the traders. I told them that I felt sure that the insiders were doing the majority of the selling and if I was right, the market must be going down. Then I gave them a little lecture on how markets are manipulated. I never knew if they caught on to the idea or not. Nor if they were in any degree convinced that the peg would be pulled. I was right, except in timing. The peg was pulled the following Thursday, instead of Monday just when Chicago wheat was having a strong rally. Winnipeg wheat declined over 15 cents a bushel from here, which was a very large drop, percentage-wise, at these low prices.

To my credit, I analyzed what was transpiring in this triangle very easily. I was catching on to the science of chart reading, the understanding of manipulation and the guided thoughts of the unwary. It was so obvious to me that the peg was rigged for the benefit of the insiders, not the farmers. They sold short to the confident speculators who had faith in their government. Probably few ever realized that they had a fast one pulled on them.

When we finished harvesting, I continued to work for 50 cents a day and board, cutting green poplar into stove wood, during the ten days I was waiting for threshing to start. I then worked with this crew for $2 a day driving a bundle team. In the meantime my wife was doing housework for a school teacher and her family at Wabamun that I had known for years, at $8 a month. They treated her like one of the family.

We were working illegally in Canada, as we were there as visitors. I did not have a guilty conscience as I felt that Canada owed me the right to earn a few dollars in return for the years of pioneering on the homestead.

After threshing ended I was idle until a small portable sawmill began operating in the open woods near my old home district, a short distance from Gainford. I landed this job only because I was well known there. My wages were 15 cents an hour. After the 75 cents per day charge for board and 10 cents for accident insurance, I had $3.15 clear for a 60-hour week. I was on the night shift and some mornings it was forty degrees below zero when we went to breakfast.

I was given the job of canting, which is rolling a log onto the carriage and turning it from time to time on signal from the sawyer. For a while after we had a thaw, snow melted and the water froze on the underside of the logs leaving a coat of ice where the warm air had failed to reach. Because of this, twice a log rolled out from under the dogs just after the first slab had been cut and the carriage had started back. The circular saw would catch the log and toss it at us. Luckily we were able to see the impending danger and avoid being struck by ducking out of its line of flight. Each time the log struck a gasoline lantern hanging above the sawyer's head.

We slept in a log shack that had been occupied the previous winter by another crew and we became lousy at once. We could only believe the lice had survived from the previous winter. The sawmill owner built a new, clean shack of green lumber and tarpaper. We boiled our clothing, moved in, and were free of lice.

In April, my wife and I hitch-hiked to Sweetgrass on the Montana border. Hitch-hiking on Alberta highways was easy in those days. In these distressed times people were quite sympathetic toward a couple heading out from these prairie towns with a couple of suitcases. We had one hitch in our hitch-hiking. American Immigration restrictions had tightened and I had insufficient proof of American citizenship. I had no birth certificate as my Danish parents had failed to register my birth in Louisiana. I sent a letter to my Mother asking her to sign an affidavit which would allow me to enter the U.S. My wife continued on by train to her parents' small farm near Big Sandy, Montana.

I now had a wait of over a week because of slow mail service to my Mother's district. I visualized this as being a very monotonous wait, but it didn't turn out that way. A fellow at the boarding house where I had already settled down in Coutts, on the Canadian side from Sweetgrass, told me that his brother the day before had mentioned that he was about to start a fencing project. He lived about thirty miles out on the main highway toward Lethbridge. His brother needed a man but did not have anyone in mind. It was now about two hours before dark and I figured that I could still make it that day. I hurriedly packed my suitcase, and five blocks later I was out of town trying to hitch a ride. I had been warned that no one would pick me up after dark, but I thought I had plenty of daylight left to make it in. Traffic was light in those days, and not one car came my way until after dark, and it would not stop. I kept on walking until about eleven o'clock. By this time I was really weary. When I saw the outline of a house ahead about two hundred yards from the road, I angled off toward it. They had no electric light and when a couple opened the door I could not see what they looked like nor see inside. At first they thought I was a motorist who had suffered a breakdown and they seemed hospitable. But when they found out I was a hitch-hiker, they froze. They didn't have an extra bed. I asked if they had a rocking chair or something I could rest in until daylight. No, they didn't have a rocking chair. I asked if they had a barn with a hayloft that I could sleep in. No, they had no hayloft. Was there a straw pile nearby where I could spend the rest of the night? No.

I headed at another angle back to the highway. Then, within two hundred feet, I spotted a straw pile in the darkness. I started to claw myself a hollow spot to lie down in when I found that this straw stack was probably at least two years old because six inches of the top surface was loaded with soil that had been blown in by these southern Alberta dry winds. I dug down to clean straw and made myself a comfortable bed. I now had an idea that was new to me. I slipped on a work shirt that I had in the suitcase, buttoning the collar button above my head and the fourth button under my chin. This at least kept the straw out of my ears. But I was unable to sleep as quickly as I wished. I had to get used to the mice rustling under my head.

I arrived at my destination in time for a late breakfast. This small rancher-farmer had not yet picked a man. He agreed to pay me $1 a day and I went right to work. This fencing job only took us five days, so I was ahead $5 in wages and saved more than that in board. I guess I learned about high finance from that!

Back at Coutts, I did not have long to wait for the affidavit from my Mother which was acceptable by the American Immigration. I now felt as if I was entering a new life.

I hitch-hiked to Shelby. From there I rode a freight train to Havre and again took to the highway to Big Sandy. It was a happy reunion with my wife and I now met her family for the first time.

Within a week I found a job helping to open up a "gopher hole" coal mine at $1.50 per day and board. Some time later my wife located herself a job as a maid with a wealthy family on a large ranch and was soon promoted to cook.

We were now able to earn some money, slowly to be sure, but could save a fair amount of it. We were quite unhappy over the fact that we were unable to live together. I was anxious to test myself in the market, any market. A chart formation on oats appeared good and I sent $125 to a broker in Great Falls with an order to buy one job of Chicago oats futures. When I received the confirmation I also received a bad scare. The broker had bought 2,000 bushels with the explanation that jobs of oats were in multiples of 2,000 instead of 1,000 as in other grains. That left me with a very narrow margin of 6-1/4 cents a bushel instead of 12-1/2. Without a stop-loss order I could have lost most of the $125 very quickly if my judgment was wrong. Oats moved up, but I made only $85 on this trade because the top was a very fast thrust type, and because of slow newspaper quotations out in the country I missed a good part of it. But this $85 profit did accomplish something besides increasing our small savings. It gave me some confidence.

I spent the latter part of the winter feeding cattle on a ranch, pitching hay from a stack into a hay rack, then, as the team of horses pulled the load across an open field, I pitched the hay onto the ground. Twice, in spite of my vigilance against the cold, I had frozen cheeks.

Between our savings and a couple of fair profits in wheat we had nearly $700 in our account with the broker in the spring of 1935. We quit our jobs and went to Great Falls with the hope that I could find steady work which would enable us to live together for a change. This bright hope had a sudden death. Ten days later, before I found work, the broker's office closed. The owner had been speculating in wheat with his customers' money and gone broke, then skipped town. We had $16 in cash and no job. We had to start all over again.

My wife quickly found work as a housemaid, and I went to an employment agency and found that a "good" tractor man was wanted on a farm. I knew I would be a good man on a tractor if given a chance. I had been around gas engines a good deal, was well acquainted with horse drawn farm implements, and was sure that tractor drawn equipment would be no problem. For the only time in my life I lied myself into a job. When I was asked what tractors I had handled, I quickly named three common makes. That did it. I was given the job.

It was too late in the day to catch the train to Square Butte and I had to wait until the next day. The only problem facing me in this work was being able to start a tractor without showing my ignorance. I went to a couple of farm implement dealers pretending I was a prospective buyer, hoping to learn something that would help me. I learned little about starting a tractor. I doubt that I appeared very genuine.

My employer turned out to be an old Dane. The first morning he helped me service the tractor and showed me exactly how to start it. I was really in luck. If, instead, he had merely pointed at the tractor and said "There it is," I would have been in trouble. He rode one round with me plowing the field and left. I made very sloppy turns on the first two corners. But from then on I had everything under control.

During the next winter I got so tired of doing nothing and baching in a small housekeeping room in Great Falls (my wife was living in the home in which she worked) that I took a job in March on a small cattle ranch up in the mountains. This turned out to be about the most miserable job I ever had. To start with, the rancher's wife was away on a long trip and the rancher was a very poor cook, and a sourpuss as well. As a conversationalist he was a complete dud.

Here I became a cowboy midwife to a bunch of half-wild Hereford cows that were dropping their calves in over a foot of snow. Some mornings it was below zero. My chore in the morning was to haul hay and spread it in an open field. If I noticed a cow standing by herself in the distance, I would later on ride horseback out there to see how the calf was doing. If it was not surviving the cold I would hang it across the horse in front of the saddle, while its mother stood wild-eyed. After mounting I would lift it back onto my lap and we would ride to the barn, over a mile distant. There is no chance of a cow, even a tame one, following you, because by now, she has lost sight of her calf. After leaving the calf in the barn, I would return for the cow. Trying to drive a half-wild cow away from where her calf was born was no easy task, especially when my horse was no better as a cowpony than I was as a cowboy. By the time I would get her in the barn, she was no longer half wild, she was all wild. And invariably so was I.

After a month of this I returned to Great Falls and in May I went to work on the construction of the spillway on the Fort Peck Dam as a laborer at 50 cents an hour. I was soon promoted to carpenter's helper at 70 cents on a crazy shift, beginning at three a.m. We lived in barracks that held thirty-two beds. With all three shifts mixed, it was a problem getting enough sleep. Because of the heat, I got very little during the day. A group of noisy young fellows working on the day shift made sleep impossible sometimes until eleven p.m. Then, eating breakfast at two a.m. I merely went through the motions.

While studying and keeping up my grain futures charts, I was exposed to the comments and occasional sarcasm of others. The usual remark after a long monotonous explanation of what the charts were for, was, "If you know how to beat the market, what are you doing working here?" My answer of course would be that I had to work in order to save money for this purpose. In those days I was not critical of anyone who was skeptical about this ability that I claimed to be developing. I certainly had no visible proof.

While working on the Fort Peck Spillway I missed most of a good rise in wheat. The top of this move turned out to be the beginning of a near perfect fifteen-week consolidation period. Following this top there was no real break in the next four weeks. But the action was the kind that worried the bulls. The three-week following rally had an action about it that did not excite them much either. It stopped just short of the previous top.

Turning down from here was the beginning of the process designed to convince the traders that it could not go up. The following weeks of this pattern became very quiet and really dulled the enthusiasm of the bulls, so much so that no doubt a great many turned bearish and sold short.

At this high level, compared to the previous summer, the price of wheat could not stay up so quietly, for so long, unless there was sound buying coming to the market. The nervous selling by the public would have pushed it down for the simple reason that there was little incentive to buy. There had to be, which meant it must be going up.

I had already recognized this situation three weeks before it was completed when I returned to Great Falls after the Fort Peck job closed down because of wintry weather. In the broker's office I found a very bearish atmosphere toward the grain market. Here are a few of the market comments from the *Great Falls Tribune* that appeared from October 19 to November 6, 1936. They were certainly designed to take the heart out of the bulls.

> "It was estimated that export taking of Canadian wheat amounted to but 500,000 bushels. Talk was current that importing countries had apparently acquired sufficient wheat to cover needs until it is more definitely known what will be the southern hemisphere's probable crop outcome."
>
> "Reports of rains benefiting wheat crops in Argentina and Australia were a notable bearish factor. One trade authority predicted that the exportable surplus from the present wheat in Argentina would be possibly 90,000,000 bushels more than the last crop."
>
> "A tendency to raise estimates of Australia's wheat this season was apparent."
>
> "One unofficial forecast issued today said returns pointed to about 11% larger winter wheat acreage in the United States than last year. Widespread rain and snow throughout the United States grain belt together with pronounced weakness in the Liverpool wheat market had considerable bearish effect too on Chicago wheat values."
>
> "Secretary Wallace's suggestion that in the United States the

coming season may produce a wheat crop of 900,000,000 bushels, a total equaled twice only in the last 10 years, received considerable notice."

"Reports are that the Argentine Government is likely to abolish the Argentine minimum price for wheat."

This last item was on the last day of a four-day shakeout—during this fifteen-week consolidation period that had positively false upper resistance level. With this outpouring of bearish comment and the manipulated actions of the market giving the appearance that the line of least resistance was down, small wonder that there was such bearish sentiment around the broker's office. These bearish implications, like mudslinging in politics, are bound to stick.

You can be sure that all these items were not written by an ordinary reporter. They were written by one who was highly skilled in the art of "How to Influence the Speculators in the Wheat Market."

These comments only backed up my opinion that the wheat market was building up a strong base as the past actions were indicating. This was the first time that I had the opportunity to "play" the market when my opinion was positive beyond all doubt.

As the wheat futures were beginning to break out on the upside, they began to undo the bearish image that they had created in the minds of the speculators. As the market rose the bullish tempo of the comments increased to such an extent that any bearish item that appeared would be totally ignored by the majority of traders.

And so, combined with the optimism generated by the fast rising market, the majority of traders will have discovered that they bought in the top range, *as usual.*

This was my first experience on this kind of formation, and luckily as a chartist I understood it perfectly. I understood it so well, and my enthusiasm was so great, that I was losing sleep while anticipating this move. Strangely, over the years, I cannot recall losing sleep when I was in trouble in the market. Sometimes when worried, I would sit up until the early morning hours (this is not what I meant by not losing sleep), studying my charts and comparing daily swings of past actions, trying to decide whether to take a loss or sit tight, or place a stop-loss order. After coming to a decision I seldom had trouble going to sleep.

I cleared over $500 on this move, which today does not seem like much. But it was a lot of money to my wife and I in those days, after the small wages we had worked for. Our future now was brightening considerably. But before the next perfect formation came up I had lost part of this profit, some of it in the stock market. I also spent another idle winter, except for doing some of the cooking and housekeeping. My wife was doing hourly work in some of the better homes, so this winter I was not baching although I did part of the cooking and housekeeping. At least we were able to settle down and live together.

On August 31, I regained my courage and bought 5000 bushels of Chicago wheat, barely getting under the wire before the close. Examine the chart on soybeans action. In studying the grain futures actions previous to the breakout of World War II, doesn't the timing of these bottom actions indicate that the insiders knew what was going to happen? The previous seven weeks' action of soybeans had a very depressing influence on the speculators. Good accumulation action. On August 24 there was heavy selling against a public buying wave, and the final shakeout developed from here when a temporary political calm set in on the European scene. Then suddenly an overwhelming buying wave developed as the war broke out, and for three days soybeans rose higher and higher with 4 cent gaps, the allowable limit, then another gap of 5 cents when the limit had been increased a cent. On Friday, September 8th the insiders sold heavily, stopping the rise, which encouraged so much pent up profit taking the next morning that

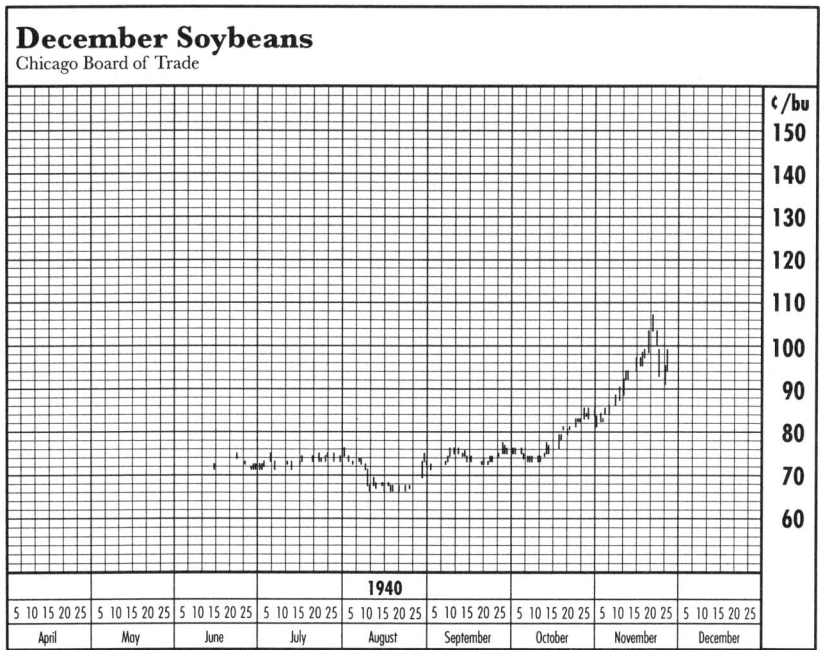

it opened down with a nearly 4 cent gap, and closed 6-1/2 cents lower after the limit move for one day had been increased to 8 cents per day. The very lack of activity which usually takes place in a top range and the quickness with which the price turned down again, was proof that this was not a distribution top. This quick reaction was brought about for the purpose of deflating the enthusiasm of the bulls. Nothing accomplishes this better than falling prices.

The following action was very discouraging to those who were long on soybeans. By now, the majority were thoroughly convinced that they had been wrong. Again, when the obvious impression was that soybeans could not go up, they did. Their uptrend began six weeks before wheat and rye. This uptrend had three short consolidations that I easily recognized.

I sold my 5000 May wheat in the top range following the fast rise. The next day, we went shopping for a new car. We decided on a new 1940, red Oldsmobile with radio and heater for $1200 cash. We had been married for over six years without owning even a jalopy. Now we had the means of enjoying some of the pleasures in life that we had been missing.

The next evening I paid for the car by check which I drew from the broker. But I overlooked endorsing it and the following day the salesman brought it to where I was working on the construction of the Civic Center Building. At the time I was stripping lumber from concrete forms high on a scaffold above the stage of the auditorium. The labor foreman tossed the end of a weighted rope up to me, and I pulled up a bucket with the check in it and endorsed it.

In Great Falls I had been keeping it a secret from friends and fellow workers that I was speculating in futures. Some of the workers had gone so far as to razz me for being too cheap to buy a car. After this check episode spread among fellow workers I happily admitted that I had just made a killing. The usual comment was, "Boy, you're lucky."

Of course it was natural for them to think of it as being luck. To some of them I took the time to admit that I was lucky. Lucky that I had a wife who was as thrifty as I, willing to work at low wages to help save money in order to speculate, willing to do without even an old car, and to attend only second-run movies. Lucky that I happened to have the opportunity to take lessons in chart reading, based on the study of market manipulation and the psychology of the public, and lucky that

I was young enough at the time to grasp this unusual type of thinking. Lucky that I was willing to study my charts far into the night at times and during the weekends. And above all I was lucky to recognize that "Fact" is a dictator and to abolish wishful thinking.

After my construction labor job we decided to spend the winter of 1940-41 in California. We settled down in Santa Monica. This was an enjoyable experience for we Northerners. I did well enough in the market that I did not go back to construction work and dropped my union membership. We loafed for the summer and went back to Montana for the Christmas holidays with my wife's parents on the farm, arriving there early in December. The morning of Pearl Harbor found us so busy dressing turkeys that we had not even turned on the radio. When a neighbor dropped in late in the day and told us the news, my thought was where will the Japanese hit next? I automatically decided that my next move would be to go into a defense plant in California. We headed for Santa Monica right after Christmas. There, Uncle Sam made an arc welder out of me and I spent the rest of the war helping to build Liberty and Victory ships at Calship on Terminal Island in Wilmington.

I knew the war was won when Hiroshima was hit by the atom bomb and I did not go back to work the next morning. About ten days later I was notified that my employment had been terminated. In other words, I was fired!

What You Should Know About Trading Futures

For those who insist on speculating in futures I will add some comment on various charts, showing some sound accumulation formations, known as head and shoulder bottoms and some triangles that when seen should not be ignored. For the person who knows his way around the futures markets, and knows how easy it is to take a loss, this portion of my book can be of real value. To the novice, I advise you to stop where you are. It is far too risky. The profit potential in commodity trading is terrific, but the odds against becoming a successful speculator are almost insurmountable. The price actions in futures are so highly manipulative that at times a trader hardly knows whether he is coming or going. Taking losses becomes a way of life and a trader literally gets to a point where he will run at the sight of his own shadow. Shakeouts and false starts invariably make him wrong at the right time. What he thinks is rationalizing, becomes just plain emotionalism.

To succeed, you should chart daily at least two options of every commodity. At times options based on different crop years will vary considerably in their actions. And periodically get long term monthly charts on futures from your broker, even though they are not up to date. They may give you a clue at times when you see one that has been down, for perhaps years. When one appears to have lost any ability to rally, you should pay close attention to it. It is from these lengthy low areas that many of the profitable large moves start. Only buy high after a proper formation such as a triangle, especially a flat-topped triangle, or a long consolidation period of many weeks, after a good sized rise having a positive resistance level established to give a false impression of the commodity being unable to go up. If you are lucky enough to have a bottom, or a good formation show up once a year among all these commodities, and play it heavily by buying on a scale-up during the early part of the move, you will become a millionaire in less time than I did. Playing for the small and intermediate moves is what kills you.

It is difficult to describe tops in the futures markets satisfactorily. They are almost always made up of violent action. That is the time to sell. But the very largest moves will have violent trading actions with its shakeouts, before the top is made. Sometimes there may be two tops, months apart. And there are so many variations. I have sold on the top range, but rarely. Once I sold rye on a top day purely by accident, because I stubbornly held on for a long term capital gain in 1951. I realized previously that the insiders, with their huge profits must try to convert them into long term capital gains as much as possible. Because of this reasoning I was able to hold on with confidence.

I bought this 40,000 bu. May rye, 5M @ 146-1/4, 5M @ 146-3/8. 30M @ 146-1/2 on the last shakeout in a triangle that broke out on the upside two days later. It sold as low as 145-3/4 on the day I bought it. If I had not been determined to hold on for a long term capital gain I may have sold it above 190 in February. Late in April it had a flurry from 199, and I sold on the top day when it hit 208. I sold it through my broker's Miami branch, 5M @ 207 and 35M @ 206-3/4, with a profit of $23,987. The insiders could hardly have made a more perfect trade. Following is a list of other long term gains I have made in futures.

Commodity	**Date Bought**	**Date Sold**	**Profit**
May Cotton	8-29-50	3-9-51	$13,005
May Rye	10-24-50	4-30-51	23,987
December Potatoes	2-6-51	9-11-51	505
March Potatoes	5-8-51	1-7-52	9,370
July Cotton	10-25-51	5-19-52	2,735
July Soybeans	10-28-58	6-4-59	2,199

July Soybeans	11-4-60	6-15-61	7,503
March Wool	1-24-61	9-11-61	4,110
		TOTAL:	$63,414

When I have told other traders that I did this, their usual comment was that it was difficult to understand how I could stay in an option that long. They probably did not believe me. Nor had they probably ever thought of holding for over six months.

Long range trend lines are not very dependable in futures compared to stock trend lines. Because futures are so speculative, there are more deceiving moves pulled in them. A perfect uptrend of a few weeks on a large move will almost certainly have a minor break which will catch many stop-sell orders that were moved up too closely. Then as the price moves up with increased momentum you can be sure there will be at least one big sell-off before the top action takes place. That is where you will have your trouble trying to decide "is this the change of trend or just a shakeout?" When there have not been enough violent swings preceding the break to appear to be distribution, then you would decide to hold for a further move. There are times the action will be such that even I cannot guess. Other times it will appear toppy before a break, then will go much higher. A certain four-day violent swing, a small setback, then a secondary rally, perhaps making a new high, with about three quieter days slightly on the downside but all within the upper range, can constitute a very good top in many futures. This type of action after a long rise is where the public buys heavily. But probably before this happens, you would have taken your profit. Whenever or wherever you sell, pick up your marbles and leave the game until you see another bottom opportunity in another commodity, or a good consolidation or triangle in the same one.

SELLING SHORT. Because tops are usually so violent and can so seldom be picked with any degree of accuracy, I advise against trying to sell short. Picking a price to sell your longs is one thing, but selling short is quite a different matter. Picking the wrong spot for a short sale can be deadly. Using stop-loss orders is fine if you have an action that might indicate to you a good spot for a stop. But too many times you may be tempted to sell short when there is no sensible spot for a stop-loss order. Invariably you will sell short too soon and panic with many of the other bears. You will find it far more difficult holding onto your short position, and more risky than hanging onto your longs if you bought them reasonably low. After all there is a reasonable limit to how low a commodity can drop, but have you ever been caught in a bear squeeze? Some bears when trapped, have probably thought the sky was the limit. Selling futures short merely because you think they are too high, will too often get you in trouble. You may be right that they are too high, but if too many bears crowd into an option, they are the very ones who give it the strength to go far higher when they panic. Selling short can be very tempting, but you have to be an exceptionally sharp trader to be able to break even.

PYRAMIDING. Pyramiding is another dangerous way of playing the futures, unless the timing is right. I favor doing so within limitations. After having bought about one-third of your purchasing ability within the latter part of a head and shoulders bottom or what appears to be an accumulation or consolidation triangle, you should buy another one-third as it breaks out on the upside, then after this when it has a reaction, place a stop buy for the other third above the last high. You now have a cushion of profit to help keep you from sweating. As the markup stage continues at a moderate pace with normal setbacks, after each advance into new high ground you can use your paper profits to buy more by placing stop buys above recent highs during a setback.

It is very common during this early markup stage for a commodity to form a nearly perfect trend line, and it is logical to think this will continue for several weeks. Don't follow too closely with stop-sell orders, if you use them, because a too-perfect trend will almost certainly be broken just as a shakeout, and to catch stop-sell orders. As momentum is gathered there may suddenly be a one-day fast rise followed by a sharp setback almost as quickly, giving a weak appearance as if it has gone too high. Don't let this fool you; it is meant to look this way. You and others are considered to be excess baggage; this was meant to dump you overboard and to discourage buying. Normally after this shakeout with the price recovering to near the recent highs, you can buy more with your paper profits if you wish, and move your stop sells to below the recent low. Remember, if you have a long base behind this move you can expect a large rise. After the next fast rise, if it continues to "boil" on the upside, it may be in a top area. From here on, you are on your own. This first violent action may be the top or it may not. I have seen tops, that appeared to be obvious as such, but I had sold long before because I had misinterpreted a previous action as a top. You may wait with patience to pick a strong appearing bottom, but when you are in, you are under pressure to pick a selling spot and there comes a time when time is short.

I have so many charts covering past actions, and so many of these are so well established in my mind, that when I see a certain action I will recall one, or several in the past, that are similar. I then dig them out and compare them. It can be very helpful. That is how you learn to anticipate future actions by studying past actions. It is important that you keep and study your old charts.

Brokers and advisory services, and of course the exchanges themselves, are quick to defend the futures markets' existence. These defenders of the legitimacy of speculating in futures, claim it is necessary. The futures markets were created so that business firms and dealers in commodities, can hedge against their stock in trade in order to protect them from wide changes in prices. The fact is that if there wasn't excessive speculation, there would be only moderate price changes, except perhaps in a perishable commodity such as potatoes. Before the days of potato futures, were the dealers going broke frequently, because of fluctuating prices? I doubt it.

It is said that speculators create a fluid market for the purpose of hedging and that without them, it would be virtually impossible to place hedges totaling millions of bushels on the grain exchanges. That is true. Hedging is selling short against commodities in trade and storage. Without speculators there could not be any hedging. So this provides an excuse for having futures markets. Why not make use of the gullible public to absorb the risks involved by wide swings in prices!

Could anyone be naive enough to believe that the real reason for our futures markets is to take advantage of the human weakness for gambling? Well, I am. When the public plays the tables of Las Vegas they know what they are up against. There remains only a dim hope that Lady Luck could smile upon them. But when people try to hit the jackpot in wheat futures, they seriously think they can do it. Any fool knows that all you have to do is read up on the latest crop reports and estimates of future yields, or follow the drought news or effects of late spring rains delaying the planting of crops, or know that there is a famine in Red China, or that Russia is opening a new agricultural district up in Siberia that will overflow the communist grain bins, or that a world surplus of wheat is bound to develop since the women of Afghanistan have accepted the fad of becoming slim and are on a strict diet and . . . But to simplify making money in futures, just ask a broker, or if you want to feel more confident, subscribe to an advisory service that admits that they have made money for years. Besides, the cost of this service is deductible against your profits, if any. And there are brokers and advisors who will gladly make all decisions and do all your trading for you. Pardon my cynicism.

Strange as it seems, after all the know-how one will seem to have acquired, and expert advice that was accepted, nearly every right decision that was made, will turn out to be at the wrong time. When a purchase was made, wasn't everybody else buying? Obviously, it had to go up. It did, but not much. All the bullish news indicated that it would go much higher. What went wrong? Simply that too many traders had the same opinion.

Sample Charts and Comments

Frozen Pork Bellies—1966

Besides the many gyrations that are meant to mislead you, here is a perfect example of what in my opinion was obviously meant to mislead.

A friend brought me an advisory letter dated June 3, 1965. After one-and-a-half pages of information and explanations pertaining to hog prices vs. belly prices, the advisor had this to say: "It is my recommendation that long positions be closed out and short sales be made at this time (in belly futures). I believe prices have overshot their relationship to value and such damage has been done to consumption while 90% of one of the largest holdings on record is yet to be merchandised that not even a $1000 per contract drop in prices can correct the situation."

The writer mentioned the $1000 in a way that made it sound about as easy as shooting fish in a barrel.

The next paragraph proves that this tip comes right from the horse's mouth.

"As in past years, I am active in the purchase, sale, and storing of actual bellies and am informed as to the condition of the cash market. I operate right on the trading floor of the Chicago Mercantile Exchange and can always apprise you of the status of the market... I am as near to you as your telephone, just call me collect at any time for information or to place an order."

After reading the letter I told my friend that this was a good indication that belly futures would be moving *higher.* They not only moved higher, they skyrocketed.

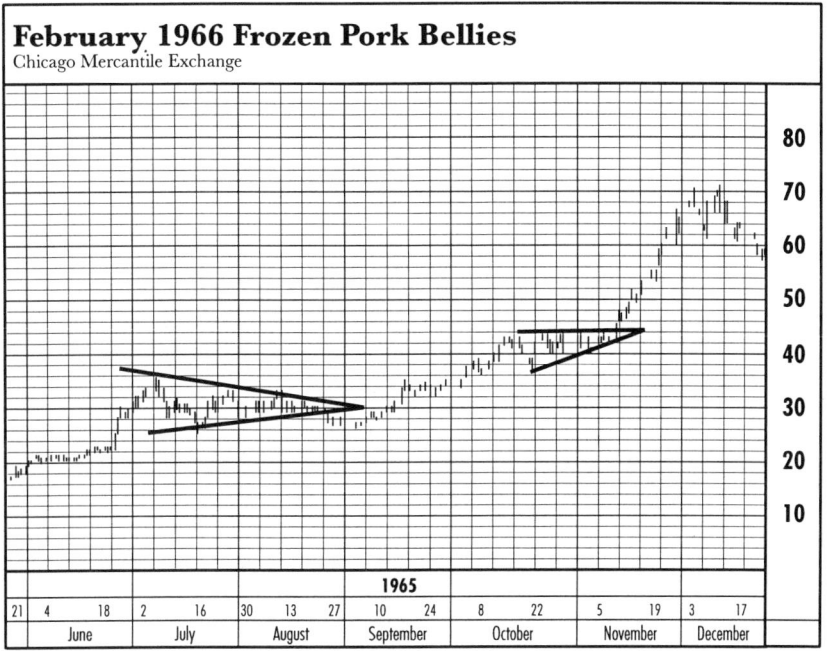

How many of these tip sheets were sent out all over the country? Were others sent out by other brokers also?

Frozen pork belly futures are not heavily traded. If only a small percentage of recipients of this mail took the bait, they helped give the price a terrific boost when they covered in their short sales at heavy losses.

I had the proper reaction to this recommendation, but I failed to do anything about it; at least I should have immediately charted belly futures back a few weeks.

If you had accepted this tip the following week, you would have sold short just above 20 cents in an extremely quiet range, and you would immediately have been taken on a wrong way ride.

I then became interested and began charting the belly futures. When I saw what I considered to be a false move or shakeouts from the eight-week triangle, in September I bought 10 contracts. On October 18, I sold out with a profit of $20,467.50.

Four weeks later belly futures completed a perfect triangle, which because of its nearly flat top, or false resistance level, was very bullish. This is the type of triangle that really turns a bull into a bear to their sorrow. To the average trader, it was obvious that it could not go up.

At the time I half expected a false move or final shakeout before the breakout on the upside. Here was a formation that appeared more sound and safe than the previous triangle and shakeout, but for some reason which I cannot begin to explain, I lacked the will "to do." Is it possible that one's subconscious mind becomes overcautious?

From this example in pork bellies, do not get the impression that as an amateur you can do this also. This commodity section is for those who have considerable experience in commodity trading and have found out the hard way how dangerous it is. I do believe that these individuals, if they will stand aside until one of these chart formations presents itself, will have a good chance of recouping their losses.

Study the following charts closely and watch for similar ones in the future. You can afford to plunge with a minimum of risk in the head and shoulders or triangles of long duration.

Beware of trying for the intermediate moves.

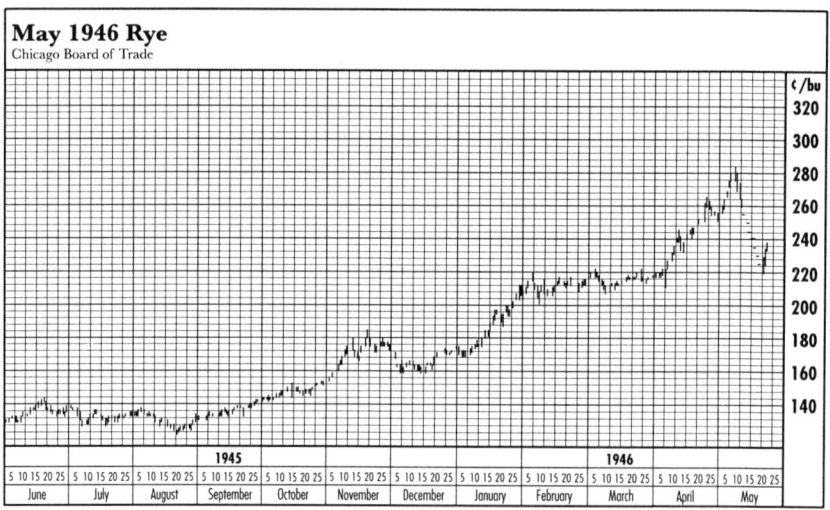

Rye—May 1946

The chart of May rye in early 1946 shows that the price of a commodity is never too high to buy, if it has the proper action. The extreme high prices in this triangle enabled me to interpret these actions more positively than if they had taken place at a much lower range, because at this price it was more attractive to the bears. Beyond all doubt, this nearly ten-week triangle had become loaded with bears.

After a large rise it turned down from $2.22 for a typical four-day selling wave that turned many traders bearish, then formed a three-week flat-topped triangle. This is not a true flat top, but at the time I considered $2.19 to be a false resistance level, even though it had sold as high as $2.22. Then came the one-day shakeout, breaking both the uptrend line and the low of the last reaction. No doubt there were many stop-sell orders on this day. Later I bought some at $2.20 and $2.23, thinking this to be the beginning of the big move. But when it turned out to be a false start, to be safe, I sold at a loss when it broke the newly formed upward trend line. This was guided into a perfect four-day shakeout, after which I bought lightly the next morning. This one really worried the bulls. If this had been a final breakdown from this high price it would have been far weaker. But it was 7 cents less than the four-day shakeout. During this slow rally, I bought more. I now drew a nearly flat line on top and an uptrend line which forms the new triangle. You don't have to understand the effect of these manipulations on the nervous traders in order to play a configuration like this successfully. Just the fact that this was a triangle was enough. It gave a reasonably positive buying point when it broke out from the upper level.

I bought more with confidence when it did this because it was obvious that the powerful bear trap was being sprung. Because this action took place so high, it meant a very large move to follow. It took powerful inside interests to support a high base like this. There could not have been a better setup for the Commodity Exchange Commission to investigate manipulation, if they had wanted to. I have never seen any noticeable inclination on their part to do much investigating. In Reno and Las Vegas only the odds are against the public. On the Chicago Board of Trade and other exchanges the cards are stacked against them as well.

Let's do some close analyzing of this bear trap. You may never see a better one. It was baited with one of the best combinations of broken trends, false moves, false resistance level, sharp shakeouts and a final sluggish rise that gave the appearance of weakness, but actually was well camouflaged technical strength. Strength derived from the potential buying power of the trapped bears and excitable bulls. From inside the triangle it rose nearly 64 cents in twenty-seven days. Notice all the 5-cent limit days it had during this move. This turned out to be one of my near perfect plays. I do not have any of my records beyond 1948. But I do remember selling very near the top.

Any chartist should positively have sold out providing he was long when the long uptrend was broken. It proved to be a mistake, but if breaking a trend like this is ignored, far worse mistakes will be made.

That slow rally impressed the traders that May rye was losing its strength when it fell back sharply from 2.22-1/2, breaking another trend line. To the average trader a definite resistance level had now appeared and this whole action was brainwashing him into thinking that if May rye could not go up, it must be going down. The bulls were induced to take a profit. Because too many bears were selling short, they were defeating their own purpose. They were the ones who were putting the teeth in this trap, from which they were unable to escape without a loss.

The last sixteen days of this action in which it remained in a closing range of 5 cents was the clincher. Because I could recognize how the manipulations in this triangle affected the average trader I could see the internal forces that were being built up here. From the trader's viewpoint, it was obvious that May rye could not go up. He does not understand that when it is obvious to him, it is obvious to the majority. And except for temporary periods, the majority are always wrong, because the insiders are on the opposing side, as in a contest. They know what they are doing and have the power to do it.

A chartist, if he did not understand nor could he interpret the actions within this triangle as I did, could interpret it just as positively, but from another viewpoint. The price of May rye just could not hold up so high, and so quietly during those last fifteen days, unless powerful buying was taking place. It is just as simple as that. If the early part of this triangle had been distribution, it would have been allowed to drop plenty after it became loaded with longs.

Wheat—May 1947

This May wheat triangle is an extremely long one. It is not as well defined as the corn triangle shown on page 300, that was completed about the same time, but it was there to be seen. And I did see it.

During the previous accumulation triangle of wheat in 1946,

President Truman made a statement on November 29 that, "We had a far bigger surplus of wheat than we had anticipated." The futures traders dumped their wheat overboard the next two days and it was no doubt picked up by very willing hands.

It was not long after this that the U.S. Government was buying wheat heavily for the Marshall plan shipments to Europe. Naturally when the speculators became aware of this, they bought heavily in the futures market. Truman "blew his top," condemning people for speculating in foodstuff, implying that they were practically taking food out of hungry mouths. An investigation followed and names were published. Truman's personal doctor, Dr. Graham, was exposed as a speculator. My name and that of another couple from an adjoining city were published in our local paper, *The Daily Breeze*. Among the list published by the *Los Angeles Times* were business firms such as The Montana Flour Mills, together with their positions in the futures market. This list showed that these companies were short millions of bushels. They were legitimately hedged against their holding of wheat and flour in their business. No doubt many people misunderstood this, instead, thinking these companies were profiteering by the big move.

What interested me in this *Los Angeles Times* list were several outfits based in Mexico City with Spanish names which gave me the impression that they were business firms. They were listed as holding millions of bushels of wheat futures. It would be very hard to convince me that any legitimate business firm in Mexico City would be long this huge amount in our futures markets. Could these have been large American interests operating under fictitious names, and tax free?

May Corn 1946-47 Triangle

This thirteen-week corn triangle coincided with the wheat triangle and head and shoulder bottom of oats. All ending at about the same time and with a final shakeout, followed by a normal slow rise and the typical increase in speed as they attracted a following of speculators.

As in wheat and oats, later options rose to new highs later in the year. These bases all proved to be exceptionally sound. Watch for similar actions in the future.

May Soybeans 1949-50

This twenty-four week combination of head and shoulders bottom and triangle in soybeans during the winter of 1949-50 was the basis for the biggest profit that I ever took out of the futures market. It is not perfectly symmetrical as was the one in 1940, but it is there to be seen and it served its purpose well, that of inducing the traders to sell. It accomplished a trick that nature can't possibly do. It turned the many bulls into bears and as far as I was aware of there had been no assistance by the government during the base, such as took place during the 1940 head and shoulders bottom.

From a chartist's point of view, this move was about as perfect from its base to its top as you can ever wish to see. After its final shakeout in February it rose step by step with its normal days of setback and consolidations for six weeks, gathering momentum as it moved up. Then on March 27th the traders became excited and pushed beans up the one day limit of 10 cents. But selling pressure forced the options to close about 2 cents down from the high of the day. The next day the price held in a quiet range. The next morning, March 29th, the Commodity Exchange Commission ordered the brokers to report all holders of soybean futures to them. This frightened many speculators and they dumped their beans overboard. They sold down the 10-cent limit, and several cents more the next morning, then quietly rallied and formed a two-week triangle. There was no doubt in my mind that it would go up from this. To start with, beans could not top out after only a one-day fast move and a quiet day following. Not enough action and time for the insiders to sell out. Then the order came for the brokers to make this report. All it was meant for in my opinion was to scare the traders. If this order had a legitimate reason, it could have been given confidentially to the brokers. But no, it came over the wires for all to see. This was a neat assist from our government.

Many traders became excited by that 10-cent rise. From the insiders' viewpoint this was too soon for the public to be getting in. Over 30 cents too soon. This order was like dousing them with a bucket of cold water. After a 30-cent rise from here, the traders fully recovered their confidence and obligingly bought heavily, taking the heavy lead off the shoulders of the manipulators that they had carried all the way up from the bottom. What a relief. The traders now of course got the best of the deal. They would be carrying this heavy burden of soybeans on a down grade. But apparently some traders balked and dumped some beans overboard, so a second run-up was necessary into even higher ground to induce them to carry their part of the load.

I refused to sell out when that mysterious order to the brokers was given. Some time later when I was not at home, a representative of the Commodities Exchange Commission called on me in person. Most of the questions asked my wife were common questions pertaining to employment, etc. One question that puzzled me was, "did I know the manager of a certain bank." I knew him only by sight. What business was it to the CEC whether I did or not? I was playing this move in beans so perfectly and heavily that perhaps someone thought a leak of inside information had developed.

I bought some contracts of beans in the bottom range then bought more when the price clearly broke the trend line on the upside, then more and more as it slowly moved upward. I have mentioned this method of buying to friends, and to them it did not sound rational. Why didn't I buy all of it at the bottom, at the lower price? This is something I learned the hard way, never to do in a futures market. Hindsight of this twenty-four week bottom now indicates I should have bought heavily to begin with, but if I had bought heavily in the bottom range, a sharp shakeout or false move would no doubt have worried me into taking a loss on part of it. It is far better to buy in as safe a manner as possible. Speculating in futures is so risky that even in the rare times when I had a positive opinion, I bought in this manner as I outlined. As the slow rise confirms your opinion from a sound base, you acquire a cushion of profit against an early shakeout. I sold out on May 3rd with over $80,000 profit.

Was there any reason for the average fundamentalist to foresee this big move ahead? Of course not.

While I caught this move so neatly, I still had a lot to learn. I went through a period of over-confidence. Before the year was over I had lost more than half of this profit by playing the minor swings. Besides soybeans, I was in and out of four other commodities. When I don't have that positive appearing formation to back up my opinion, I seem to be frightened too easily. Apparently I do not have the right type of temperament for this kind of trading. In fact, I am sure there are many that do not, chartists or fundamentalists.

Index of Stock Charts

Abbott Laboratories, 187
Admiral Corp., 75
A.J. Industries, 240
American Can Co., 51
American Snuff Co., 110
Anaconda Co., 21
Anchor Hocking Glass Corp., 57
Armstrong Cork Co., 19
Associated Dry Goods Corp., 22, 32
Atlantic Thrift Centers, Inc., 77

Bayuk Cigars, Inc., 56, 169
Beatrice Foods Co., 57
Belding Hemingway Co., 144
Boeing Co., 48
Bond Stores, Inc., 102
Borg-Warner Corp., 33
Boston and Maine Railroad, 80
Briggs and Stratton Corp., 62
Burlington Industries, Inc., 82

California Packing Corp., 85
Canadian Pacific Railway Co., 45

Carrier Corp., 39
Central Soya Co., 44
Chadbourne Gotham, Inc., 253
Checker Motors Corp., 252
Chicago Yellow Cab Co., Inc., 27
Chock Full O'Nuts Corp., 199
Chris-Craft Industries, Inc., 25
Chromally Corp., 58
Chrysler Corp., 66, 116
Coca Cola Co., 60
Collins and Aikman Corp., 59, 90
Columbia Broadcasting System, 63
Continental Oil Co., 51
Corn Products Co., 58, 138
Crescent Corp., 84
Crown Cork and Seal Co., 59
Crown Zellerbach Corp., 38
Curtiss Wright Corp., 11, 137

Dana Corp., 145
Douglas Aircraft Co., 246
Dow Jones Trends, 122
Dr. Pepper Co., 63, 107, 134, 135

Eagle-Picher Co., 44
Eastman Kodak Co., 52
Endicott Johnson Corp., 247
Evans Products Co., 76
Ex-Cell-O Corp., 35

Firestone Tire & Rubber Co., 41
Ford Motor Co., 64
Foster Wheeler Corp., 168
Freeport Sulphur Co., 184, 242
Fruehauf Corp., 243

General Cable Corp., 36, 108
General Cigar Co., Inc., 82, 109
General Motors Corp., 37
Gimbel Bros., Inc., 12, 13
Goodrich (B.F.) Co., 89
Greyhound Corp., 64, 182

Heinz, (H. J.) Co., 185
Hershey Chocolate Corp., 60
Hotel Corp. of America, 79

Illinois Power Co., 246
International Business Machines, 183
International Packers, Ltd., 49

Julius Kayser & Company, 251

Kalamazoo Stove, 87
Kelsey-Hayes Co., 45
Kresge (S.S.) Co., 245
KVP Sutherland Paper, 43

Laboratory for Electronics, 81
Lionel Corp., 75
Lion Oil Co., 55
Litton Industries, 185

Marquette Cement Mfg. Co., 200
Mead Corp., 40

Metro-Goldwyn-Mayer, Inc., 25
Microwave Assoc. Inc., 79
Monogram Industries, Inc., 62
Monon Railroad Co. "B", 61
Mueller Brass Co., 249

New York Central Railroad Co., 43

Outboard Marine Corp., 184

Papercraft Corp., 78
Parmelee Transportation, 14, 17
Pfeiffer Brewing Co., 31
Polarad Electronics Corp., 78
Powdrell & Alexander, Inc., 16

Reichhold Chemicals, Inc., 118
Republic Steel Corp., 50, 183
Revlon, Inc., 186
Royal Crown Cola Co., 108

Schenley Industries, Inc., 30
Seaboard World Airlines, Inc., 166
Seeman Bros. Inc., 145
Servel, 81
Spiegel, Inc., 186
Standard Oil Co. of Ohio, 140
Studebaker Corp., 24
Sunshine Biscuits, Inc., 15

Thor Power Tool Co., 68, 69
Tractor Supply Co. "A", 118

Union Bag-Camp Paper Corp., 144
United Shoe Machinery Corp., 48

Vanadium Corp., 23

Wiebolt Stores Inc., 77
Woodward Iron Co., 42

Xerox Corp., 52

Index of Commodity Charts

Corn, May, 1947, 300

Frozen Pork Bellies, February, 1966 — Chicago, 295

Rye, May, 1946 — Chicago, 296

Soybeans, December, 1940 — Chicago, 285
Soybeans, May, 1950 — Chicago, 300

Wheat, December, 1932-33 — Winnipeg, 276
Wheat, May, 1933 — Chicago, 272
Wheat, May, 1947 — Chicago, 299